FLAVORS *of the* SUN

FLAVORS *of the* SUN

The Sahadi's Guide to Understanding, Buying, and Using Middle Eastern Ingredients

CHRISTINE SAHADI WHELAN
PHOTOGRAPHS BY KRISTIN TEIG

CHRONICLE BOOKS
SAN FRANCISCO

SPECIALTY FOODS
SAHADI IMPORTING CO.
187-189
SAHADI'S
718.624.4550
SAHADIS.COM

ATLANTIC
AVENUE
IDDLE EASTERN
DI'S
187-189
189
718.624.4550
SAHADI'S
187-191

Library of Congress Cataloging-in-Publication Data available.

ISBN 978-1-4521-8245-2

Manufactured in China.

Food styling by **CAITLIN HAUGHT BROWN.**
Prop styling by **NIDIA CUEVA.**
Design by **LIZZIE VAUGHAN.**
Typesetting by **HOWIE SEVERSON.**
Typeset in Caslon, Copperplate, and Brandon Grotesque.

10 9 8 7 6 5 4 3 2 1

Chronicle Books LLC
680 Second Street
San Francisco, California 94107
www.chroniclebooks.com

HERBS & SPICES
SUMAC
KABOB
BAHARAT
TANDOORI
5 SPICE
HAWAIJ
ZAATAR
PEPPER
7 SPICE
SHAWARMA

SAHADI'S

To Uncle Richie, who taught me
to trust my sense of taste and
travel the world through food.

[4705]

[4815]
15]
[4825]

SAHADI'S
SAHADI'S
EXIT

ALMONDS
NATURAL
$7.50 / LB
[4045]

CONTENTS

INTRODUCTION

Sumac. Aleppo peppers. Date molasses, za'atar, preserved lemons. Until fairly recently, it required time and ingenuity to track down these staples of Middle Eastern cooking, most of which were rarely seen outside of ethnic markets in communities with large immigrant populations.

How things change! Today, hummus is a lunchbox staple, and pomegranate molasses can be found on most supermarket shelves next to the balsamic vinegar. At Sahadi's we've had a bird's-eye view of—and perhaps more than a little hand in—the explosion in popularity of the foods and flavors of the Middle East. As New York City's oldest continually operating specialty food store, we've been importing and selling Middle Eastern provisions and prepared foods for more than a hundred years. We take enormous pride in knowing that we have helped generations of cooks who immigrated from Syria, Lebanon, Israel, Jordan, and beyond keep cherished family traditions alive, while at the same time introducing a new generation of chefs and home cooks to unfamiliar and exciting new flavors.

As the fourth generation of Sahadi to work in the family business, we have found it fascinating to watch the evolution of our customer base. Where we once catered primarily to an immigrant population seeking the raw ingredients for home cooking, we now feed thousands each week from our prepared food counters and cater to a diverse mix of shoppers from every possible cultural background. We've expanded our offerings to keep pace with changing tastes and food trends, but it's the Middle Eastern specialties—dry goods, olives, nuts, and spices—that continue to define what makes us unique in a city that's hardly lacking in food choices.

In recent years, I've seen the public appetite for these flavors grow by leaps and bounds, fueled in no small part by the recipes of acclaimed chefs like Yotam Ottolenghi, Michael Solomonov, and Paula Wolfert, as well as adventuresome cooks perennially in search of the next new thing. I always know when the *New York Times* or *Bon Appétit* magazine has published a new Middle Eastern–inflected recipe because the store is inundated with customers clutching a clipping or peering at their phones as they peruse the shelves looking for ras el hanout or orange blossom water. While I'm happy to sell them these trendy "new" ingredients—most of which we've been carrying for decades—I know that once they've busted out that special dish for their next dinner party, those sought-after ingredients are likely to languish at the back of the pantry, forgotten and unused. I've lost count of the times I've been asked "What can I do with the rest of the date molasses I bought?" or "What else is Urfa pepper good for?"

I wrote this book to answer questions like those and dozens more, with both simple, family-friendly recipes you'll want to add to your weekly rotation as well as food prompts and no-recipe recipes that will have you scraping the bottom of those jars before you know it.

Sahadi's packages and sells over 150 different spices and seasoning blends—all with their own loyal constituencies—as well as specialty, gourmet, and artisanal products from six continents. But for the purposes of this book, I've chosen to drill down on a relatively small handful of versatile, essential flavorings and ingredients, and show lots of different ways to use them rather than present a showcase for every single seasoning we carry. I want to be sure you never have to skip one of my recipes just because it requires a special trip to the store or worry that you might end up with dozens of single-use ingredients. All the ingredients I'm spotlighting here can be used lots of different ways and in both sweet and savory dishes.

In that same spirit, I've arranged the recipes in this book by the broad flavor profiles that characterize Middle Eastern cooking: Bright, Savory, Spiced, Nutty, and Sweet, with a range of recipes for every course of the meal in each category. Although it's a little bit unconventional to structure a cookbook this way, my hope is that it accomplishes two things.

First, it illustrates how in many cases the ingredients in each of these categories can be substituted for one another or even used interchangeably. For example, if you like the subtle perfume of rose water but not the flavor, orange blossom water will give a similar effect. If you're looking for the citrus zing of pomegranate molasses but don't want to add more liquid to your recipe, a teaspoon or two of sumac or ground hibiscus can help you achieve the same result. Feta cheese, cured olives, and capers all add a savory salty tang to a dish, so if your recipe calls for one and you only have the others, go ahead and substitute. Play around with spice blends like berbere, shawarma, or harissa; in so many cases they can be used exactly the same way, or substitute for other blends, like curry powder and even pumpkin pie spice! Tahini can provide the earthiness and richness of nuts in baking or in salad dressings. You get the idea. By my grouping these ingredients together, I hope you will see the potential for swapping them in and out of recipes as your mood and the state of your pantry dictate.

Second, I find that these categories reflect the way I go about pulling together a menu on any given day. Gray and gloomy outside? Sounds like the perfect occasion for a vibrantly seasoned Hummus with Moroccan Spices and Preserved Lemon (page 40) or a serving of Classic Fattoush (page 49). Seeking comfort food when life feels challenging? Check out the rich and nutty Chicken Soup with Pine Nuts (page 238) for stick-to-your-ribs satisfaction. Round out your game-night buffet with Whipped Feta Spread (page 103) or pomegranate-spiked Sweet-and-Sour Beef Hand Pies (page 76). I find that the most exciting meals hit a number of different flavor notes, leaving no taste bud unstimulated. Choosing dishes from across these five categories (or using one of the menus on page 336) will help you achieve just the right balance.

ABOUT THE RECIPES

I've written this book to give you the information, inspiration, and recipes to make these ingredients that my family and I have championed for three generations a part of your everyday repertoire, whether you are cooking up a Middle Eastern feast or just looking for a way to add new life to an old favorite.

I grew up in a Lebanese household eating mostly traditional foods prepared by my mother and aunts. My mother, Audrey, always cooks like she's expecting six hundred guests, and several times each year we turn out feasts that would do any Aleppo housewife proud. Likewise, the majority of the foods we prepare and sell at Sahadi's have their roots in the classic recipes of Syria and Lebanon, and I love hearing our American born-and-raised customers casually throwing words like fettoush or kibbeh into conversation as they plan their upcoming parties.

When I cook for my family at home, though, tradition matters less to me than *flavor*. When I married my husband, Pat, whose background is Italian and Irish, I began incorporating the flavors I love into dishes that brought together the best of Middle Eastern, Mediterranean, and American cuisines. I made fewer of the long-simmered, heavy dishes I'd been raised on, reserving those for holiday meals and family gatherings, and instead leaned in to the lighter side of Middle Eastern cuisine: grilled foods, interesting salads and vegetable dishes, and grain bowls topped with highly seasoned legumes and condiments.

As our kids grew and weekends were devoted to outdoor activities and get-togethers with friends, I realized just how perfectly so many of these foods, made to be served warm or at room temperature, were suited to casual entertaining. Because the weather throughout the Middle East is temperate for the majority of the year, much of life is lived outdoors. Many restaurants don't even have indoor seating; diners gather at the tables, conversing with neighbors as they stroll by and stop to chat. Platters of salad, breads, and grilled meats are passed around so everyone can create their own meal, tucking bits of spicy condiments, fresh mint, or pickled vegetables into a pita sandwich as they like. It's a leisurely way of eating that can go on for hours. At our home in Brooklyn we try to emulate this lifestyle, and my neighbors know they will find me in the backyard, tending my pepper plants, grilling up a mess of harissa shrimp or vegetable skewers, or enjoying a twilight cocktail, from May through October. We have sought to re-create this communal culture at our second outpost in Brooklyn's Industry City, where diners gather at a long table to eat grain bowls with grilled meats and pickled vegetables, or snack on a pastry and strong coffee, any time of day.

The recipes in this collection reflect all of those influences. Some are essentially faithful renditions of Middle Eastern classics, dishes that have been bestsellers at the Atlantic Avenue store for decades. Others I've developed more recently to please the palates of my young adult children—who like almost everything better with a jolt of za'atar or harissa—as well as our globe-trotting customers. These recipes don't necessarily reflect the cuisine of one particular region or country; like the menu at Sahadi's, they illustrate the common threads that run throughout the cuisines of Lebanon, Syria, Israel, Jordan, Greece, Turkey, and North Africa. I hope they will help you add some diversity to your weeknight cooking and simplify your entertaining menus.

Sahadi Brand HONEY
$5.75
5 Pound Jar
The Honey With The Middle East Flavor
SAHADI
PURE
HONEY
PISTACHIO NUTS
YERBA MATE
FLOR DE LIS
SESAMETTES
SAFFRON
575
275
325
140
285
265
190
165
225

A SHORT HISTORY OF SAHADI'S

The story of Sahadi's begins as so many American food stories do: with the dream of a better life and the remembered flavors of a homeland far away.

In the late nineteenth century, Arab Christians left the Middle East by the thousands, fleeing wars and economic insecurity. Between 1880 and 1920, about fifty thousand immigrants from areas now known as Lebanon, Syria, Israel, and Palestine arrived in New York City, settling in a neighborhood on Manhattan's Lower West Side that would come to be called Little Syria. The first Sahadi's store, located just a block off the Hudson River, was opened by my great-great uncle Abrahim Sahadi, one of five siblings from Zahlé, Lebanon, a river town and historically a center of Lebanese trade and agriculture. Abrahim immigrated to America in the late 1800s, leaving behind his three brothers and a sister in hopes of finding work to help support them and his parents. In 1895 he decided to open a store where fellow Arabs could buy the dry goods, olive oil, and Turkish pistachios they were accustomed to enjoying back home. With the assistance of Khalil, a brother back home, Abrahim began importing bulk goods and selling them primarily to fellow Middle Eastern immigrants.

In 1919, Abrahim was joined by his eighteen-year-old nephew, Wade Sahadi—my grandfather. Gedu Wade was an affable and welcoming salesman who began nearly every transaction by inviting a customer into the back of the store to drink coffee, eat pastry, have a smoke, and trade news.

In 1941 Wade decided to strike out on his own, purchasing a narrow brick building not far from the Brooklyn waterfront. Grandpa Wade had to wait two years for the barber shop occupying the ground floor of 187 Atlantic Avenue to finish out its lease, but in 1948 the Sahadi Importing Company opened its doors. It quickly became an anchor for Brooklyn's burgeoning Middle Eastern population and remains the face of our business today.

While the new store became a gathering place for Brooklyn's Arab immigrant community, Wade was also building an extensive web of international suppliers. He not only stocked the store's shelves with hard-to-find ingredients from the Middle East but also began distributing these goods to communities across the United States, becoming a lifeline to the old country for hundreds of thousands of Arab Americans from coast to coast.

SAHADIS ON ATLANTIC AVE, 1960S
The tin walls and ceilings of the original storefront remain to this day; the 1960s prices (5 pounds of honey for $5.95) sadly do not.

Through it all, Sahadi's has always been a family-run business. Grandpa Wade continued to run the store and delight our customers until his death in 1967, when my father, Charlie, and his brothers, Ritchie and Bob, took the reins. In 1978, we bought the two adjoining storefronts, eventually breaking through the walls to create a maze-like warren of connected shopping spaces, something like a modern-day version of a Middle Eastern bazaar. In addition to packaged goods from Europe, South America, and local artisanal producers, we added bakery cases lined with pastries and cookies, a flatbread station, and a counter offering a changing roster of prepared foods for takeout.

For me, my siblings, and our cousins, weekends and summer vacations were spent "helping" at the store; by the time I was eight, I was earning pocket money filling quart containers with tahini from a fifty-gallon vat. And now, in the store's seventh decade, my brother Ron and I are steering the ship, making Sahadi's the longest continually operated specialty food store in New York. Since 2000, we've been joined by my husband, Pat, who left his finance job to help us expand our reach even further, distributing premium-quality Middle Eastern goods to wholesale customers in all fifty states. Our vast warehouse in nearby Sunset Park handles more than two thousand products sold across the country. And most recently we've launched a second location featuring a market, café, and event space in Brooklyn's Industry City.

Over time, both the product mix and the customer base at Sahadi's have evolved, reflecting the changing nature of our neighborhood. Many of our second-generation immigrant customers, looking for a less urban lifestyle, have moved away from Brooklyn. In their place have come families in search of more spacious housing than they could afford in Manhattan, as well as artists priced out of Greenwich Village and financiers who appreciate the easy commute to Wall Street. As the other Middle Eastern stores that once lined our stretch of Atlantic Avenue have faded away, Sahadi's remains, at once a neighborhood fixture and a magnet for food writers, professional chefs, and adventurous cooks who know they can always find something new on our shelves to expand and excite their culinary palates. Today, a crock of homemade kimchi sits beside the turmeric-pickled cauliflower in the olive case. Each year we prowl the aisles of international food festivals to bring in new products before they're available anywhere else. And I look forward to seeing how the next generation of Sahadis keeps the store vital and growing in the coming decades.

What many consumers don't realize is that nearly everything we stock, from powdered za'atar to figs to olives and olive oil, is a commodity with a limited season. It's our job to purchase just enough to get us through to the

"THE HOUSE OF QUALITY"

SAHADI'S "EL AHRAM" BRAND

TAHINI

1 lb. net in tin cans	$ .19 per can
2 lb. net in tin cans	.35 per can
4 lb. net in tin cans	.70 per can
8 lb. net in tin cans	1.35 per can
42 lb. net in tin cans	.15 per lb.
500 lb. net in drums (approx.)	14½ per lb.

SHELLED SESAME SEEDS

200 lb. bags 1st quality	per lb.
200 lb. bags 2nd quality	per lb.
200 lb. bags toasted	per lb.

UNSHELLED SESAME SEEDS

200 lb. bags white	$ .10 per lb.
200 lb. bags yellow	.14 per lb.

Turkish Delight and Marmalade Candy
Quotations On Request

Prices Quoted Subject To
Change Without Notice

"THE HOUSE OF QUALITY"

STANDARD PACKING OF HALWA

Cut Halwa 72's	12 boxes to ctn.
Cut Halwa 120's	8 boxes to ctn.
Halwa 2-6's loaves	6 boxes to ctn.
Halwa Nibs 72's	12 boxes to ctn.
Half Moons 36's	10 boxes to ctn.
Half Moon's 90's	10 boxes to ctn.
Imp. Style 1 lb. boxes	24 boxes to ctn.
Imp. Style 4 oz. pkgs.	12 boxes to ctn.
Half 'N' Half 14 oz. boxes	24 boxes to ctn.

We Also Manufacture
"MELISSA" Brand PASTEL HONEY BAR

24-5c bars to box .... per box
24 boxes to a carton

TERMS:
Trade Discount 5%
Cash Discount 2%-10 days
ON HALWA ONLY

All Prices Quoted F.O.B. New York

"THE HOUSE OF QUALITY"
Established 1895

JOBBERS'
PRICE LIST
Season 1941-42
SAHADI'S "EL AHRAM"
BRAND HALWA

SAHADI
EL-AHRAM
BRAND
HALWAH

A. Sahadi & Co., Inc.
Manufacturers—Importers
61 WASHINGTON STREET
New York, N. Y.
Telephone: BOwling Green 9-8674

A 1941 wholesale price list for my Grandfather Wade and Uncle Abrahim's importing business featured their exclusive El Ahram brand of halva (available in plain or marble!).

next crop without running short—or sitting on an oversupply. That way we never have to sell a stale nut or tough, dry apricot—but when we're out, we're out, until the new crop comes in.

We've operated that way since the beginning, and we think our customers can tell the difference. Buying direct from the growers lets us know exactly what we are getting, and our relationships with many of these family-owned farms go back for generations. Great-Great Uncle Abrahim would have been dazzled by the array of imported goods we now carry, but he'd also be gratified to know our customers can still buy the same Turkish figs, harvested the same way, that we have been importing for more than a century.

Lately we've been supporting a number of Middle Eastern women's cooperatives, who supply us with traditional products rarely seen in the United States, like apple and green fig jam, apricot syrups, and date compote with almonds. We love making these unique treats available—and supporting these women in roles they never have had the opportunity to experience before. And when we opened our café, we began importing wine produced in Lebanon to showcase the winemaking strengths of the region.

With every bite, our customers know they are getting not just something good to eat, but something the Sahadi family would be proud to serve you in their own home. Good food, after all, is made with love—a timeless family value that knows no borders.

Above: The original storefront at 187 Atlantic Avenue doubled in size when we broke through the wall connecting our building to 189 Atlantic. In 2012 we expanded to our current footprint by annexing 191 Atlantic as well. **Opposite:** Our catalogs and price sheets, like this Christmas 1967 edition, were a homemade affair. A local artist created all the illustrations; my mother typed up the prices and taped down the layouts by hand.

1 BRIGHT

TART, TANGY, CITRUSY

HIBISCUS

POMEGRANATE MOLASSES

PRESERVED LEMONS

SUMAC

PICKLED VEGETABLES

Of all the spice blends and flavorings we carry, I find this group of ingredients has been embraced most enthusiastically by chefs and, more recently, home cooks. Like a squeeze of lemon juice or a splash of vinegar, these tangy, sometimes puckery seasonings add liveliness and acidity that instantly wake up heavier, fattier, or just plain bland preparations. And they perform this feat of culinary magic without contributing extra fat or calories (or, in the case of pomegranate molasses, just a negligible amount)—a pretty nifty trick.

You'll be especially inclined to reach for ingredients from this category during the summer because they are just so clean and refreshing, like a tall glass of cold lemonade on a sultry day. In the Middle East we are crazy for barbecuing. Even here in Brooklyn, where the temperatures don't quite reach the stratospheric heights that they do throughout most of the Middle East, I cook outdoors as much as I possibly can, and I serve foods either warm off the grill or at room temperature. Because Middle Easterners often serve meals at room temp, we gravitate toward leaner meats like lamb and chicken that are less likely to congeal as they cool. The downside is that these meats can be less flavorful (fat is a great conveyor of flavor), especially at room temperature. Tangy complements with a bit of acidic bite, including vinegar-preserved vegetables like the Pickled Turnips on page 53 or bits of preserved lemon (page 43), do wonders to bring these foods alive.

But don't push these seasonings to the back of the spice cabinet once your grill goes back into storage. Many winter dishes benefit from a brightening touch, too. Think of the way a sprinkle of gremolata—that Italian blend of parsley, lemon zest, and garlic—cuts the richness of a plate of osso buco, or how a final dash of vinegar sparks up the earthy flavor of a good borscht. Any of the ingredients in this section will have the same effect on braised and roasted meats, stews and soups, and winter vegetables (especially squash).

I find most of these flavors pair well with rich, fatty, or mild foods, like yogurt and oats. And don't discount the visual appeal that a sprinkle of sumac, a dusting of hibiscus sugar, or a swirl of pomegranate molasses contributes to your plates.

PICKLED
VEGETABLES
SUMAC

HIBISCUS
POMEGRANATE MOLASSES
PRESERVED LEMONS

Hibiscus

If you've ever sipped a cup of Red Zinger tea, you are familiar with the sunny, tart flavor of the dried hibiscus flower, as well as its brilliant bright red color. Steeping the blossoms in hot water is still one of the most popular ways to use hibiscus, and in the winter I find a cup of hot hibiscus tea sweetened with organic honey very soothing; it's also perfect iced, needing only a touch of sweetener to balance its slight bitter edge. However, hibiscus is also well-suited to many dessert applications, and it's especially pretty in holiday desserts. Generally, the blossoms need to be steeped in a liquid to release their flavor. You can also infuse vinegar with hibiscus and use it to make a hot-pink vinaigrette to serve over a salad of baby spinach, feta, strawberries, and slivered almonds.

WHAT TO LOOK FOR • Choose hibiscus petals that are dry but not brittle and have a deep brownish-red color. You want large pieces, not small, dusty fragments. Keep hibiscus away from heat and sunlight, which can fade its color, and store up to 3 months in an airtight container, as you would any kind of tea; after that its flavor will be less potent.

SERVE IT WITH • Many fruits—especially red fruits like cherries, strawberries, and raspberries—partner well with hibiscus. Hibiscus sugar is a great way to use it; an exception to the steeping rule, it is made by grinding the dried blossoms with sugar. You can roll cookies in it, sprinkle it on a cake, or use it to rim a glass for a cocktail or lemonade.

Pomegranate Molasses

If you were to take a gallon of fresh squeezed pomegranate juice and boil it for several hours until it had reduced to a thick, slightly viscous syrup, you'd have homemade pomegranate syrup, more commonly called pomegranate molasses. Or you can cut to the chase and buy a bottle of this bright magenta elixir, a tangy flavor enhancer that can be used in any number of refreshing ways.

You might be surprised not to find this product in the sweet category with its cousin, date molasses, but all-natural pomegranate molasses balances its fruit notes with a tart bite that pairs beautifully with savory ingredients and sweet ones. To be sure, many of the pomegranate products on the market can be quite sweet and thick. However, these tend to contain added sugar (or high-fructose corn syrup) to make a cheaper product. The pure, unsweetened, all-natural version has a sweet-and-sour taste much more reminiscent of the fresh fruit itself. If you want a sweeter, thicker glaze you can always cook it down with a bit of sugar as you would to make a balsamic vinegar glaze.

WHAT TO LOOK FOR • Opt for the all-natural, unsweetened product whenever possible. Avoid any that are labeled "glaze" rather than pure pomegranate molasses, as that most certainly indicates the addition of sweeteners and other extenders. Otherwise, scrutinize the ingredient list and reject any that include preservatives or added sugars. Pomegranate molasses is shelf-stable and can be kept unrefrigerated for six months or more.

SERVE IT WITH • I keep it on the shelf next to the honey and add a dash whenever a dish needs more zing. The fruit's inherent sweetness makes a nice counterpoint to salty cheeses like feta or Pecorino, and its slight acidic tang cuts the richness of fatty foods, including salmon, avocado, and lamb. The tart freshness it imparts also sparks up everything from yogurt to grain salads—I especially like to use pomegranate molasses in conjunction with fresh pomegranate seeds when the fruit is in season, to underscore the brightness and pop of the seeds. Reach for pomegranate molasses whenever you might use a raspberry purée.

Preserved Lemons

A specialty of North Africa, preserved lemons have found their way into the kitchens of many different regions. Preserved lemons were not traditionally used in Lebanese cuisine, but today our food cultures are so intertwined they have become one of my very favorite ingredients. They have a depth of flavor that is salty and savory and complex; think of the difference between a cucumber and a pickle. In addition to brightness, they add a funky earthiness that contributes a singular taste to a wide range of preparations.

Unlike sumac or lemon juice, even finely minced preserved lemon retains its own character rather than blending in, announcing itself with a burst of sharp flavor. They are most typically sold in jars, packed tightly with a brine of either pure lemon juice or salt water. The lemons are split or quartered and heavily salted before being tucked into their jars; for this reason, most recipes make use of only the softened rind, discarding the super-salty flesh. If you make your own at home (page 43) and store them in the refrigerator, you can use less salt, making the entire fruit usable, flesh and all.

WHAT TO LOOK FOR • If you don't preserve your own lemons, be choosy about the quality of the prepared ones you buy. The process of sealing them in a jar involves heat, which can alter their texture and flavor, and if they remain in the jar a long time they will become soft (and can even eat right through the jar!). We find the preserved lemons that we import from Morocco to be of consistently good quality, and we sell them loose from crocks so you can see what you're getting. If you are buying them prepacked, look for firm, well-shaped lemons that are not mushy or mashed too tightly into their jars. Both homemade and commercially prepared lemons will keep in their brine for several months in the refrigerator, taking on a deeper pickled flavor and softer texture over time. Shake the jar now and then to keep the lemons moist; otherwise the salt may rise to the top and form a crust. If this happens, just scrape off the salty rime.

SERVE WITH · Because preserved lemons are both tangy and salty, they are a one-and-done way to season and brighten just about anything bland, from grains to beans, and the minced bits add an extra pop of flavor when you bite them. Preserved lemons have an affinity for fish; blend them into a compound butter and slip a pat onto a piece of broiled or grilled fish. Slivered bits of preserved lemon rind go incredibly well with green olives, too, as both are cured and salty, and the citrus flavor mitigates the oiliness of the olives. Mince some into a salsa or stir a bit into a seafood salad.

Sumac

One of the most ubiquitous souring agents used throughout the Middle East, sumac is made from the red berries of the sumac bush, which are first dried and then ground. Most of the sumac sold in our store comes from Turkey, although at one time Syria was a large producer, as are parts of the Mediterranean. It's a versatile ingredient that can be cooked into a dish or used as a finishing element. Sumac brings a lot of what a squeeze of lemon juice does to the party, with the advantage that it doesn't add moisture or water down your sauces the way juice does. In fact, sumac will actually draw liquid from vegetables like cucumbers and tomatoes, so wait to add it to your dishes just before serving, or it will dilute the flavors.

WHAT TO LOOK FOR · Because ground sumac is the product of a single berry, not a blend of seasonings, it can vary in potency and flavor from year to year, so always taste after adding sumac to see if you need to adjust the quantity up or down, depending on how strong the flavor is. Whole berries are rarely imported to this country, so most of what you find will be preground. Ground sumac can get a bit clumpy, so some spice merchants mix salt into their sumac to keep the grains separate. We prefer a bit of moisture to overly salty sumac, so ours never contains added salt. (Be sure to read the label when you buy so that you can adjust the seasonings in your dish if you are not able to find pure, unsalted sumac.) The color of the sumac berries can change from season to season and region to region, ranging from bright red to a deeper brick or burgundy color, but this color variation doesn't affect the flavor. Some importers color their sumac; if your sumac bleeds in water or turns your food pink, that's a dead giveaway that it has been artificially dyed. Store sumac in a tightly sealed jar to keep it as moisture-free as possible; if it does get damp, spread it on a baking sheet to dry thoroughly, then return it to the sealed jar.

SERVE WITH • Sumac has a very bright, savory flavor that makes it a good foil for fatty or rich foods. Its granular texture also adds a nice contrast to creamy, soft dishes, giving them some body and a toothsome bite. It's great with fish and shrimp and just about any kind of grilled meats, including beef and lamb. It also goes well with mild-flavored foods like beans and dips. I keep mine on the counter next to the Aleppo pepper so I can sprinkle a pinch onto veggies, soups, and anything else that needs a hit of color and a touch of tartness.

Pickled Vegetables

Because spoilage is an omnipresent concern in the region's warm climate, pickling has been a common way to preserve fresh produce for centuries throughout the Middle East. Beets, small Persian cucumbers, and turnips are among the most common, but just about anything and everything that grows is pickled.

Kitchens typically have a jar of pickling solution at the ready, and any bits of vegetable leftovers go into the jar to become a piquant accent for another meal.

It's not surprising, therefore, that pickles are a ubiquitous presence at most meals, especially with grilled meats or anything that is rich and fatty, like meze. Middle Easterners add pickles to sandwiches as others use lettuce and tomato, to add a bit of freshness and tang.

WHAT TO LOOK FOR • While pickles remain safe to eat for months, they become soft and taste too strongly of brine after a few weeks, so when purchasing pickled vegetables, freshness is key. They should be crisp and contain no additives aside from salt, vinegar, and spices. I am especially wary of pickles that have been artificially colored. You should still be able to detect the flavor profile of the vegetable itself, while not being overpowered by garlic, onions, or other additions.

SERVE WITH • Pickled vegetables go with everything, but especially grilled foods and kebabs, sandwiches, grain bowls—anything that needs a little punch of salty, savory brightness. They add dimension to dishes that can be one-note, like rice lentils, and their pungency is especially appreciated during fasting season, when meals are meat free and on the spartan side.

THE
MEDITERRANEAN ROSE
page 39

POMEGRANATE
CRANBERRY SANGRIA

Pomegranate Cranberry Sangria

Falling somewhere between a traditional sangria and a mulled wine, this jewel-toned pitcher drink is a wonderful centerpiece for a fall or holiday gathering. It is sweet, tart, spicy, and earthy all at once—the perfect foil for a robust charcuterie plate.

SERVES 8 TO 10

1 mandarin orange or clementine

1 cup [140 g] fresh cranberries

¼ cup [50 g] sugar

1 Tbsp pomegranate molasses

1 cinnamon stick

¼ cup [60 ml] brandy

One 25.4 oz [750 ml] bottle full-bodied red wine, such as cabernet sauvignon or merlot, chilled

½ cup [120 ml] pomegranate juice

1 cup [174 g] pomegranate seeds

Seltzer or club soda

1 orange, sliced into rounds, for garnish

Sprigs of fresh mint, for garnish

Using a large, very sharp knife, slice the rind off the orange in strips, avoiding as much of the pith as possible. Cut the rind into long strips. Peel or slice off as much of the remaining pith from the fruit as you can and dice the flesh.

Put both the orange rind and flesh in a saucepan over medium heat and add the cranberries, sugar, pomegranate molasses, cinnamon stick, and 2 Tbsp of water. Stir well and bring to a simmer. Continue to simmer just until the cranberries begin to pop, about 5 minutes. Set aside to cool completely. Stir in the brandy, transfer to a pitcher, and refrigerate overnight to allow the flavors to develop.

To serve, stir in the wine and pomegranate juice and seeds. Pour into ice-filled glasses, top with seltzer, and garnish with an orange wheel and mint sprig.

A BROOKLYN
TRADITION

The Mediterranean Rose

Hibiscus-infused vodka gives this cocktail (pictured on page 36) its lovely pink hue, but it gets its name (and delicate fragrance) from a bit of rose water. Serve it in a martini or coupe glass to highlight the color and sugared rim. Unlike many infused vodkas, this one is ready to use in just a few hours, so you can brew up a batch for an impromptu gathering any time! This looks like a lot of steps, but they are all extremely easy, and all the components can be made ahead of time and stored at room temperature.

MAKES 1 COCKTAIL

Hibiscus Vodka

One 1.5 liter [51 oz] bottle unflavored vodka

2½ oz [70 g] dried hibiscus blossoms (2 cups)

Rosewater Simple Syrup

1 cup [200 g] sugar

1 Tbsp fresh lemon juice

2 tsp rose water

Hibiscus Sugar

4 Tbsp [50 g] sugar

½ oz [15 g] dried hibiscus blossoms

Lemon wedge, for serving

Club soda, for serving

Organic rose petals, for garnish (optional)

To make the hibiscus vodka: Combine the vodka and hibiscus in a large jar or bottle and shake to combine. Set aside to infuse until the vodka is bright magenta. It will start to take on color almost immediately, deepening over time. After 12 hours (or as little as 1 hour if you are pressed for time) strain the vodka into a clean container, discarding the hibiscus.

To make the rosewater simple syrup: In a saucepan bring the sugar to a boil with 1 cup of water. Reduce the heat and simmer for 5 minutes, or until the sugar is completely dissolved. Let the syrup cool to room temperature, then stir in the lemon juice and rose water.

To make the hibiscus sugar: Combine 1 Tbsp of the sugar and the hibiscus blossoms in a food processer and whir together until the hibiscus is finely ground. Transfer to a shallow bowl and stir in the remaining 3 Tbsp of sugar.

To serve, rub the rim of a martini glass with the lemon wedge to moisten. Dip the rim in the hibiscus sugar. Set aside for a minute to dry (you can do this in advance if you like).

In a cocktail shaker, mix 1 oz [30 ml] of the infused vodka with 1 Tbsp of the simple syrup. Add 2 ice cubes and shake vigorously. Strain into the rimmed martini glass and top off with club soda. Garnish with an edible rose petal.

Hummus with Moroccan Spices and Preserved Lemon

A few years ago, we decided to offer a hummus tasting at a street fair in our Brooklyn Heights neighborhood. We set up a station in front of the store with five new varieties we created especially for the event, asking the passersby to vote for their favorite. When the results were tallied, this sassy blend won in a landslide. It is now a fixture in the deli case as well as on the café menu. I'm guessing it will find a permanent place in your snack and party rotation as well.

MAKES 2 CUPS

2 cups [320 g] cooked chickpeas, drained, liquid reserved (see Note)

2 garlic cloves

¼ cup [55 g] tahini

¼ cup [60 ml] fresh lemon juice

½ tsp sea salt

1 Tbsp diced preserved lemon rind, plus more for garnish, store-bought or homemade (page 43)

½ tsp ras el hanout, plus more for garnish

Extra-virgin olive oil, for drizzling

Put the chickpeas in a blender or food processor with 3 Tbsp of the reserved liquid. Add the garlic, tahini, lemon juice, and salt and blend until smooth. Check the consistency; if too thick, add more of the reserved chickpea liquid by the teaspoon. Add the preserved lemon rind and ras el hanout and purée. Taste for seasoning and let stand, covered, for 30 minutes or so to combine the flavors.

Serve drizzled with a bit of oil and topped with minced preserved lemon rind and a sprinkle of ras el hanout. The hummus can be stored in the refrigerator in a covered container for 4 or 5 days.

NOTE

If you prefer to cook your own chickpeas, start with ¾ cup [135 g] dried chickpeas. To speed cooking, you can presoak them in water to cover by 1 in [2.5 cm] for 2 or 3 hours. For presoaked, bring the water to a boil, lower the heat, and simmer for about 25 minutes, or until tender. For dried, add enough water to cover by 1 in [2.5 cm], bring to a boil, lower the heat, and simmer for about 1 hour, until tender. When you drain them, save at least ¼ cup [60 ml] of the cooking liquid.

SPICED SALT
page 157

Preserved Lemons à la Paula Wolfert

I first learned how to make these powerful flavoring agents from famed cookbook author Paula Wolfert, who was among the first to introduce them to cooks and diners in the United States. When you make your own at home you have more control over the end product than buying them ready-made. Preserved lemons get stronger, more pungent, and softer the longer they sit at room temp, so once they are ready, store them in the fridge. Refrigerating the lemons also allows me to use far less salt than in traditional recipes, which had to stand up to desert heat, so both the flesh and the rind are usable. I always opt for organic fruit, since you will be eating the peel.

8 lemons, preferably organic

6 Tbsp [110 g] fine sea salt

2 thin dried hot peppers, such as Thai bird's eye chiles

Juice 4 of the lemons. Cut an *X* into the stem end of the remaining 4 lemons, cutting about halfway through each. Stuff 1 Tbsp of salt into the slits in each lemon.

Sprinkle 1 Tbsp of salt into the bottom of a wide-mouthed quart jar, then arrange the 4 salted lemons on top. Pour the juice into the jar, then sprinkle the remaining 1 Tbsp of salt on top. Weight down the lemons (a smaller lid works well) and press down to get the juices flowing. Let stand overnight, then press on the lemons again to release more juice. The lemons should be fully submerged (if not, add more lemon juice or water). Let the lemons stand undisturbed at room temperature, ensuring they remain covered in juice.

After 4 days, cut off a small piece of rind to test. If the lemons are ready they will be very aromatic, slightly softened, intensely flavored, and a bit salty, like a pickle. If not, reweight the lemons and let them continue to steep in the brine, testing every day or so. They will usually be fully preserved after 7 days, sooner if the weather is warm. Cover the jar and refrigerate for up to 3 months.

TEN MORE WAYS TO USE PRESERVED LEMONS

·1·

Preserved Lemon Purée

The easiest way to use preserved lemons is also the simplest: Quarter 1 or 2 preserved lemons and pick out any seeds. Purée the quarters in a food processor until smooth. Transfer to a tightly covered jar and use by the spoonful to season soups, stews, dressings, and potato salads. It will keep for 1 month.

·2·

Summer Vinaigrette

Stir 1 Tbsp of chopped shallot into ¼ cup [60 ml] of white wine vinegar. Add 2 or 3 Tbsp of finely chopped fresh summer herbs—whatever you have on hand or are growing in the garden—mint, chervil, parsley, chives, and basil are all great. Season with ¾ tsp of salt and 1 Tbsp of finely minced preserved lemon rind. Slowly beat in ¾ cup [180 ml] of extra-virgin olive oil until emulsified.

·3·

Citrusy Pilaf

Rice and grain pilafs can taste a bit flat. For a more lively take, stir 2 tsp of very finely minced preserved lemon rind and 2 to 3 Tbsp of chopped fresh dill into 2 cups [200 to 400 g] of freshly cooked grains. Add chopped cooked shrimp or chicken and some chopped green olives or cubes of feta for a one-dish meal that is good warm or at room temperature.

·4·

Broiled Fish Piquante

Chop the rind of ½ preserved lemon and add to 1 cup [240 g] of labneh, 1 Tbsp of Dijon mustard, and 1 or 2 dashes of liquid harissa or other hot sauce. Spread a thick layer on a fillet of striped bass, cod, or other firm white fish and broil until the fish flakes and the topping is browned and bubbly, 5 to 7 minutes, or until cooked through. Sprinkle with chopped parsley or mint and serve hot.

·5·

Preserved Lemon Compound Butter

Compound butters like this one are a quick way to elevate the everyday to something a bit more special with just a trip to the freezer. Keep a couple of varieties stashed away, labeled with date and flavoring. Mash together ½ cup [110 g] (1 stick) of unsalted butter with the finely minced rind of 1 preserved lemon and ¼ cup [10 g] of chopped flat-leaf parsley. Form into a log and chill or freeze. This is enough to top 10 to 12 servings of fish, asparagus, or chicken cutlets.

·6·

Lemon-Ginger Simple Syrup

Combine 1 cup [200 g] of sugar and 1 cup [240 ml] of water in a saucepan. Add the rind of 1 preserved lemon and a 2 in [5 cm] piece of fresh ginger, peeled and chopped, and bring to a simmer. Cook until the sugar has completely dissolved, then set aside to infuse and cool. Strain the syrup into a glass jar and store in the refrigerator, then use as a bar mixer with vodka or tequila, a splash of soda, and a mint leaf.

·7·

Spicy Seafood Dipper

Do tartar sauce one better with this sprightly, lighter mixture: combine 1 cup [240 g] of mayonnaise with 1 Tbsp of finely chopped preserved lemon rind, 1 Tbsp liquid harissa, and salt. It's especially tasty with fried seafood like clams, oysters, or calamari, and also great with grilled or steamed shrimp.

·8·

Poaching Liquid

When you are preparing seafood for a cold salad or seafood platter, use this lemony court bouillon for an extra burst of flavor. To 2 qt [2 L] of water, add 1 whole hot chile, 3 or 4 stems of cilantro, ½ white onion, 2 sliced garlic cloves, and the flesh of ½ preserved lemon plus salt. Bring to a simmer, add your seafood, and cook gently until firm and just opaque. Toss the cooked seafood with the slivered rind of the preserved lemon, chopped celery, chopped parsley, and a splash of extra-virgin olive oil.

·9·

Rich Risotto

Give your risotto a dairy-free burst of flavor by substituting 2 Tbsp of finely chopped preserved lemon peel (or 1 Tbsp of puréed preserved lemon) for the usual Parmesan cheese. It is especially good with a vegetarian risotto of asparagus, fava beans, green garlic, ramps, leeks, or snap peas. Pescatarians can add shrimp or scallops.

·10·

And Don't Throw Out the Pulp!

Pick out and discard any seeds or stringy membranes, then purée until smooth. Transfer to a pitcher, sweeten with agave nectar or simple syrup, then mix with club soda for a subtle and sophisticated lemonade.

Crostini with Green Almond Relish

Green almonds are a seasonal specialty with a distinctive crisp, fresh flavor—a taste like spring, which is when they are available. They come and go in a matter of weeks, so if you happen to come across them, snatch them up or you will miss them! You use the entire soft nut, both the fuzzy pod and the kernel inside. To make the most of their delicate taste and texture, I like to serve this relish on a small crouton atop a dollop of fresh ricotta cheese with cocktails; you could also pair it with any mild cheese or even poached fish.

SERVES 6 TO 8 AS AN APPETIZER

1 cup [140 g] fresh green almonds (about 6 ounces), sliced

2 garlic cloves, sliced

1 dried chile, such as Thai or Tabasco

½ cup [120 ml] extra-virgin olive oil

1 cup [140 g] pitted olives, such as Castelvetrano, Sicilian, or Kalamata, sliced

2 Tbsp caperberries, sliced, or small whole capers

2 tsp finely chopped preserved lemon rind, store-bought or homemade (page 43)

¼ cup [10 g] chopped parsley

1 baguette

1 cup [240 g] fresh ricotta cheese, at room temperature

Preheat the oven to 350°F [180°C].

Combine the almonds, garlic, and chile in a saucepan and cover with the oil. Bring to a simmer over medium heat, then cook gently over low heat for 8 to 10 minutes, or until the almonds are becoming tender. Remove from the heat.

While the mixture is still hot, stir in the olives, caperberries, and preserved lemon rind. Cover the pan and set aside for 10 minutes. Stir in the parsley.

While the flavors of the chutney bloom, cut the baguette into ½ in [12 mm] diagonal slices and arrange on a rimmed baking sheet. Toast the slices, turning once, until lightly toasted, about 12 minutes.

To serve, spread each piece of toast with 2 Tbsp of ricotta. Top with a generous tablespoon of the almond chutney and serve warm.

Turmeric-Pickled Cauliflower

Not only do these tangy morsels taste bright, they *are* bright, a brilliant saffron yellow that will do wonders for a grain bowl in the winter months when the options at the produce counter are limited. I also love to tuck them into sandwiches or add a little bowl of them to an antipasto platter, much as you would serve jardiniere with olives and cheese.

MAKES 2 QT [2 L]

2 Tbsp whole black peppercorns

1 Tbsp fennel seeds

2 tsp mustard seeds, yellow or black or a combination of both

1 tsp coriander seeds

2 small dried hot chiles, such as Thai bird's eye chiles, or 1 tsp dried red pepper flakes

¾ cup [150 g] sugar

¼ cup [75 g] fine sea salt

2 tsp ground turmeric or 1 tsp ground turmeric plus a 1 in [2.5 cm] piece fresh turmeric, cut into thin coins

6 cups [1.4 L] cider vinegar

6 medium garlic cloves, thickly sliced

1 sweet onion, thinly sliced

1 large head cauliflower, cored and broken into florets

5 baby sweet peppers, sliced into rings

Toast the peppercorns, fennel seeds, mustard seeds, coriander seeds, and the chiles in a dry skillet, shaking frequently, for 2 minutes, or until fragrant. Transfer to a saucepan. Add the sugar, salt, and turmeric and mix well, then stir in the vinegar. Add 1 cup [240 ml] water and bring to a boil.

While the brine heats, put the garlic, onion, cauliflower, and peppers in a large, deep heatproof bowl (a tempered glass bowl works well). Pour the boiling liquid over the vegetables and put a plate on top to keep the vegetables completely submerged in the brine; weight the plate with a heavy can if needed. Pickle at room temperature for 24 hours, then transfer to jars and refrigerate for up to 4 weeks. Remove the garlic cloves after a few days, as they will discolor.

Classic Fattoush

Fattoush, the bread salad that is Syria's answer to tabbouleh, is a dish at the heart of every Syrian and Lebanese household, and sumac is at the heart of every good fattoush, serving to lift and brighten the fresh vegetables. My mom's family is from Syria, and this salad was on our table for every big event as far back as I can remember. We still serve it at all traditional family gatherings, and it is a crowd pleaser. The crispy pita chips soak up the lemony sumac dressing and contribute great texture, but don't add them in advance, as they will become too soft.

SERVES 6 TO 8

½ cup [70 g] chopped Persian cucumbers
2 romaine hearts, chopped
½ cup [70 g] halved grape tomatoes
½ cup [60 g] chopped celery
½ cup [60 g] chopped yellow bell pepper
½ cup [60 g] chopped red bell pepper
½ cup [70 g] chopped red onion
½ cup [60 g] chopped radishes
½ cup [20 g] chopped fresh parsley
2 Tbsp chopped fresh mint

½ cup [120 ml] extra-virgin olive oil
2 Tbsp fresh lemon juice
2 Tbsp red wine vinegar
1 garlic clove, minced
2 tsp sumac, plus more for garnish
1 tsp sea salt
½ tsp freshly ground black pepper
½ tsp Aleppo pepper
2 cups [90 g] pita chips (recipe follows)

Combine the cucumbers, romaine, tomatoes, celery, bell peppers, onions, and radishes in a large bowl and toss to mix well. Sprinkle the parsley and mint on top.

In a small bowl, whisk together the oil, lemon juice, vinegar, garlic, sumac, salt, and black and Aleppo peppers. Drizzle over the salad and toss gently to combine. Top with the pita chips and a sprinkle of sumac and serve immediately.

HOMEMADE PITA CHIPS

Middle Easterners insist their pita breads be fresh, fresh, fresh, which is why we have them delivered daily. Any we don't sell by day's end are recycled into salads like fattoush, ground into crumbs for breading, or baked into chips. To make your own pita chips, heat the oven to 325°F [160°C]. Separate each pita bread into two layers and cut each round into ten or twelve wedges. Spread in a single layer on a large baking sheet or two and toast, turning once, until crisp, dry, and golden in places, about 20 minutes. Store in an airtight container for up to 4 weeks.

Summer Quinoa Salad with Shrimp

Quinoa is a great choice for room-temperature salads because the grains stay separate and fluffy even after they are dressed. At the store we use it to make this substantial entrée salad. It has plenty of protein thanks to both the quinoa and the black beans as well as the shrimp, and the lime juice and Aleppo pepper in the dressing keep things lively. This version has a bit of a southwestern vibe, but you could easily swap out the cilantro for basil or mint and substitute olives for the black beans to take it in a Mediterranean direction. Another plus: it tastes even better made ahead and chilled for up to 24 hours. Once the weather turns warm, this is one of our top sellers, week in, week out.

SERVES 6 TO 8

Quinoa Salad

1 cup [180 g] quinoa, white or red

1½ lb [680 g] cooked small or medium shrimp

½ cup [70 g] chopped red onion

1 medium green bell pepper, cored, seeded, and chopped

1 medium red bell pepper, cored, seeded, and chopped

One 15-ounce [320 g] can black beans, drained and rinsed

2 cups [280 g] corn kernels, either frozen and thawed or steamed and cut off the cob

2 cups [320 g] cherry tomatoes, quartered

¼ cup [10 g] chopped fresh parsley

¼ cup [10 g] chopped fresh cilantro

Dressing

2 to 3 Tbsp extra-virgin olive oil

2 Tbsp fresh lemon juice

1 Tbsp fresh lime juice

2 tsp Aleppo pepper, plus more for garnish

1 tsp minced garlic

½ tsp salt

½ tsp freshly ground black pepper

½ tsp ground cumin

To make the quinoa salad: Combine the quinoa and 2 cups [480 ml] of water in a saucepan and bring to a boil. Reduce the heat, cover the pan, and simmer until the water is absorbed and the grains are tender but not mushy, about 15 minutes. Uncover and let cool.

While the quinoa cools, prep the remaining salad ingredients and combine in a large bowl.

To make the dressing: Combine the dressing ingredients in a jar and shake until well combined.

Pour the dressing over the shrimp and veggies and stir to coat. Add the quinoa and toss again, distributing the vegetables and shrimp evenly. Cover and refrigerate for at least 6 hours and up to 24 to allow the flavors to marry. Serve sprinkled with a bit of Aleppo pepper for color and a little kick.

Everyday Swiss Chard

Maybe we should have called this *every day* Swiss chard, because at our house we eat simple steamed greens—chard, spinach, mustard greens, kale, or escarole—with nearly all our meals. Feta and a shake of sumac lift the flavor without masking the essential earthiness of garden-fresh leafy vegetables, and this is equally good hot or at room temperature. Substitute any greens you like best for the chard, and make this your go-to vegetable side, too (pictured on page 54).

SERVES 6

2 lb [910 g] Swiss chard, either green or rainbow
¼ cup [60 ml] extra-virgin olive oil
6 garlic cloves, sliced
1 tsp fine sea salt
1 tsp Aleppo pepper
½ cup [60 g] imported feta cheese, diced or crumbled
1 tsp sumac
½ tsp Aleppo pepper flakes (optional)

Wash the chard thoroughly but do not dry. Cut the stems from the leaves and cut the stems into ½ in [12 mm] pieces. Keep the stems and leaves separate.

Heat the oil in a large skillet over medium heat. Add the chard stems, garlic, salt, and Aleppo pepper and sauté until the stems are softened and the garlic is fragrant, about 4 minutes. Add the chard leaves and sauté a few minutes longer to wilt a bit and coat them with the flavored oil.

Add ¼ cup [60 ml] of water to the pan, cover, and cook until the leaves are completely softened, about 7 minutes. Transfer to a serving bowl and top with the cheese. Sprinkle with the sumac and red pepper flakes, if using. Serve warm or at room temperature.

Pickled Turnips

You will find a jar of pickled vegetables like these (pictured on page 30) in every Middle Eastern household, ready to add a tart, bright contrast to savory foods like falafel or shawarma. If you choose tender young turnips, you won't need to peel them, and they also pickle more quickly. When I am lucky enough to find golf ball–size Japanese hakurei turnips in my CSA box, I toss them directly into the brine, and they are ready to eat in about 12 hours! They last virtually indefinitely in the refrigerator but will continue to pickle as they stand; I think the texture and flavor are best when eaten within a couple of weeks.

MAKES 2 QT [2 L]

1⅓ cups [320 ml] white vinegar
¼ cup [75 g] fine sea salt
2 lb [910 g] small white turnips, unpeeled
1 small beet, about 4 oz [113 g]

In a pitcher, combine the vinegar and salt. Add 2¾ cups [660 ml] of water and stir until the salt is completely dissolved.

Cut the turnips and beets into wedges and place in a large bowl. Pour the salt and vinegar brine over all, making sure all the vegetables are submerged. (If necessary, make an additional batch of brine using the same proportions.) Place a plate on top and weight with a can or other heavy object to keep the vegetables covered in the brine. Let stand uncovered at room temperature for 3 to 5 days, or until the turnips have turned light pink. Transfer to tightly covered jars and store in the refrigerator for up to 1 month.

BARLEY PILAF WITH PRESERVED LEMON AND GARLIC RELISH
page 60
TURMERIC-PICKLED CAULIFLOWER
page 47
CHICKEN KEBABS WITH TOUM
page 71
EVERYDAY SWISS CHARD
page 52
ZA'ATAR BREAD
page 98

PICKLED TURNIPS
page 53

CLASSIC FATTOUSH
page 49

Summer Squash with Pomegranate Glaze

When the summer squash is coming in fast and furious, this is a great way to use the overflow and a lot more interesting than the usual grilled squash slabs. But don't limit it to summer spreads; I find it's just as good made in the broiler, and it adds a bit of zip to heavier winter meals. Cousa is a pale green squash that resembles a stripy zucchini; zucchini is a fine substitute as long as you choose young specimens with relatively few seeds.

SERVES 4

⅓ cup [80 ml] extra-virgin olive oil

1 tsp crushed fresh garlic

½ tsp flaky sea salt

½ tsp freshly ground black pepper

½ tsp Urfa pepper or Aleppo pepper

5 medium (2 lb [910 g]) light green squash (cousa) or young zucchini, cut into ¾ in [2 cm] diagonal slabs

2 Tbsp pomegranate molasses

2 Tbsp fresh mint leaves, coarsely chopped

Whisk together the oil, garlic, salt, and peppers in a large bowl. Add the squash and turn to coat in the marinade. Marinate at room temperature for ½ hour or in the refrigerator for up to 12 hours.

Prepare a grill or preheat the broiler. If grilling, place the squash pieces over the hot part of the grill and cook until tender and browned on both sides, turning occasionally, about 10 minutes.

If broiling, line a baking sheet with foil and arrange the squash in a single layer. Broil, turning once after 3 to 4 minutes, until browned and tender on both sides.

Arrange the squash on a platter and drizzle with the pomegranate molasses. Sprinkle with the mint and more flaky salt.

Pomegranate-Roasted Beets with Goat Cheese

Pomegranate molasses brings out the natural sweetness of beets while tempering the earthy flavor that some people don't love. I like to serve this salad on a bed of lightly steamed beet greens because (a) it's a nice textural contrast, (b) it looks really pretty, (c) the greens are full of good nutrients that shouldn't go to waste, and (d) they are free! How many more reasons do you need? I always prefer to serve beets in their skins, as they contain lots of flavor and nutrients as well, but if you do the same, make sure to choose small, tender beets. The skins of older, bigger beets are too tough. This looks best made with a mix of yellow, red, and Chioggia beets.

SERVES 6 TO 8

Pomegranate Vinaigrette

¾ cup [180 ml] extra-virgin olive oil

¼ cup [80 g] pomegranate molasses

½ tsp kosher salt

½ tsp freshly ground black pepper

1 tsp Aleppo pepper

Beets

3 bunches small young beets with greens (about 12 beets)

2 Tbsp fresh thyme leaves or 1 tsp dried

½ cup [90 g] fresh pomegranate seeds

4 oz [115 g] firm fresh goat cheese

4 or 5 chives, chopped

Preheat the oven to 350°F [180°C].

To make the pomegranate vinaigrette: Whisk together the oil, pomegranate molasses, salt, and black and Aleppo peppers.

To make the beets: Separate the beets from the greens and wash both well, scrubbing the beets with a brush. Place the whole beets on sheets of heavy-duty foil (if using a mix of varieties, use a separate sheet for each color). Drizzle each pile of beets with a few tablespoons of the vinaigrette and sprinkle with the thyme. Fold the foil up and over them to seal tightly. Put the packets on a rimmed baking sheet and roast for about 1 hour, or until the tip of a knife pierces a beet easily. Let the beets cool in their packets.

While the beets are roasting, cut the beet greens and about 3 in [7.5 cm] of the stems crosswise in thin strips. Bring ½ in [12 mm] water to a boil in a saucepan and add the greens. Cook until just wilted, about 2 minutes, turning with tongs to ensure they cook evenly. Drain the greens and arrange them on a large platter.

Once the beets are cool, cut off the pointed tips and stem ends, and cut the beets into wedges, leaving the skins on. Arrange them over the beet greens. Sprinkle with the pomegranate seeds and crumble the goat cheese over all. Drizzle with the remaining pomegranate vinaigrette and garnish with the chives.

Barley Pilaf with Preserved Lemon and Garlic Relish

A mixture of fresh garlic, preserved lemon, and bell peppers stewed together in oil adds a ton of flavor to a simple stovetop pilaf (pictured on page 54) made with barley, a grain that is not seen often enough on tables in the United States. The remaining relish can be enjoyed on slices of toasted country bread, with or without a schmear of mild goat cheese.

SERVES 6

Relish

1 cup [100 g] sliced garlic from about 2 whole heads of garlic

1¼ cups [300 ml] extra-virgin olive oil

½ cup [70 g] pitted Kalamata olives, sliced

¼ cup [35 g] finely diced sun-dried tomatoes

¼ cup [45 g] drained small capers

¼ cup [65 g] small-diced preserved lemon, rind only, store-bought or homemade (page 43)

¼ cup [55 g] finely diced roasted red peppers

¼ cup [35 g] currants

½ cup [20 g] chopped fresh parsley

Fine sea salt and freshly ground black pepper

Pilaf

2 cups [400 g] pearled barley

4 cups [960 ml] vegetable or chicken stock

To make the relish: Put the garlic in a heavy saucepan and cover with the oil. Cook over low heat until the garlic softens, about 10 minutes. Remove from the heat and add the olives, sun-dried tomatoes, capers, preserved lemon, roasted peppers, and currants. Mix well and set aside to cool to room temperature. When cool, add ¼ cup [10 g] of the parsley along with a sprinkling of sea salt and 1 tsp black pepper. Adjust the seasoning and transfer to a jar, making sure all the ingredients are submerged in oil. If not, add a few more tablespoons of oil. (The relish can be made 3 or 4 days in advance and refrigerated. Bring to room temperature before using.)

To make the pilaf: Drain 2 Tbsp of oil from the relish and heat the oil in a large saucepan. Add the barley and toast, stirring, until coated with oil and fragrant, about 2 minutes. Add the stock and bring to a boil. Reduce the heat and simmer until the stock has been absorbed and the barley is tender, 25 to 30 minutes.

Drain off any remaining liquid from the barley and add 1½ cups [360 g] of the relish. Toss well. Add the remaining ¼ cup [10 g] of parsley and toss again. Serve warm or at room temperature.

Grilled Whole Snapper with Preserved Lemon Vinaigrette

Don't be intimidated by the prospect of working with a whole fish. Believe it or not, they are much simpler to cook than fragile fillets—and also less likely to overcook. Plus, a whole fish just looks so badass when you bring it to the table. It's also a snap to double the recipe to serve 4 or more. Practice filleting the fish tableside with family before you attempt it in front of company, but even if you don't remove the fillets completely intact, rest assured that every little morsel will be delicious. Whole black sea bass or a pink snapper would be great in this dish as well; just choose whichever looks freshest and has bright, unclouded eyes. This is particularly good with asparagus that was grilled alongside the fish and bathed in the vinaigrette. Note: the vinaigrette can be made 1 or 2 days in advance; the fish can be stuffed and marinated in the refrigerator a few hours before you need to grill it.

SERVES 2 TO 3

Preserved Lemon Vinaigrette

2 preserved lemons, store-bought or homemade (page 43)

1 cup [240 ml] extra-virgin olive oil

2 tsp harissa spices or 1 tsp Aleppo pepper

1 garlic clove, minced

1 tsp sea salt

½ tsp ground coriander

½ tsp ground fennel

½ cup [20 g] chopped fresh parsley, plus more for garnish

½ cup [20 g] chopped fresh cilantro, plus more for garnish

Snapper

1 whole red snapper, 2 to 3 lb [0.9 to 1.4 kg], cleaned and scaled

½ small red onion, cut into slices

1 Fresno chile, cut into slices

Aleppo pepper, for garnish

Flaky sea salt, for garnish

Continued

To make the preserved lemon vinaigrette: Scoop out and discard the flesh from 1 of the preserved lemons and mince the rind finely. Place in a medium bowl with the oil, harissa, garlic, salt, coriander, and fennel. Add ¼ cup [10 g] each of the parsley and cilantro and toss to combine. Set the vinaigrette aside at room temperature or refrigerate for up to 2 days; bring to room temperature and stir to recombine before serving.

To make the snapper: Slice the remaining preserved lemon thinly. Stuff the cavity of the fish with the lemon slices, the remaining ¼ cup [10 g] each of the parsley and cilantro, and a few slices of red onion and chile. Place in a large roasting pan and drizzle with half of the vinaigrette, reserving the rest for serving. Turn the fish to coat the outside well and set aside to marinate at room temperature for 1 hour, or cover with plastic and refrigerate for up to a few hours.

Preheat a grill, creating a hot zone on one side and a medium-hot zone on the other. Oil the grill grates well using tongs and a paper towel saturated with oil. Place the fish on the hot side of the grill, cover the grill, and cook until the skin is well browned and crisp, 10 to 12 minutes. Carefully turn and cook on the second side for another 10 minutes; don't worry if some of the skin pulls away when you turn the fish.

When the fish is beautifully charred, move it to the medium-hot side of grill, cover the grill again, and cook for 10 to 15 minutes longer, or until the flesh flakes easily away from the bone but is still moist. Transfer to a serving platter and drizzle with the remaining vinaigrette. Serve hot, sprinkled with Aleppo pepper, flakly sea salt, parsley, and cilantro.

SERVING TIP

To portion the fish, use a sharp chef's knife to make a vertical cut just behind the head and another right before the tail, cutting down to the bones but not all the way through the fish. Holding your knife parallel to the fish and pressing it against the spine as you go, cut smoothly from tail to head, separating the flesh from the bones. Use a spatula to lift off the fillet in one or two pieces and transfer to serving plates. Now that you have exposed the skeleton, grasp the tail and gently lift off the bones and head in one piece, exposing the remaining, boneless (!) fillet. Easy!

Grilled Sea Scallops with Charred Scallions and Sumac

Sumac is my go-to spice when I need to brighten up a dish. Its tart, almost lemony flavor is an ideal complement to any fish or poultry that finds its way onto my grill. While scallops are quite delicate, I find that the extreme heat of grilling brings out their sweetness even better than pan frying, giving them a lovely caramelized crust that can stand up to this earthy puréed sauce.

SERVES 4

Sea Scallops

1 lb [455 g] sea scallops
2 Tbsp extra-virgin olive oil
1 Tbsp ground sumac
1 garlic clove, minced
½ tsp sea salt
½ tsp freshly ground black pepper
½ tsp Aleppo pepper

Scallion Sumac Sauce

1 bunch scallions, trimmed
2 garlic cloves
¼ cup [10 g] chopped fresh parsley
2 Tbsp extra-virgin olive oil
Juice of 1 lemon (about 2 Tbsp)
1 tsp ground sumac
1 tsp Aleppo pepper
½ tsp sea salt

¼ cup [10 g] chopped fresh cilantro or dill
1 bunch chives, with chive blossoms if in season, chopped

To make the scallops: Dry the scallops thoroughly and use a sharp knife to pull off the tough strips of muscle on the side of each. Combine the oil, sumac, minced garlic, salt, and black and Aleppo peppers in a medium bowl. Add the scallops and toss to coat, then cover with plastic and refrigerate for 15 to 45 minutes.

When ready to serve, prepare a barbecue grill or preheat a ridged grill pan until very hot. Use an oil-saturated paper towel and tongs to oil the grates thoroughly. Thread the scallops onto pairs of skewers (this keeps them from spinning).

To make the sauce: When the fire is hot, place the scallions and the 2 garlic cloves in a grill basket and grill, turning often, until they start to char in a few spots, 5 or 6 minutes. Transfer the scallions and garlic to a blender and add the parsley, oil, lemon juice, sumac, Aleppo pepper, and salt. Purée until smooth, then transfer to a small bowl.

Place the scallops over the hottest part of the fire and sear on one side until they are nicely marked and release easily, about 3 minutes. Turn and grill the second side just until barely cooked through, 1 or 2 minutes longer. Do not overcook.

Transfer the scallops to a platter and sprinkle with the chopped herbs. Serve with the sauce.

Sheet Pan Chicken with Sumac and Winter Squash

Herby and garlicky, with a bright jolt of sumac, this is everything you want in a one-pan meal. Squash, which can be a bit bland, absorbs so much flavor from the chicken and herbs. Kabocha and delicata squash are good options because they doesn't need to be peeled, but acorn squash or butternut work, too. I sometimes use a couple of different kinds for visual interest. Either way, you'll have folks wanting to eat directly from the pan the second you take this out of the oven!

SERVES 6

4 lb [1.8 kg] chicken pieces, any combination

3 Tbsp sumac

1 tsp fine sea salt

½ tsp dried thyme

½ tsp dried oregano

2 garlic cloves, grated with a rasp

1 cup [240 ml] extra-virgin olive oil

1 kabocha squash (or ½ kabocha squash and 1 acorn squash)

1 bunch fresh oregano or thyme

3 red onions, peeled and quartered

1 lemon, thinly sliced

Pat the chicken pieces dry and, if you are using breasts, cut each in half to make 2 smaller pieces.

Whisk together 2 Tbsp of the sumac with the salt, dried thyme, dried oregano, and garlic in a large bowl. Add the oil and stir until well blended. Add the chicken pieces to the bowl, turning to coat them with the mixture, then cover with plastic wrap and refrigerate for 1 to 2 hours or up to overnight.

Preheat the oven to 350°F [180°C]. Cut the squash in half through the stem end and remove the seeds. Cut the squash into ½ in [12 mm] thick slices and arrange them in a single layer (or overlapping slightly) on a large baking sheet. Scatter the herb sprigs on top, reserving a few for serving. Arrange the chicken on top of the squash, skin-side up, leaving a bit of room between the pieces and tucking in red onion chunks here and there. Dot the lemon slices around the pan. Pour any remaining marinade over everything.

Roast in the center of the oven for 30 minutes. Baste the chicken and squash with pan juices and continue to cook for 15 minutes, or until the skin is browned and the chicken is cooked through. Sprinkle with the remaining 1 Tbsp of sumac and the reserved herb sprigs. Serve directly from the baking sheet.

TEN MORE WAYS TO USE

SUMAC

·1·

Onion Relish

Halve and thinly slice 1 small red onion and soak overnight in water to soften. The next day, drain the onions and stir in ½ cup [20 g] of chopped fresh parsley and 2 Tbsp of sumac. Season with ½ tsp of salt. Store in the refrigerator for up to 1 week. This is like a Middle Eastern gremolata, a simple way to brighten up meat dishes, especially those that are rich or heavy, but I also use it to top sandwiches, dips and spreads (it's great on guacamole!), and bean soups.

·2·

All-Purpose Chicken Marinade

Season ½ cup [120 ml] of extra-virgin olive oil with 1 Tbsp of ground sumac; 2 garlic cloves, minced or grated; and 2 Tbsp each of chopped fresh marjoram or parsley and fresh oregano (or fresh za'atar). Store in a covered jar in the refrigerator for up to 2 weeks. Use it to marinate chicken pieces before tossing them on the grill; rub it onto a whole chicken before roasting, or drizzle it onto a carved rotisserie chicken.

·3·

Bagel Topper

Not a cream cheese lover? Brush a halved bagel with melted butter and sprinkle with sumac. Crisp in a 350°F [180°C] oven for 15 minutes, or until golden. Serve topped with slices of smoked salmon and a sprinkle of chives or parsley.

·4·

Brighter Braises

Many midwinter stews benefit from a jolt of uplifting freshness. Stir 1 or 2 Tbsp of sumac into your osso buco, pot roast, or veal stew when they are about 15 minutes shy of done to allow the flavors to meld.

·5·

Fresh Fish Grill

Use this with fish of any kind; it's especially nice with a fattier fish like bluefish or mackerel, which can stand up to the strong flavors. Stir together ½ cup [5 g] of chopped dill or fennel fronds, ½ cup [120 ml] of orange juice, ¼ cup [60 ml] of extra-virgin olive oil, 2 Tbsp of ground sumac, and 1 tsp of salt in a bowl until combined. Set aside ½ cup of the mixture for serving and use the rest to marinate a whole fish. Stuff the fish with a few slices of Cara Cara orange, grill until done, and serve with the reserved marinade on the side for drizzling.

·6·

Tangy Chicken Salad

To give some zest to a salad without making the binder watery, mix ¾ cup [180 g] of labneh or unflavored Greek yogurt with 1 Tbsp of ground sumac, ½ cup [60 g] of diced fennel or celery, ½ cup [70 g] of diced cucumber, ½ cup [70 g] of dried cranberries (optional), 1 Tbsp of chopped parsley or mint, and 2 cups [250 g] of cubed cooked chicken. Serve atop lettuce or in a pita sprinkled with more sumac.

·7·

Margs, My Way

Sumac adds so much more to a classic margarita than a plain rim of salt. Mix 3 Tbsp of ground sumac with 2 Tbsp of coarse salt on a shallow plate. Rub the rim of a tall glass with the cut surface of a lime and dip it in the sumac mixture to coat. Set aside for a few minutes to set, then fill with ice and your favorite margarita mixture.

·8·

Sumac Eggs

For a carb- and guilt-free take on eggs Florentine, poach 1 or 2 eggs and serve atop a mound of steamed spinach, chard, or other greens. Sprinkle liberally with ground sumac, flaky salt like Maldon, and a few grinds of fresh black pepper.

·9·

Cheesy Crackers

Every cook who entertains should have a log of these slice-and-bake treats in the freezer for unexpected guests. Mix together 1 cup [140 g] of all-purpose flour; ½ cup [70 g] of cornmeal; 1 cup [80 g] of grated white Cheddar; 4 Tbsp [60 g] of cold butter, grated; 2 Tbsp of ground sumac; 1 tsp of salt; and ½ tsp of Aleppo pepper. Mix to combine, then add 2 Tbsp cold water. Form into a mass, then roll in plastic wrap to form a 2 in [5 cm] diameter log. Freeze until needed, then slice ½ in [12 mm] thick and bake on a lined baking sheet at 375°F [190°C] for 15 minutes, or until golden.

·10·

"Lemony" Potato Wedges

Toss wedges of Yukon gold potatoes with olive oil, black pepper, sumac, and a few sliced garlic cloves. Spread on a baking sheet and roast at 425°F [220°C] for 20 to 25 minutes, or until the edges are crispy, turning once or twice.

Chicken Kebabs with Toum

Even those of us who cook for a living resort to takeout now and then, and when I do, I invariably wind up grabbing a rotisserie chicken at Karam, a Middle Eastern deli-grill near our home in Brooklyn. The chicken is always perfectly cooked and juicy, but the real draw is their addictive toum. Native to Lebanon, toum is an egg-free cousin of aioli, with a much more potent punch of garlic. It keeps well in the refrigerator, so don't be tempted to halve the recipe; you'll find plenty of ways to use any extra, from salads to seafood to sandwiches. Leftover chicken makes a perfect lunch folded into a flatbread with some lettuce, onions, a bit of pickled vegetable, and, of course, plenty of that garlicky toum.

SERVES 6 TO 8

Chicken

2½ to 3 lb [1.2 to 1.4 kg] boneless, skinless chicken breasts, cut into 1 in [2.5 cm] chunks

½ cup chopped fresh parsley, plus more for garnish

¼ cup extra-virgin olive oil

2 garlic cloves, crushed

1 tsp fine sea salt

1 tsp Aleppo pepper, plus more for garnish

1 tsp smoked paprika

½ tsp ground cumin

½ tsp ground black pepper

Toum

¼ cup [60 ml] fresh lemon juice

2 Tbsp crushed fresh garlic

1 tsp fine sea salt

2 cups [480 ml] extra-virgin olive oil

1 lb [455 g] red or yellow baby bell peppers or full-size peppers, cut into quarters

2 cups [320 g] cherry or grape tomatoes

To make the chicken: Put the chicken chunks in a large bowl. Add the parsley, extra-virgin olive oil, garlic, salt, Aleppo pepper, smoked paprika, cumin, and black pepper. Mix well, cover, and refrigerate for at least 2 hours and up to 12 hours.

To make the toum: Put the lemon juice, garlic, and salt in a food processor. With the motor running, slowly pour in the oil in a steady stream until fully emulsified and fluffy like mayonnaise. Store in the refrigerator in a tightly covered container.

When ready to cook, preheat a barbecue grill, ridged grill pan, or the broiler until very hot. Wipe the grill grates or grill pan with an oil-soaked paper towel to prevent sticking. Thread the chicken chunks onto long metal skewers, alternating with the bell peppers and tomatoes.

Grill the skewers over high heat, turning once, until well browned and cooked through, 10 to 12 minutes total. Garnish with parsley and Aleppo pepper, and serve with lots of toum.

Spatchcocked Chicken with Preserved Lemon Marinade

A Middle Eastern take on a beloved classic, chicken under a brick, this is equally enticing cooked over a hot grill or on a stovetop grill pan. Many grocery stores now sell whole chickens with the backbone removed and flattened for grilling. If yours doesn't, use a sharp pair of shears to cut along either side of the backbone to flatten it, or simply substitute leg-and-thigh quarters. Marinate this overnight if you have the foresight; if not, 30 minutes at room temperature will still impart a lovely herbaceous and citrus flavor.

SERVES 4

1 cup [240 ml] extra-virgin olive oil

1 Tbsp Aleppo pepper, plus more for garnish

1 Tbsp Preserved Lemon Purée (page 44)

4 or 5 sprigs fresh lemon thyme or Greek oregano, plus more for garnish

1 tsp minced garlic

Freshly ground black pepper

Fine sea salt

One 3 to 3½ lb [1.4 to 1.6 kg] chicken,
backbone removed and flattened, or 4 whole leg quarters

1 lemon, cut in wedges, for serving

Combine the oil, Aleppo pepper, lemon purée, herbs, garlic, and black pepper in a mixing bowl or sealable plastic bag. Adjust the salt; depending on your preserved lemons, you may not need to add any.

Add the chicken and turn to coat with the marinade. Cover or seal and refrigerate overnight or let stand at room temperature for 30 to 45 minutes.

When ready to cook, heat a barbecue grill or ridged grill pan until very hot. Place the chicken on the grill, skin side down, and place a heavy skillet on top. Weight the skillet with a few cans or a brick to ensure the chicken is well-pressed and making contact with the grill grates. Grill for 15 minutes, or until the skin is crisp and nicely marked.

Turn the chicken, move it slightly away from the hottest part of the grill (or reduce the heat to medium), and cover. Cook until done, another 15 to 20 minutes, or until an instant-read thermometer registers 160°F [75°C] in the thickest part of the thigh.

Transfer to a cutting board, cover with foil, and let rest for 10 minutes before cutting into serving pieces and arranging on a platter. Garnish with herb sprigs and Aleppo pepper, and serve with the lemon wedges.

Minted Baby Lamb Chops with Pomegranate Glaze

Adding a pomegranate glaze makes something that's already delicious—in this case, tender, dainty rib lamb chops—even more special with almost no effort. I like to prepare these on the grill, but indoors, a ridged grill pan will do the job nearly as well and makes this a great year-round option. This will serve 4 to 6 people, depending on appetites and budget; if you want serve a larger group, use the same rub and glaze on a boned and butterflied leg of lamb, applying the glaze just before the meat comes off the grill to give it a lustrous sheen. A dollop of Tzatziki (page 199) complements the minty notes of the marinade.

SERVES 4 TO 6

¼ cup [5 g] crushed fresh mint leaves
2 Tbsp extra-virgin olive oil
1 tsp kosher salt
1 tsp Aleppo pepper
½ tsp freshly ground black pepper
Twelve ½ in [12 mm] thick lamb rib chops (about 2 lb [910 g] total)
¼ cup [80 g] pomegranate molasses

Combine the mint, oil, salt, and Aleppo and black peppers in a mini food processor or blender and whiz to make a paste, adding a bit more oil if needed to loosen the mixture.

Scrape out the paste into a large bowl, add the chops, and toss to coat all over with the mixture. Cover the bowl and set aside at room temperature to marinate for 30 minutes while you fire up the grill or preheat a grill pan over medium-high heat.

Arrange the chops on the hot grill or pan, placing them over the hottest part of the fire. Sear for about 2 minutes or just until browned, then turn and sear the second side. Brush the tops of the chops with the pomegranate molasses. Turn again, brushing the second side with the molasses, then turn one last time. Cook no more than 30 seconds per side after glazing, just long enough to caramelize it without overcooking the meat.

Transfer to a serving platter, cover loosely with foil, and let the chops rest for 5 minutes or so before serving.

Sweet-and-Sour Beef Hand Pies

A bit of pomegranate molasses and warm spices in the meat mixture give these little pockets a wonderful sweet/sour tang that is especially appealing to kids. They are as perfect in a lunchbox as they are in a picnic hamper, and they freeze well, too, so you can defrost one or more in the fridge overnight for a grab-and-go the next day. When my kids were little, they would often pack up a few extras to share with friends.

MAKES 10 PIES

1 Tbsp extra-virgin olive oil
½ cup [70 g] chopped onion
1 lb [455 g] lean ground beef or lamb, or a combination
1 tsp fine sea salt
½ tsp ground black pepper
½ tsp ground allspice
¼ tsp ground cinnamon
2 Tbsp pomegranate molasses
1 recipe Basic Bread Dough (page 98)

Preheat the oven to 350°F [180°C]. Line a rimmed baking sheet with parchment paper.

Heat the oil in a large skillet over medium-high heat. Add the onions and cook, stirring, until soft and translucent, about 5 minutes. Add the meat, salt, pepper, allspice, and cinnamon and cook, breaking up the meat with a wooden spoon, until fully cooked and crumbly, about 10 minutes. Stir in the pomegranate molasses, then set aside to cool for 10 or 15 minutes.

Divide the dough into 10 equal portions, about 1½ oz [40 g] each. Dust a work surface with flour. Working with one portion at a time, roll it into a small flat circle. Place a spoonful of the meat mixture in the center, then bring the dough up and over the filling from 2 sides. Pinch the edges together firmly to seal in a half-circle. Place on the baking sheet. Repeat with the remaining portions and filling.

Bake the meat pies for 15 minutes, or until slightly puffed and well browned. Let them stand on the baking sheets for 10 minutes before serving hot, or let cool to room temperature. These are best eaten the day they are made, but if you have leftovers, wrap them in plastic while still warm and refrigerate for up to 3 days or freeze for up to 1 month.

TEN MORE WAYS TO USE
POMEGRANATE MOLASSES

•1•

Pomegranate Mimosa

For an easy, super-pretty drink that is perfect for weddings or a festive brunch, drizzle about 1 to 2 tsp of pomegranate molasses down the sides of a champagne flute and let it set for a few minutes. Drop 5 or 6 pomegranate seeds into the glass and fill with champagne. If you are serving a crowd, you can prep the glasses ahead of time, and feel free to substitute a reasonably priced cava or prosecco for the champagne.

•2•

Scarlet Salad Dressing

This snappy blend will pep up a simple green salad. It's particularly good combined with thinly sliced cucumbers, feta, and sweet white onion; or a leafy green salad topped with avocado and pomegranate seeds. In a measuring cup, combine 2 Tbsp of pomegranate molasses with 2 Tbsp of champagne or rice wine vinegar (be sure to use a mild white vinegar to preserve the color). Season with ½ tsp of fine sea salt and a generous pinch of Aleppo pepper. Whisk in ½ cup [120 ml] of good extra-virgin olive oil until well combined.

•3•

Pomegranate Poke Cake

Prepare your favorite butter, lemon, or pound cake recipe according to directions. Let the cake cool in the pan for about 10 minutes, then invert onto a cooling rack. Immediately use a wooden or metal skewer to poke deep holes all over the top of the cake, then drizzle with ¼ cup [80 g] of pomegranate molasses, allowing it to sink into the cake. Cool completely, then spread with a glaze of 2 cups [200 g] of confectioner's sugar mixed with 3 Tbsp of lemon juice, or enough to make it fluid.

•4•

Rainbow Roasted Carrots

Scrub 1 lb [455 g] of small carrots, preferably multicolored. Toss on a rimmed baking sheet with 2 Tbsp of extra-virgin olive oil, ¾ tsp of sea salt, ½ tsp of freshly ground black pepper, and 1 tsp of Aleppo pepper. Roast at 425°F [220°C] for 25 to 30 minutes, until just beginning to brown, then flip and glaze with 2 Tbsp of pomegranate molasses. Continue to roast until tender and shiny, another 10 minutes. Serve garnished with toasted pumpkin seeds (pepitas).

·5·

Grilled Glazed Salmon

Stir together equal amounts of soy sauce, pomegranate molasses, and extra-virgin olive oil and brush onto salmon steaks or center-cut fillets before grilling over a hot fire. Turn once or twice to keep the glaze from burning. Before serving, sprinkle the fish with a pinch of Aleppo pepper for color. Garnish with lime wedges.

·6·

Avocado Toast

Toast a slice or two of seeded multigrain bread and spread with fresh ricotta cheese. Top with a few slices of ripe avocado and a handful of toasted sunflower seeds. Drizzle with pomegranate molasses and sprinkle with flaky salt.

·7·

Pomegranate Glaze

For decorating desserts or drizzling over cheese, combine 1 cup [320 g] of pomegranate molasses with ¼ cup [50 g] of sugar in a small saucepan. Bring to a boil, stirring to dissolve the sugar, then continue to cook at a brisk simmer until reduced by half. Cool and store in the refrigerator in a covered jar for up to 3 months.

·8·

Rosy Oatmeal

To shake up a bland morning routine, stir 2 tsp of pomegranate molasses and 1 Tbsp of chopped dates into 1 cup [80 g] of cooked oatmeal. Top with a dollop of Greek yogurt and a sprinkle of chopped almonds.

·9·

Boosted Baba Ghanoush

Perk up store-bought baba ghanoush with 1 Tbsp or more of pomegranate molasses. Stir well, spread on a plate, and top with a drizzle of olive oil and a handful of fresh pomegranate seeds. Finish with 1 or 2 pinches of sumac or Urfa pepper.

·10·

Pom-Roasted Eggplant

In a large bowl, whisk together 1 part pomegranate molasses to 4 parts olive oil. Season with salt, pepper, and a good pinch of Aleppo pepper. Add 1 large eggplant, cut in chunks or ½ in [12 mm] slices, and toss to coat. Roast on an oiled baking sheet at 450°F [230°C] for 12 to 15 minutes, turning once or twice as they roast, until browned on the outside and creamy inside. Serve hot or at room temperature, sprinkled with fresh pomegranate seeds.

White Chocolate Cranberry Cookies with Sumac Glaze

These pink-flecked cookies became a staff favorite the first time I made them. The tart glaze contrasts with the sweet white chocolate to make a great flavor combination. These would be a beautiful addition to a holiday table or a pretty springtime dessert.

MAKES 24 COOKIES

Cookies

2½ cups [350 g] all-purpose flour

2 tsp ground sumac

¼ tsp fine sea salt

¼ tsp baking powder

1 cup [220 g] (2 sticks) unsalted butter, at room temperature

1 cup [200 g] granulated sugar

1 egg

1 tsp vanilla extract

1 cup [140 g] dried cranberries

1 cup [180 g] white chocolate chunks or chips

Glaze

½ cup [60 g] confectioner's sugar

2 tsp whole milk

1 tsp fresh lemon juice

½ tsp ground sumac

Preheat the oven to 350°F [180°C]. Line 2 rimmed baking sheets with parchment paper and set aside.

To make the cookies: In a medium bowl, whisk together the flour, sumac, sea salt, and baking powder. Set aside.

Combine the butter and sugar in the bowl of a mixer and beat on medium speed until light and fluffy. Add the egg and vanilla and mix well. Reduce the speed to low and beat in the flour mixture until nearly combined. Stir in the cranberries and white chocolate chunks by hand until well distributed.

Form the cookie dough into 2 Tbsp balls and arrange on the prepared baking sheets. Bake for 10 to 12 minutes, or until the cookies are just beginning to brown around the edges. Let the cookies cool on the pan for 5 minutes, then transfer to wire racks to cool completely.

To make the glaze: Combine all the ingredients in a small bowl and stir until smooth—the glaze will be quite thick.

Drizzle the glaze over the cooled cookies and let stand for 30 minutes to set. Store the cookies in an airtight container for 3 or 4 days.

Hibiscus Shortbread Icebox Cookies

With just six ingredients, this versatile dough is so easy to make, and it's all done in the food processor. It bakes up a pretty pale fuchsia with a sweet/tart flavor reminiscent of raspberries. You can keep the wrapped logs of dough in the freezer for bake-anytime cookies, or if you prefer, roll out the dough and cut it with cookie cutters. If you love the look of a traditional shortbread, press the crumbs into a pie pan and score the top in wedge shapes. It would even make an outstanding crust for a fruit tart or lemon bars. Rolling the logs in hibiscus sugar or chopped nuts is optional but makes an even prettier, more finished-looking cookie.

MAKES 2 DOZEN COOKIES

½ cup [100 g] granulated sugar
½ cup [18 g] dried hibiscus blossoms
1 vanilla bean, cut into ¼ in [6 mm] pieces
1½ cups [210 g] all-purpose flour
¼ cup [35 g] cornstarch
1 cup [220 g] (2 sticks) unsalted butter, very cold, cut into small pieces
1 egg, beaten (optional)
Hibiscus sugar (page 39) or finely chopped pistachios (optional)

Combine the sugar, hibiscus, and vanilla bean in a food processor. Cover the top of the food processor with plastic wrap (this keeps the powdered sugar mixture from wafting around your kitchen), then replace the top as usual. Process the mixture until almost fully powdered, about 5 minutes, then let the mixture settle for a minute before opening the top. Discard the plastic wrap.

Add the flour and cornstarch to the processor and pulse until combined. Add the butter and pulse until the mixture looks like coarse meal and is starting to clump around the edges. Add about 1 tsp of water and pulse a few more times until it has mostly come together in large clumps, adding another teaspoon of water if necessary.

Divide the dough into two portions and form each portion into a 2 in [5 cm] thick log. Wrap tightly in plastic and refrigerate for at least 1 hour or until firm.

Preheat the oven to 350°F [180°C] and line two rimmed baking sheets with parchment paper.

If desired, brush the logs all over with the beaten egg and roll in your choice of hibiscus sugar or pistachios. Use a large, sharp knife to cut the logs into ¼ in [6 mm] thick slices, turning the log after each cut to keep it round. Place the slices on the prepared baking sheets, leaving ample space between them, as the cookies will spread as they bake. Bake until just beginning to brown slightly at the edges, about 12 minutes, reversing the positions of the sheets once to ensure even baking.

Allow the cookies to cool on the pan for about 5 minutes, then carefully transfer to a wire rack to cool completely. The cookies will be quite delicate. Store in a tightly covered airtight container for up to 5 days.

STRAWBERRY-
POMEGRANATE
REFRIGERATOR JAM
APRICOT HOT
PEPPER JELLY
page 153

Strawberry-Pomegranate Refrigerator Jam

Strawberries and pomegranate have a wonderful affinity for each other, and in combination they make a delicious preserve to serve on toast, yogurt, or labneh. Unlike traditional preserves, which are cooked down with lots and lots of sugar and pectin, these are thickened with chia seeds and have only a touch of added sweetener, so it's not only a beautiful color, it's a healthy indulgence. Note, however, that the jam must be stored in the refrigerator and used within a week or two.

MAKES TWO 8 OZ [230 G] JARS

1½ cups [210 g] chopped fresh strawberries

½ cup [90 g] pomegranate seeds

2 Tbsp honey or agave nectar

1 Tbsp pomegranate molasses

1 Tbsp fresh lemon juice, preferably Meyer lemon

3 Tbsp chia seeds

Combine the strawberries and pomegranate seeds in a 4 qt [3.8 L] saucepan. Place the pan over low heat and cook, covered, until the fruits release their juices, 5 to 10 minutes, removing the lid occasionally to stir and crush the fruits with a wooden spoon. Remove from the heat and stir in the honey, pomegranate molasses, and lemon juice. Taste for sweetness and add a bit more honey if desired.

Add the chia seeds and mix well to distribute them thoroughly. Allow the mixture to cool a bit, then transfer to jars, and refrigerate uncovered. It will thicken and set up after a few hours. Cover the containers tightly and refrigerate until ready to use.

2
SAVORY

EARTHY, SALTY, HERBACEOUS

FETA CHEESE

NIGELLA

ZA'ATAR

OLIVES

MINT

This chapter is for those who like their food highly seasoned but not necessarily spicy hot. With their briny tang and strong herbal tones, the flavors covered here represent the cooler side of the Middle Eastern flavor spectrum. Mint, in particular, lifts every dish it appears in with an unexpected pop of interest yet contributes no heat (or fat!). Middle Easterners tuck it into sandwiches, blend it into salads, and use it as a ubiquitous garnish.

When fresh herbs are not available, or when a dish needs an earthier herbal note, sesame-enriched za'atar is an all-star. This multipurpose seasoning blend is favored from Israel to Iran and appears as an ingredient in marinades, braises, and baked goods as well as a finishing touch straight from the jar. You'll soon find it's a workhorse in your kitchen as well, providing verdant herbal flavor all year long. And nigella, actually a seed, has a unique, hard-to-define flavor that quietly lifts sauces, dressings, and baked goods with its cool, herbal presence.

Salty ingredients like olives and feta are so often the answer when a dish just seems to need *something*, and they add richness as well as salinity. No shrinking violets, they can subtly boost the underlying flavors of a dish when used as an accent. Whether ground into tapenade, melted into a sauce to incorporate into a dish, or dotted on top for added visual and textural interest, these savory ingredients are the easiest ways to add a fresh, fragrant note that elevates even simple recipes.

DRINKS AND STARTERS

SALADS AND SIDES

ENTRÉES

SWEETS

MINT
OLIVES
NIGELLA

FETA CHEESE
ZA'ATAR

Feta Cheese

When it comes to versatility, I would place feta second only to Parmigiano-Reggiano in the canon of workhorse cheeses, and it is used throughout the Mediterranean, Middle East, and beyond. With its briny tang, crumbly texture, and excellent meltability, it does multiple duty as a seasoning, a garnish, and, of course, a delicious ingredient in its own right. We probably sell more feta at Sahadi's than all other cheeses combined—hundreds of pounds per week.

Feta is of course most associated with Greece, but it is produced worldwide, primarily from sheep's milk, but also from cow's and goat's milk, or a combination, depending on the region. Whichever dairy is the base, the cheese curds are pressed into a form and then pickled in brine for two months, giving feta its distinctive salty flavor. It is ready to eat at that point, but feta can also be aged, with the texture becoming drier and crumblier the longer the cheese stays in its brine.

We source our feta from Bulgaria, France, Egypt, and the United States, but to my palate the best is the barrel-aged feta from Greece. It's 100 percent sheep's milk, with a pleasant tang and firm texture. It's a matter of taste, though, so try a few and see which you like best. You may also want a younger, smoother feta if you are blending or melting it, and a crumblier aged feta for sprinkling on salads and pilafs. Either way, you'll find it adds just the right touch of sharpness and richness to a wide variety of foods.

> **WHAT TO LOOK FOR** • Whenever possible, purchase feta in block form, not precrumbled (which generally indicates a lower-quality, mass-produced cheese). Look for cheese with clean, sharp edges rather than roughened, broken edges, and clear brine rather than cloudy brine—both indicate cheese that has been properly stored and has not started to disintegrate. Feta will keep for a good long time in the refrigerator if you change the salted water it's stored in every few days.
>
> **SERVE WITH** • Feta has an affinity for other sharp, acidic flavors like lemon, olives, and tomatoes, and can also be used as a salty accent for milder ingredients like poultry and seafood, grains, and greens.

Nigella

Nigella, a tiny black seed that looks like sesame and is sometimes labeled black caraway, lends a distinctive flavor and aroma to baking and cheese dishes. It is one of many seasonings in our dukkah blend. The taste has hints of onion and herbs; in fact, it's a bit like "everything" seasoning wrapped up in one tiny little package. At the store we use it to flavor twisted cheese, a Syrian specialty similar to mozzarella, and sprinkle it on vegetable hand pies.

WHAT TO LOOK FOR · These are sold whole and may be labeled black caraway, black cumin, or even onion seeds, probably due more to their flavor than to any botanical connection.

Store nigella seeds in a covered container away from light and heat to preserve their potency.

SERVE WITH · Nigella seeds add both flavor and an attractive finishing accent to many baked goods and breads, much as a sesame seed or poppy seed would. They have an affinity for grain salads, vegetable dishes, and potatoes, and can be added to dressings or sprinkled directly onto green salads for a bit of crunchy texture.

Za'atar

The term za'atar is used to describe both a green herb native to the Middle East and the eponymous seasoning blend that features it prominently. At Sahadi's we sell it in plus-size jars because those who know and love it use it the way others use salt and pepper: generously and on just about everything.

The recipe for za'atar seasoning varies from region to region and even from family to family. In Jordan, za'atar contains cumin; Syrians put a lot more sumac in theirs, making it appear more red than green. Aside from these local variations, za'atar always includes sesame seeds, sea salt, and some amount of sumac, for a blend of salty, tangy, and richness, plus lots of dried za'atar, which provides the herbal punch. This spiky-leaved herb falls somewhere between thyme and oregano in taste. In the agricultural regions of the Bekaa Valley, Lebanon, where it is grown in abundance, many small family farms sell their crops to a cooperative that blends them together to sell on the side of the road. It is not grown commercially in this country, so we import dried, powdered za'atar (we're the only American spice seller to do so) by the shipping container and make our own proprietary blend. The proportions are different each year because we never know how potent a particular crop will be until we get the container open; mixing it ourselves is the only way to ensure a consistent product.

WHAT TO LOOK FOR · Check the ingredient label to see what's in the blend you're considering. I find za'atar without cumin more versatile, but it's a personal and family preference. Always buy za'atar from a reputable company, as less-scrupulous merchants have been known to "extend" the more costly ingredients with anything green—including grass clippings! If possible, take a sniff of the blend, and if it smells like a fresh-cut lawn, pass it by. Use your za'atar within three to six months of opening it, and store it in a cool, dark place to preserve its flavor.

SERVE WITH • Za'atar is an all-purpose seasoning that is a boon to any one-dimensional ingredient like potatoes or eggs. In fact, it is best paired with things that *don't* have a lot of flavor of their own, so they don't compete. Except for the sesame seeds, it is fat free, so you get a lot of bang for your buck, calorie-wise.

Olives

Olives are some of the most popular items in our store, and we take special pride in sourcing ours direct from growers on three continents. I often see customers standing over the olive bar, baffled by the variety, but there are no bad choices; it's really a matter of personal taste. If you're uncertain, buy a container of mixed olives and see which you like best, both for eating out of hand and as a seasoning ingredient. In general, green olives are meatier and milder than black, and oil-cured more intense than brined, but olives vary in flavor and texture based on many factors: country of origin, variety, curing method, and the preferences of the grower when preserving their crop. We carry the broadest array of olives we can find, with a combination of house-cured and purchased products. We love it when members of our multicultural staff introduce us to products cured in their homelands; it keeps the assortment seasonal and interesting.

WHAT TO LOOK FOR • Good olives should have a fairly firm texture; clear, clean brine; and a fresh, shiny look. Avoid any that are discolored or wrinkled (unless they are oil-cured) or, it should go without saying, canned. Merchants who love olives take immense pride in curating their olive department, so try to buy from a purveyor that keeps the olive bar well stocked and cared for. Store olives in their brine in the refrigerator and use within two to three weeks of purchasing for best flavor and texture.

SERVE WITH • Along with pickled vegetables, olives are the basis for many of our cheese boards and Mediterranean party platters, as they go with so many salty and sweet flavors. Combining different colors and textures, not to mention flavors, will give your appetizer spreads more dimension. Use anywhere you need a punch of flavor or color.

Mint

Mint is probably the fresh herb used most widely throughout the Middle East, as indispensable as parsley is in American kitchens for finishing cooked dishes and sparking up salads. Because it is considered a digestive aid, it is often served along with fatty foods—grilled meats in particular seem to call for the cool, vibrant flavor of fresh mint. You will see mint piled onto platters alongside skewers of grilled meat so that each diner can take a bit of the bracing herb along with the savory meat morsels. Its crinkled leaves also make a beautiful garnish, and at our house, everyone knows to strip off only the leaves at the bottom of the stem for cooking, as I save the perfect sprigs at the top to dress up fruit salads, cocktails, and more.

More than any other herb I can think of, mint represents the taste of summer and, unlike fresh basil (to which mint is closely related, botanically), it is readily available year-round. It's far more versatile than most cooks realize, and I consider it quite underused in Western kitchens. Reach for it when you would otherwise use basil or parsley, and you will be very pleased with the results. Fortunately, it is one of the easiest herbs to grow. Planted out in the garden, it will spread season after season to consume more of your garden patch each year if you let it. Pots will contain the spread and allow you to grow a variety of distinct kinds. I grab handfuls from my yard right up until the first frost. Whatever is left at the end of the season I dry, but honestly, the taste of the fresh is so far superior that I don't worry about saving much for the colder months.

WHAT TO LOOK FOR • The mint used throughout the Middle East is the variety usually labeled spearmint (or occasionally "mojito mint") in the United States; peppermint, which has darker stems and smoother, more pointed leaves, is stronger and too biting to eat raw. Choose mint with crisp leaves and a good aroma when rubbed between your fingers; avoid any with black spots or edges, a sure sign the entire bunch is past its prime. Fresh mint doesn't keep for more than a few days in the refrigerator, but you can prolong its life for a day or two by wrapping the stems in a damp paper towel and enclosing the bunch in a sealed plastic bag.

SERVE WITH • Mint works equally well with sweet and savory foods and is especially good in its raw state; cooked (or dried), it tends to lose its impact. It has an affinity for olives, chocolate, and most meats and dairy. In short, it is a do-it-all, serve-with-anything herb that provides an unexpected pop of flavor and freshness in a wide variety of dishes.

SERVE IT WITH • In the summer, mint is a sprightlier alternative to parsley or basil in most kinds of vegetable and potato salads, and it is *the* essential ingredient in fattoush (page 49), the bread salad that is Lebanon's answer to tabbouleh. Mint is also what gives the cooling, lively mixture of yogurt, garlic, and cucumber known as tzatziki its zip. It pairs well with chocolate, another rich food, as well as fresh berries and melon.

Za'atar Bloody Mary

What brunch is complete without a Bloody Mary? For our Industry City café, we knew we needed a killer version that featured classic Middle Eastern flavors. Adding za'atar and Aleppo pepper makes our version a little peppery, with just the right amount of herbal punch. We used canned tomatoes in purée for a cleaner, brighter tomato flavor, but if you prefer to use tomato juice, just omit the water from the recipe. We think you'll agree that our bloody base is good enough to drink on its own, especially when you give it some time in the fridge to develop the flavors.

MAKES 8 COCKTAILS

3 cups [600 g] chopped tomatoes in purée or 3 cups tomato juice

1 large celery stalk, sliced

1 scallion, both white and green parts, sliced

1 garlic clove, chopped

2 Tbsp liquid harissa or zhug

Juice of 1 large lemon

2 Tbsp plus 2 tsp za'atar

1 Tbsp prepared horseradish

3 tsp Aleppo pepper

3 tsp fine sea salt

1 tsp ground black pepper

1 lemon, sliced

1½ cups [360 ml] vodka

Celery sticks and cucumber spears, for garnish (optional)

In a blender, combine the tomatoes and their purée with the celery, scallion, garlic, harissa, lemon juice, 2 Tbsp of the za'atar, horseradish, 1 tsp of the Aleppo pepper, 1 tsp of the salt, and the black pepper. If using canned tomatoes, add ½ cup [120 ml] of water (do not add water if using tomato juice). Blend until thoroughly puréed. Add more horseradish, salt, pepper, or lemon juice as needed. Refrigerate the mixture overnight or up to 3 days to blend the flavors.

To serve, stir together the remaining 2 tsp of za'atar, 2 tsp of Aleppo pepper, and 2 tsp of salt on a small plate or piece of wax paper. Use one of the lemon slices to rub the rim of 8 highball glasses and dip the rim in the spices. Fill the glasses with ice and add 3 Tbsp of vodka to each. Add about ½ cup [120 ml] of the tomato mixture, stir, and garnish with a lemon slice and a celery stick or cucumber spear.

Za'atar Bread

Our bestselling flatbread pizza, what we call "The Sahadi Special," is really just our basic za'atar bread (pictured on page 54) topped with a relish of olives and tomatoes. You'll use this multipurpose dough to make pastries, hand pies, and the meat and nut-topped flatbread on page 234.

MAKES 4 LARGE FLATBREADS

Basic Bread Dough

2 cups [280 g] bread flour

1 tsp salt

1 tsp dry active yeast

½ tsp sugar

¾ cup [180 ml] warm water

1 Tbsp extra-virgin olive oil

5 Tbsp [35 g] Lebanese za'atar

¼ cup [60 ml] extra-virgin olive oil

To make the dough: Combine the flour, salt, yeast, and sugar in the bowl of a stand mixer. With the mixer on medium, add the water and the 1 Tbsp of oil and mix until the dough comes together in a ball. Turn out the dough onto a work surface, wrap in plastic, and set aside in a warm place to rest for 30 to 60 minutes. The dough will not double in size, but it will lighten and appear a bit puffed.

When you are ready to bake, preheat the oven to 525°F [275°C], or as close as your oven goes. Lightly grease a rimmed baking sheet. Combine the za'atar with the remaining ¼ cup [60 ml] of oil in a small bowl.

On a floured work surface, divide the dough into four equal portions. Use a rolling pin to roll out each portion into a thin 8 in [20 cm] round and place on the baking sheet. Spread each dough circle with 2 Tbsp of the za'atar mixture, covering it completely. Use a fork to prick the dough all over.

Bake for 1 minute. Open the oven and use a spatula to rotate the breads quickly on the pan to help them brown evenly. Bake for another 30 seconds or until the bottoms are lightly browned. If any pockets or bubbles develop, you can pierce them with a fork or leave them as is. Eat warm or at room temperature.

VARIATION

To make "The Sahadi Special" (pictured opposite), divide the dough into eight equal portions. Roll, top, and bake. While still hot, top each flatbread with 2 Tbsp of chopped green olives, 2 Tbsp of finely diced onion, and 2 Tbsp of diced tomato. Return to the oven for another 30 seconds.

TEN MORE WAYS TO USE

ZA'ATAR

·1·

Rice Pilaf

For every cup of rice you plan to cook, sauté 1 tsp of za'atar in 1 Tbsp of oil; warm it just until the sesame seeds start to sizzle. Stir in the rice and toast for 1 to 2 minutes, then add liquid as usual and cook over low heat until tender. Sprinkle additional za'atar on the rice before serving.

·2·

Finish a Salad

Straight from the jar, za'atar adds a bit of crunch and texture to almost any kind of salad, whether mayonnaise based or tossed with a vinaigrette. It's a little bit tart from the sumac and a touch salty from the sea salt.

·3·

Savory Yogurt

Flavor 1 cup [240 g] of plain yogurt with 1 or 2 tsp of za'atar. Serve on a hot day as a refreshing accompaniment to meats or fish, or enjoy on its own with the addition of diced cucumber.

·4·

Dipping Oil

For the easiest of all appetizers, pour oil onto a shallow dish and season liberally with za'atar and a few hot chiles. Serve with warmed pita breads for dipping.

·5·

Za'atar Eggs

Sprinkle directly onto a hard-cooked egg for snacking, or make a simple egg salad with a bit of full-fat yogurt, chopped red bell pepper, parsley, chopped celery, and za'atar.

·6·

Minimalist Marinade

Season extra-virgin olive oil generously with za'atar and toss to coat chicken pieces. Grill or bake until golden and cooked through, then serve on a bed of bitter greens with some good French bread and a tomato salad.

·7·

Seasoned Spuds

Za'atar does wonderful things for potatoes. Use it to jazz up a plain baked potato with sour cream, or toss whole baby potatoes with olive oil, chopped garlic, and za'atar and roast until tender. Sprinkle the hot potatoes with chopped fresh parsley.

·8·

Labneh Spread

Blend labneh with za'atar and spread on a grilled chicken pita sandwich.

·9·

Olive Oil and Za'atar Popcorn

Warm a few tablespoons of fruity olive oil in a large heavy pan with a lid over medium heat. When hot but not smoking, add ¼ cup [50 g] of popcorn kernels and heat, shaking continually, until the popping has stopped. Add za'atar and a sprinkle of Aleppo pepper, if you like.

·10·

Za'atar Paste

Combine equal amounts of extra-virgin olive oil and za'atar to make a thick, chunky paste. Smear it onto a warmed pita and eat as is, or top with a crispy fried egg.

Our World-Famous Olive Medley

My favorite way to eat olives is directly from the barrel, but when I want to get a bit fancier, I bring home a pint of our house-made marinated olives (pictured on page 105). Most retailers sell mixed olives that arrived premixed and seasoned, but we like to mix and match our own, using olives from different continents. We then season them in small batches. Our customers seem to approve, as this cocktail blend is one of the most popular items in the store. I think it looks and tastes best when the olives are left whole and unpitted—just be sure to provide a small bowl for the pits.

MAKES ABOUT 1 QT [960 ML]

½ cup [120 ml] extra-virgin olive oil
3 strips of lemon peel, removed with a vegetable peeler
1 shallot, thinly sliced
4 garlic cloves, thinly sliced
1 cup [160 g] Kalamata olives
1 cup [160 g] Castelvetrano olives
1 cup [160 g] French Provençal olives, black or green
¼ cup [40g] capers, drained
1 tsp za'atar
1 tsp Aleppo pepper
½ cup [110 g] chopped roasted red peppers
¼ cup [10 g] chopped parsley

In a medium saucepan, heat the oil over medium-low heat until it just begins to get hot. Add the lemon peel, shallot, and garlic and heat until the shallot is sizzling and the lemon peel just begins to curl; do not let it brown. Add the olives, capers, za'atar, and Aleppo pepper and toss for 1 minute over the heat to warm through. Remove the pan from the heat, cover, and set aside to cool to room temperature, 15 to 20 minutes.

Add the roasted peppers and parsley and stir until well combined. Serve immediately or transfer to a covered container and refrigerate for up to 1 week. Allow the olives to return to room temperature before serving.

Whipped Feta Spread

If you like feta cheese, everything for this knockout spread (pictured on page 109) is probably in your fridge and pantry already, making it a very useful recipe to have up your sleeve when unexpected company drops by. I spread it on crostini and top with a bit of black or green tapenade (the one on page 106 would be ideal), but you could easily substitute paper-thin slices of cucumber or radish, or even bits of rare beef filet. Toss leftover feta spread with hot pasta and roasted or sautéed shrimp for a super-simple supper.

MAKES ABOUT 1¼ CUPS [300 G]
SERVES 8 TO 10 AS PART OF A COCKTAIL SPREAD

6 oz [170 g] Greek feta cheese, cut into ½ in [12 mm] cubes

½ cup [120 g] labneh or Greek yogurt

½ cup [110 g] roasted red pepper strips

2 Tbsp chopped fresh parsley

2 tsp extra-virgin olive oil

1 tsp Aleppo pepper

Combine the cheese, labneh, and red pepper strips in a food processor and pulse on and off a few times to break them up a bit. Don't make a smooth purée; you want some texture to remain. Add the parsley, oil, and Aleppo pepper and continue to pulse until the mixture just starts to become creamy, with a few chunks of cheese and pepper still visible.

Store in a covered container, refrigerated, for up to 2 weeks.

Spiced Beet Dip with Za'atar, Goat Cheese, and Pistachios

A classic recipe from Yotam Ottolenghi inspired this vivid pink dip, and I enjoy it as much for the color it brings to a meze spread as for its earthy, tangy flavor. Caña de Cabra is a soft goat cheese; you can substitute any similar cheese, like Bûcheron. Pistachios look especially festive with the beet-tinted dip, but toasted pine nuts or chopped toasted hazelnuts would be great here as well.

MAKES 4 CUPS [450 G]

1¾ lb [800 g] beets (about 6 medium)
1 cup [240 g] plain labneh
1 small red chile, seeded and minced
2 small garlic cloves, minced
3 Tbsp extra-virgin olive oil
Juice of 1 lemon
2 Tbsp za'atar
1 Tbsp pomegranate molasses
1 tsp fine sea salt
1 tsp Aleppo pepper
1 tsp sumac
2 scallions, both white and green parts, thinly sliced
2 oz [55 g] soft goat cheese, such as Caña de Cabra, crumbled
3 Tbsp coarsely chopped roasted, salted pistachios
Endive leaves or pita chips, for serving

Trim the greens and long tails from the beets but do not peel. In a large pot, cook the beets in 1 in [2.5 cm] of boiling water until just tender. Drain thoroughly, and when cool enough to handle, slip off the peels.

Cut the beets into large dice and add them to the bowl of a food processor with the labneh, chile, and garlic. Purée until smooth, stopping to scrape down the sides a few times. Add the oil, lemon juice, za'atar, pomegranate molasses, salt, Aleppo pepper, and sumac and blend again.

To serve, turn out the dip onto a plate or platter. Top with the scallions, cheese, and pistachios. Serve with your preferred dippers.

SPICED BEET DIP

OUR WORLD-FAMOUS OLIVE MEDLEY
page 102

Great Green Tapenade

Once you get in the habit of making tapenade, you will wonder how you ever got along without it—it's that versatile. Spread it on crostini or serve with cheese and crackers for instant cocktail nibbles; give a salad or pasta dish a savory flavor boost; or do as my husband does and scoop it up with pita chips for a quick snack. I make both black and green tapenade year-round, sometimes throwing in minced sun-dried tomatoes or roasted peppers along with whatever herbs are growing in my garden to change it up. This version (pictured on page 109), made with meaty Castelvetrano olives and lots of bright citrus, is a standout. Pair it with a lemony hummus, some grilled bread, and a nice white wine for a low-key aperitif.

MAKES 2 CUPS [540 G]

2 garlic cloves
2 anchovy fillets
1½ cups [210 g] pitted Castelvetrano olives
¼ cup [40 g] capers
¼ cup [10 g] chopped fresh parsley
2 Tbsp fresh lemon juice
1 Tbsp chopped preserved lemon (rind only)
2 tsp herbes de Provence
1 tsp grated lemon zest
1 tsp freshly ground black pepper
1 tsp Aleppo pepper
½ tsp fine sea salt

In a food processor, pulse the garlic and anchovy until chopped finely. Add the remaining ingredients and pulse until well mixed but not puréed; there should still be visible bits of olive. Let stand for at least 1 hour to blend the flavors. Leftover tapenade can be topped with a few tablespoons of olive oil in a tightly covered jar and refrigerated for up to 2 weeks.

Cheesy Hand Pies

Cheese pies are so fragrant—you can smell them almost as soon as they hit the oven. Nigella seeds give the filling its appealing fragrance and flavor, but if you don't have them, you can simply omit them, or substitute another seasoning, such as hot pepper flakes. We always fill ours with a mixture of cheeses so you get a combination of gooey, creamy, and fluffy textures in every bite, and we coat the pies with toasty sesame seeds for extra crunch. Like most of the hand pies we sell, these can be eaten at room temperature, but I especially like them piping hot, when the cheese is all molten and the seasonings are extra savory. Pair them with a bowl of hot tomato soup for a perfect cold-weather meal.

MAKES 10 PIES

4½ oz [130 g] string cheese, cut into chunks (about ¾ cup)
4½ oz [130 g] Syrian cheese or queso fresco, cut into chunks (about ¾ cup)
4½ oz [130 g] Greek feta cheese, cut into chunks (about ¾ cup)
¼ cup [10 g] chopped fresh parsley
1 Tbsp nigella (black caraway) seeds
1 Tbsp dried oregano
½ tsp fine sea salt
1 recipe Basic Bread Dough (page 98) or 1 lb [455 g] premade pizza dough
1 egg, well beaten
¼ cup [35 g] toasted sesame seeds

Combine all three cheeses in the bowl of a food processor and pulse until finely chopped. Stir in the parsley, nigella seeds, oregano, and salt.

Preheat the oven to 350°F [180°C]. Line two rimmed baking sheets with parchment paper.

Flour a work surface well. Divide the dough into ten equal portions (about 1½ oz [40 g] each). Working with one portion of dough at a time, roll the dough into a disk about 6 in [15 cm] across. Place a spoonful of cheese mixture in the center. Fold opposite sides up and over the mixture and pinch the edges together to seal, making a half-moon-shaped pie.

Brush the pie all over with the beaten egg wash and sprinkle with the sesame seeds. Place on the prepared baking sheet. Repeat with the remaining dough balls and filling.

Bake for 15 minutes, or until slightly puffed and well browned. Let stand for 10 minutes before serving hot, or cool to room temperature. These are best eaten the day they are made, but if you have leftovers, wrap them in plastic while still warm and refrigerate for up to 3 days, or freeze.

BOLD AND SPICY HUMMUS
page 156

CHEESY HAND PIES
page 107

GREAT GREEN
TAPENADE
page 106
WHIPPED
FETA SPREAD
page 103

Antipasto Salad

At the store we call this a salad, but it's really more like a meze in a bowl, with chunks of marinated peppers, cheese, olives, and sausage. It can be made well ahead of time, which really allows the flavors to bloom. Serve it with toothpicks or pita triangles for scooping.

SERVES 4 TO 6

8 oz [230 g] salami, pepperoni, or other dried, cured sausage, cut into ½ in [12 mm] chunks

½ cup [70 g] mixed pitted olives

3 oz imported feta, cut into ½ in [12 mm] cubes (about ¾ cup)

¼ cup [55 g] roasted red pepper strips

¼ cup [45 g] pepperoncini

¼ cup [60 ml] extra-virgin olive oil

¼ cup [10 g] shredded fresh mint leaves, plus more for garnish

2 tsp za'atar, plus more for garnish

Put the salami chunks in a large bowl. Add the olives, feta, red pepper strips, and pepperoncini, and toss gently to combine, taking care not to break up the feta.

In a small bowl, stir together the oil, mint, and za'atar. Pour over the antipasto mixture and toss again just to coat the ingredients with the dressing. Set aside for at least 30 minutes at room temperature or refrigerate for up to 2 days. Serve at room temperature, sprinkled with fresh mint leaves and za'atar.

Herbed Egg Bites (Ejjeh)

This humble recipe is one you will find yourself coming back to for its versatility, ease of preparation, and big, fresh flavor. Ejjeh (pronounced "ej-ee") are traditionally made in a pan with small, round indentations, similar to an ebleskiver pan (which is a good substitute). My mom has been known to make two hundred at a time for her church group—quite a production! At the store, we cook the mixture on a rimmed baking sheet, allow it to cool to room temperature, then cut it into small, dense squares. Our catering team makes these by the hundreds as a bite-size appetizer. In the summer, I like it in a pita with slices of ripe tomato and yogurt sauce.

SERVES 6

2 Tbsp extra-virgin olive oil

1 large onion, diced

1 bunch scallions, both white and green parts, thinly sliced

1 Tbsp chopped garlic

12 eggs

1 cup [40 g] chopped fresh parsley

1 bunch chives, sliced

2 Tbsp chopped fresh mint or 1 tsp dried

1 tsp fine sea salt

1 tsp Aleppo pepper

½ tsp freshly ground black pepper

Sliced tomatoes, for serving

Pita bread, for serving

Preheat the oven to 350°F [180°C]. Grease a 9 by 12 in [23 by 30 cm] baking pan with olive oil.

Heat the oil in a large skillet over medium heat. Add the onions, scallions, and garlic and sauté until just softened, about 5 minutes. Remove from the heat and set aside to cool.

Whisk the eggs in a mixing bowl until blended. Stir in the parsley, chives, mint, salt, and Aleppo and black peppers and combine well. Add the cooled onion mixture and mix again to distribute.

Pour the mixture into the prepared pan and bake until golden brown, about 30 minutes, or until a toothpick inserted in the center comes out clean.

Let the ejjeh cool in the pan for 30 minutes before cutting into squares. Serve with sliced tomatoes and pita bread.

VARIATION

To make individual round ejjeh, oil and preheat an ejjeh pan or ebleskiver pan over medium heat. Add ½ tsp of baking powder to the ejjeh batter.

Ladle the batter into the depressions in the heated pan and cook until browned on the bottom, 2 to 3 minutes. Carefully use a fork or the tip of a knife to turn the ejjeh browned-side up and continue to cook until crisp and set throughout.

Savory Salad Topper

Our house-made granolas are among our most popular packaged goods. We make six varieties in small, hand-mixed batches, ranging from sweet to savory, and each one has its partisans. This savory blend with herbs, Urfa pepper, and olives is one of the more unique combos, but once you get past the idea of olives in your granola, you'll find a ton of ways to use it. The salty-sweet flavor is particularly good with labneh, on cooked beans or grains, or simply sprinkled over a green salad.

MAKES ABOUT 6½ CUPS [1 KG]

2¾ cups [275 g] old-fashioned rolled (not quick) oats
1 cup [100 g] sliced almonds
½ cup [80 g] flax seeds
2 tsp herbes de Provence
1 tsp fine sea salt
1 tsp Urfa pepper
½ cup [170 g] honey
⅓ cup [80 ml] extra-virgin olive oil
1 cup [160 g] diced dried apricots
1 cup [140 g] pitted oil-cured olives, patted dry with paper towels (see Note)

Preheat the oven to 350°F [180°C] and line a rimmed baking sheet with parchment paper.

In a large bowl, mix the oats with the almonds, flax seeds, herbes de Provence, salt, and Urfa pepper. In a smaller bowl, whisk together the honey and oil. Pour over the oats and stir well to coat all the dry ingredients with the oil mixture.

Turn the granola onto the baking sheet and spread as thinly as possible. Bake for 10 minutes, then remove from the oven and stir and turn with a metal spatula. Spread out the granola again and return to the oven for 10 to 12 minutes longer, or until browned. Set aside to cool on the baking sheet until crisp.

Add the apricots and olives and mix well, leaving some bigger chunks. Transfer to airtight containers and use within 1 or 2 months.

NOTE

Be sure to pat the olives dry as thoroughly as possible, or they will make the granola soggy. If they are very moist, add them to the granola mixture as it toasts for the last 5 minutes; this will dry them out a bit.

Millet Pilaf with Almonds and Feta

You may have spotted small yellow buckshot-like grains of millet in a loaf of whole-grain "health" bread, but it doesn't appear on the dinner table all that often, which is a shame. Cooked like rice, the tiny round grains bloom into a terrific simple side dish or salad grain. Toasting the millet gives it great flavor and helps keeps the grains fluffy and light.

SERVES 4

½ cup [90 g] millet
½ cup [20 g] chopped fresh parsley
½ cup [50 g] sliced almonds, toasted
¼ cup [12 g] sliced scallions, both white and green parts
¼ cup [30 g] crumbled feta cheese, preferably Greek
1 Tbsp fresh lemon juice
2 tsp extra-virgin olive oil
1 tsp grated lemon zest
1 tsp sumac
½ tsp sea salt
Lemon wedges, for serving

In a medium skillet over medium heat, toast the millet until the grains begin to pop, about 5 minutes, stirring to brown them evenly. Add 1½ cups [360 ml] of water and bring to a boil. Cover the pan, lower the heat to a simmer, and cook for 20 to 30 minutes, or until the millet is dry and fluffy. Transfer to a mixing bowl.

Add the parsley, almonds, scallions, and feta to the millet. Stir together the lemon juice, oil, lemon zest, sumac, and salt and drizzle over the pilaf. Toss to combine and serve hot, warm, or at room temperature with lemon wedges.

TEN MORE WAYS TO USE

FETA

•1•

Marinated Cheese

For a zesty addition to a cheese tray or an unusual salad topper, cut firm feta into ¾ in [2 cm] cubes and toss with 1 or 2 whole dried red chiles, Aleppo pepper, capers, chopped parsley, and a generous drizzle of extra-virgin olive oil. Serve at room temperature with toothpicks or pita wedges.

•2•

Red Pepper and Feta Dip

Blend 8 oz [230 g] of feta with a roasted red pepper, 1 Tbsp of yogurt, ½ tsp of grated garlic, and ½ tsp of Urfa pepper (or 1 tsp of chopped fresh red chile).

•3•

Broiled Feta

For an unusual starter or dessert-cum-cheese course, cut a block of firm feta into ½ in [12 mm] slabs and arrange on a parchment paper–lined baking sheet. Broil the cheese until warmed through and lightly browned, and serve drizzled with honey and sprinkled with toasted sesame seeds.

•4•

Cheesy Dressing

A few tablespoons of feta will give any salad dressing more body and substance, much as blue cheese does, without the aggressive (and polarizing) flavor. Depending on how you plan to use it, either stir in a handful of crumbles or blend the dressing until smooth and creamy, as you prefer.

•5•

Grilled Shrimp with Melted Feta

Thread shrimp and cherry tomatoes onto skewers and grill over a hot fire (or on a grill pan) until the shrimp are pink throughout and the tomatoes are warm. Remove from the skewers and, while still hot, toss together with cubes of feta, letting the feta melt to create a sauce. Stir in chopped fresh oregano or parsley and a drizzle of olive oil.

•6•

Orzo with Feta

Toss hot cooked orzo with a bit of extra-virgin olive oil, chopped raw tomatoes, cubed or crumbled feta, and a generous 1 or 2 Tbsp of chopped fresh oregano or basil. Serve at room temperature.

•7•

Fet-ata

Crumble some feta into a bowl with chopped steamed spinach, beaten eggs, and salt and pepper. Stir to combine and cook in a nonstick skillet until set and browned on the bottom. Either invert the frittata onto a plate and slip it back into the skillet to finish cooking, or place the skillet under the broiler for 1 to 2 minutes to brown the top. Serve warm or at room temperature.

•8•

Watermelon-Feta Salad

If you haven't tried this classic combination yet, don't let another summer go by without it. Toss together cubes of melon and feta with thinly sliced fresh mint, a teeny drizzle of olive oil, and a grind of black pepper. For a more sophisticated presentation, cut the melon and cheese into triangular shards and pile them attractively on individual plates.

•9•

Tomato Salad

For a twist on the more predictable caprese salad, slice good summertime tomatoes—preferably a combination of red, yellow, and green varieties—and arrange on a plate. Crumble feta over the top, then dribble 1 or 2 Tbsp of pesto and a bit of really good oil over all. Finish with a sprinkle of caperberries or capers.

•10•

Feta Pinwheels

Roll 8 oz [230 g] of purchased pizza dough into a square. Scatter the dough generously with crumbled feta, then add bits of chopped olives, roasted red peppers, or cured meat. Roll into a log and brush with a beaten egg. Sprinkle the outside of the log with nigella or sesame seeds if desired, then cut into 1 in [2.5 cm] slices. Bake the slices on a parchment paper–lined baking sheet at 350°F [180°C] until golden, about 15 minutes.

Layered Bulgur, Fennel, and Mint Salad with Pine Nuts

If you like tabbouleh, you will *love* this make-ahead salad, which has even more green herbs and veggies, and lots of interesting textures and flavors in each bite. The salad is made a day (or even two) ahead of time and assembled in layers so the grains absorb the dressing but the herbs and vegetables stay crisp and fresh. Once combined, it can stand out at room temperature for an hour or two.

SERVES 6 TO 8

1 cup [160 g] coarse bulgur or cracked wheat
1 cup [240 ml] fresh lemon juice, plus more as needed
½ cup [120 ml] extra-virgin olive oil
4 garlic cloves, minced
1 tsp fine sea salt
½ tsp freshly ground black pepper
½ tsp sumac
½ tsp Aleppo pepper
8 scallions, both white and green parts, thinly sliced
1 cup [40 g] chopped fresh flat-leaf parsley
½ cup [5 g] chopped fresh dill
½ cup [20 g] chopped fresh mint
4 Persian cucumbers, cut into ½ in [12 mm] dice
½ cup [60 g] pine nuts
1 large fennel bulb with fronds

Put the bulgur in a large salad bowl. In a small bowl, whisk together the lemon juice, oil, garlic, salt, pepper, sumac, and Aleppo pepper. Drizzle the dressing over the bulgur.

Arrange the scallions, parsley, dill, mint, and cucumbers in this order in layers atop the bulgur. Cover with plastic wrap and refrigerate for at least 24 hours or up to 48 hours.

Put the pine nuts in a dry skillet over medium heat. Toast the nuts, tossing frequently and watching carefully to ensure they don't burn, until lightly browned, about 4 minutes. Immediately transfer to a plate to cool.

Just before serving, bring the salad to room temperature. Cut the fennel bulb in half lengthwise, then slice the halves crosswise into paper-thin slices (a mandoline is helpful). Chop ¼ cup [10 g] of the feathery fennel fronds and add them to the salad along with the fennel slices and toasted pine nuts. Toss well to combine and season with additional salt, pepper, Aleppo pepper, and lemon juice as needed.

Quinoa Tabbouleh with Chickpeas

I've upgraded this beloved herb-packed salad from side to main event by adding chickpeas and cubes of salty feta, making it a completely satisfying vegetarian entrée. Quinoa is a more delicate and nutty-tasting alternative to the traditional bulgur wheat, and also delivers more protein. Add bits of grilled chicken or lamb for a truly all-in-one summer lunch or supper. This holds extremely well for up to 5 days in the refrigerator.

SERVES 6

½ cup [120 ml] plus 2 Tbsp extra-virgin olive oil
1½ cups [270 g] quinoa
2 cups [320 g] grape tomatoes, halved or quartered if large
2 Persian cucumbers, finely diced
3 cups [120 g] finely chopped fresh parsley, packed, plus more for garnish
1½ cups [60 g] finely chopped fresh mint, packed, plus more for garnish
1 bunch scallions, both white and green parts, thinly sliced (about 1½ cups)
½ cup [120 ml] fresh lemon juice
1 tsp Aleppo pepper, plus more for garnish
½ tsp sumac
½ tsp sea salt
½ tsp freshly ground black pepper
1 cup [160 g] cooked chickpeas
6 oz [170 g] Greek feta cheese, diced

In a large saucepan, heat the 2 Tbsp of oil until hot. Add the quinoa and toast over medium heat for 2 or 3 minutes, stirring frequently. Add 2 cups [480 ml] of water and bring to a boil. Cover the pan, lower the heat, and simmer for 15 minutes, or until the water is absorbed and the quinoa is tender. Spread the quinoa on a rimmed baking sheet to cool completely.

Scrape the cooled quinoa into a large bowl and add the tomatoes, cucumbers, parsley, mint, and scallions. Toss to combine. In a small bowl, whisk together the lemon juice, remaining ½ cup [120 ml] of oil, Aleppo pepper, sumac, salt, and black pepper. Pour the dressing over the salad, mixing gently but thoroughly. Fold in the chickpeas and feta. Serve chilled or at room temperature, sprinkled with additional parsley, mint, and Aleppo pepper.

Mediterranean Couscous Salad

All of the flavors of a great Greek salad are present here, but a couscous base gives it more heft, making it a nice summertime vegetarian entrée. Because it's packed with vegetables, it looks and tastes light, but the chickpeas give it real staying power.

SERVES 6 AS A MAIN DISH, OR 8 TO 10 AS A SIDE

½ cup [120 ml] plus 1 Tbsp extra-virgin olive oil
2 tsp fine sea salt
1 tsp dried oregano
½ tsp freshly ground black pepper
½ tsp dried basil
¼ tsp ground cinnamon
1¼ cups [225 g] couscous
1 cup [160 g] cooked chickpeas
½ cup [60 g] diced radishes
½ cup [75 g] diced Persian cucumber
4 oz [115 g] feta cheese, diced
½ cup [80 g] halved grape tomatoes
½ cup [24 g] sliced scallions, both white and green parts
½ cup [110 g] roasted red peppers, cut into strips
½ cup [110 g] drained, chopped marinated artichoke hearts
¼ cup [2 g] chopped fresh dill
Juice of 1 large lemon
1 tsp Aleppo pepper

In a large saucepan, combine 3 cups [720 ml] of water with the 1 Tbsp of oil, 1 tsp of the sea salt, and the oregano, black pepper, basil, and cinnamon. Bring to a boil over high heat. Remove the pan from the heat, add the couscous, and stir to combine. Cover the pan and set aside for 5 minutes, or until the water has been absorbed. Fluff the couscous with a fork and let cool completely.

Transfer the couscous to a large bowl. Add the chickpeas, radishes, cucumber, feta, tomatoes, scallions, roasted peppers, and artichoke hearts, and toss to combine. Combine the remaining ½ cup [120 ml] of oil with the dill, lemon juice, the remaining 1 tsp of salt, and the Aleppo pepper. Drizzle over the couscous mixture and toss gently. Serve at room temperature.

Roast Fingerlings with Burrata and Mint Salsa

On Easter Sunday my family and I host an open house for brunch, with at least forty people coming to celebrate the holiday in our home. Along with the usual platters of eggs and a gigantic applewood-smoked ham, I like to offer at least one dish that serves as a vegetarian main course, and this platter of lemony potatoes topped with creamy cheese fits the bill perfectly. It's good warm or cold and is also a beautiful way to round out a summer menu of grilled steak and tomatoes. Use multicolored potatoes if you can find them; it's so much prettier.

SERVES 6

Roast Fingerlings

1 to 1½ lb [455 to 680 g] baby or fingerling potatoes

2 garlic cloves, minced

Juice and zest of 1 lemon

½ tsp fine sea salt

1 tsp Aleppo pepper

½ tsp freshly ground black pepper

¼ cup [60 ml] extra-virgin olive oil, plus more for drizzling

Mint Salsa

4 cups [48 g] lightly packed fresh mint leaves

2 garlic cloves, minced

½ cup [120 ml] extra-virgin olive oil

¾ tsp fine sea salt

1 tsp Aleppo pepper

½ tsp freshly ground black pepper

8 oz [225 g] burrata cheese, torn into irregular pieces

Juice of 1 lemon

To make the roast fingerlings: Preheat the oven to 450°F [230°C]. Place the potatoes on a large baking sheet and sprinkle with the garlic, lemon juice and zest, salt, and Aleppo and black peppers. Drizzle with the oil, then toss with your hands to coat the potatoes evenly with the oil and seasonings.

Spread the potatoes in a single layer and roast for 20 minutes. Toss the potatoes with a spatula, then return them to the oven until golden and crisp, another 20 to 25 minutes.

To make the mint salsa: While the potatoes roast, combine the mint and garlic in a food processor. Pulse three or four times to coarsely chop the mint, then, with the motor running, add the oil in a steady stream. Purée until finely chopped but not completely puréed. Season with the salt and Aleppo and black peppers.

To serve, arrange the potatoes on a platter and top with the burrata. Drizzle the salsa over the potatoes and cheese, top with a squeeze of lemon juice, and serve warm or at room temperature.

Za'atar-Roasted Vegetables

I have gotten in the habit of keeping a covered container of these roasted veggies in the fridge, and they never go to waste. We serve them at room temperature as an instant side dish, tuck them into sandwiches, and dice them into grain salads. You can adapt this basic method to any seasonal vegetables you have on hand, from wedges of cabbage and sliced leeks to tender summer squashes and quartered radishes.

SERVES 6 TO 8

¼ cup [60 ml] extra-virgin olive oil
2 Tbsp za'atar
1 tsp Urfa pepper
½ tsp fine sea salt
1 small cauliflower, cut into florets
1 large broccoli crown, cut into florets
1 tsp Aleppo pepper

Preheat the oven to 475°F [240°C].

In a mixing bowl, whisk together the oil, za'atar, Urfa pepper, and salt. Add the cauliflower and broccoli and toss to thoroughly coat the veggies with the seasonings. Turn the vegetables onto a large rimmed baking sheet and spread them in a single layer.

Roast, turning the vegetables two or three times to ensure they cook evenly, until they are nicely browned and just cooked, about 20 minutes. Transfer to a serving bowl and sprinkle with the Aleppo pepper for a little more kick and color. Serve hot or at room temperature.

Clams Steamed with Za'atar and Herbs

A big pot of steamed clams is a wonderful dish for entertaining because it is deceptively easy to prepare and brings so much briny, fresh flavor to the table. In the summer, make this on the grill in a disposable aluminum pan or cast iron skillet with a cover. Then spend the evening dipping bread into the savory broth, sipping rosé, and enjoying the sunset.

SERVES 4

3 dozen topneck or littleneck clams
¼ cup [60 ml] extra-virgin olive oil
2 shallots, thinly sliced
6 garlic cloves, sliced
1 cup [240 ml] dry white wine
1 Tbsp za'atar
¼ cup [10 g] chopped fresh mint
¼ cup [10 g] chopped fresh parsley
Country bread, for dipping

Scrub the clams well and set aside in a bowl of water to soak.

Heat the oil in a large pot over medium heat just until hot. Add the shallots and garlic and sauté for 5 minutes, or until aromatic but not brown. Add the wine and za'atar, bring to a boil, and cook for 5 minutes to reduce slightly.

Add the clams and 1 cup [240 ml] of water and return to a boil. Reduce the heat to low, cover the pan, and cook, shaking the pan now and then, for 10 minutes, or until the clams have opened. If one or two haven't opened, remove the opened clams to a serving bowl and keep warm. Continue to cook the unopened clams for 1 to 2 more minutes. If any haven't popped open by that point, discard them.

Stir the mint and parsley into the broth, then pour the broth over the clams. Serve with bread for dipping.

Spaghetti with Burst Cherry Tomatoes, Pancetta, and Feta

Mozzarella might be more expected in a dish like this, but feta gives it a different character entirely. It's both lighter and fresher tasting, with plenty of punch from garlic and chiles, and it's extremely quick to put together. It's important to use a good sheep's milk feta; those made from cow's milk, like many supermarket brands, will not emulsify into the sauce properly to produce the smooth texture you're after.

SERVES 6

2 Tbsp extra-virgin olive oil
4 to 5 oz [115 to 140 g] pancetta, diced (about 1 cup)
2 shallots, minced
6 garlic cloves, minced
4 cups [640 g] cherry tomatoes
1 tsp Urfa pepper
1 tsp freshly ground black pepper
½ tsp fine sea salt
1 lb [455 g] spaghetti
4 oz [115 g] imported feta, cut into small cubes (about 1 cup)
1 cup [40 g] chopped fresh parsley

Bring a large pot of salted water to a boil.

In a large skillet, heat the oil over medium heat. Add the pancetta, shallots, and garlic and sauté without browning until softened and aromatic. Add the cherry tomatoes and sauté until they just burst and start to release their juices, 6 to 8 minutes. Season with the Urfa and black peppers and the salt and remove from the heat.

While the tomato mixture is cooking, add the spaghetti to the boiling water and cook according to the package directions to just al dente. Drain the spaghetti, reserving 1 cup [240 ml] of the cooking water.

Add the spaghetti to the skillet with the tomato mixture and toss over medium heat until well combined. Add the feta and the reserved pasta water and toss until the feta begins to melt and the sauce is creamy and thickened. Toss with the parsley and serve immediately.

Flounder Fillet with Fennel, Orange, and Olive Salad

The combination of fennel, orange, and olives is a classic of Moroccan cuisine, and I think it works even better as a salsa-like topping for baked fish. Flounder is readily available, but it tends to be pretty mild. Here, I have given it a head start on flavor with a spicy herbed marinade and a lot more texture thanks to the salsa topping. The bright salsa also cuts through any "fishy" flavors that might raise objections at your table.

SERVES 6

¼ cup [30 g] garlic cloves

1 mild hot red chile, such as Fresno, stemmed, seeded, and sliced

Zest and juice of 2 medium lemons

1 Tbsp ground cumin

1 Tbsp paprika

1 tsp ground cinnamon

1 tsp sea salt

1¼ cups [300 ml] extra-virgin olive oil

1 bunch cilantro, chopped

1 bunch parsley, chopped

1¾ lb [800 g] flounder fillets

1 large fennel bulb, thinly sliced, fronds reserved

2 large oranges, preferably Cara Cara

1 red onion, sliced into thin half moons

4 oz [115 g] Moroccan oil-cured olives

¼ cup [60 ml] white balsamic or prosecco vinegar

1 tsp Aleppo pepper

Combine the garlic, chile, lemon zest and juice, cumin, paprika, cinnamon, and salt in a blender or food processor and purée until smooth. Drizzle in ½ cup [120 ml] of the oil and blend thoroughly. Add the cilantro and parsley and pulse on and off until combined but not fully puréed.

Put the fish in a bowl or resealable plastic bag. Pour three-quarters of the herb mixture over the fillets and turn to coat. Cover the bowl or seal the bag and refrigerate for at least 3 hours, preferably overnight. Refrigerate the remaining marinade in a covered container.

When ready to serve, preheat the oven to 375°F [190°C] and oil a large baking pan. Place the flounder in the pan in a single layer and bake for 15 to 20 minutes, or until the fillets flake easily with a fork. Set aside to cool thoroughly.

Put the sliced fennel in a large bowl. Chop the fronds and reserve for garnish. Use a large, sharp knife to slice the skin and pith off of the oranges. Halve the oranges lengthwise, then cut the halves crosswise into half moons; don't slice them too thinly or the slices will break apart. Add the oranges, red onion, and olives to the fennel mixture.

Flake the flounder into large pieces and add them to the fennel salad. Stir the remaining ¾ cup [180 ml] of oil into the reserved marinade. Add the vinegar and whisk well. Pour half of the vinaigrette over the salad and toss gently, breaking up the flounder as little as possible. Taste and add more vinaigrette if necessary. Sprinkle with the Aleppo pepper and the reserved fennel fronds. Pass the remaining vinaigrette at the table.

Salmon Kebabs with Nigella

Like many families, mine is eating less red meat and more salmon these days. As a result, I'm always looking for new ways to prepare it. Much as I love Slow-Roasted Harissa Salmon (page 193), I might like this dish even better—and not just because there's virtually no cleanup when I cook the fish on the grill. I find cumin pairs really well with salmon, giving the dish a gutsy, hearty flavor that appeals especially to the carnivores in the crowd. Serve it over pilaf, in a pita drizzled with Pomegranate Vinaigrette (page 58), or atop a bed of arugula dressed with the same vinaigrette for a sweet/sour contrast.

SERVES 6

2 lb [910 g] center-cut skinless salmon fillet, cut into 2 in [5 cm] chunks
2 Tbsp chopped fresh parsley
2 Tbsp chopped fresh mint
2 Tbsp chopped fresh chives
2 tsp Aleppo pepper
1 tsp ground cumin
1 tsp fine sea salt
½ tsp freshly ground black pepper
½ tsp nigella seeds
½ cup [120 ml] extra-virgin olive oil
1 red onion, cut into wedges
1 lemon (Meyer lemon, if available), cut into wedges

Put the salmon in a resealable plastic bag. Combine the parsley, mint, chives, Aleppo pepper, cumin, salt, black pepper, and nigella in a small bowl. Add the oil and stir to moisten. Pour the herb mixture over the salmon, turning the chunks to coat. Seal the bag and marinate for 2 hours in the refrigerator.

Prepare an outdoor grill or preheat the broiler. Thread the salmon onto metal skewers, alternating with pieces of red onion. Grill or broil for 2 to 3 minutes per side for a slightly pink interior or to your preferred degree of doneness.

Serve hot with the lemon wedges.

Grilled Chicken Paillard with Roasted Pepper and Kalamata Olive Salsa

The beauty of a dish like this one is that it can be served warm, right off the grill, or at room temperature as part of a picnic buffet or a pack-along lunch. If you prefer to substitute boneless, skinless chicken thighs for the breast cutlets, go right ahead; just allow a few extra minutes of cooking time.

SERVES 4

Chicken Paillard

4 boneless, skinless chicken breast halves

¼ cup [60 ml] extra-virgin olive oil

¼ cup [10 g] chopped fresh cilantro

1 tsp fine sea salt

1 tsp freshly ground black pepper

1 tsp Aleppo or Urfa pepper

2 medium garlic cloves, crushed with the side of a knife

Roasted Pepper and Olive Salsa

½ cup [70 g] Kalamata olives, sliced

½ cup [110 g] roasted red peppers, diced

5 scallions, both white and green parts, sliced

1 fresh jalapeño pepper, minced

4 garlic cloves, thinly sliced

¼ cup [10 g] chopped fresh cilantro

2 Tbsp minced preserved lemon rind, store-bought or homemade (page 43)

2 Tbsp extra-virgin olive oil

1 Tbsp fresh lemon juice

1 tsp freshly ground black pepper

1 tsp Aleppo or Urfa pepper, plus more for garnish

Fine sea salt

To make the chicken: Using a large, sharp knife, carefully slice each chicken breast in half horizontally to make 2 thin cutlets.

In a large bowl, stir together the oil, cilantro, salt, black and Aleppo peppers, and the crushed garlic. Add the chicken cutlets and toss to cover with the mixture. Cover the bowl and refrigerate for at least 2 hours and up to 12 hours.

To make the salsa: In a medium bowl, combine all the salsa ingredients thoroughly, reserving some of the scallion greens for garnish. Set the salsa aside at room temperature to blend the flavors together or refrigerate, covered, for up to 3 days (let it return to room temperature before serving).

When ready to cook, prepare a hot fire in a barbecue grill or preheat a ridged grill pan until quite hot. Oil the grates or ridges well. Grill the chicken over high heat just until browned on each side, 2 to 3 minutes per side. Don't overcook or the chicken will be tough.

Spoon some of the salsa over the chicken and garnish with the reserved scallion greens and a few pepper flakes. Serve hot or at room temperature. Pass the remaining salsa at the table.

Make-Your-Own Za'atar Chicken Bowl

We get a big lunch crowd at our Industry City café and market, and za'atar chicken is far and away the most-ordered item on the menu. The chicken itself is really simple, but served over a freekeh or greens bowl and topped with your choice of extras, from Greek barrel-cured feta to Kalamata olive slices or house-cured turnips and cauliflower, it becomes more than the sum of its parts. Green Tahini and Date Balsamic are the dressings of choice, and a bit of red onion relish completes the meal perfectly.

SERVES 4

½ cup [120 ml] extra-virgin olive oil

¼ cup [30 g] za'atar

2 lb [910 g] boneless, skinless chicken thighs

Roasted red pepper strips, crumbled feta cheese, chopped tomato, sliced Persian cucumbers, Kalamata olive slices, and pickled vegetables, for toppings

Green Tahini Dressing or Date Balsamic Dressing (recipes follow)

Onion Relish (page 68)

4 cups [80 g] mixed greens

4 cups [480 g] cooked freekeh or quinoa, at room temperature (optional)

Stir the oil and za'atar together in a bowl. Add the chicken and turn to coat in the herbed mixture. Cover and refrigerate for at least 4 hours and up to 24 hours.

Heat a ridged grill pan until very hot and oil the grill. Add the chicken and cook without moving until it releases from the ridges and is starting to char here and there, about 8 minutes. Turn the chicken pieces and cook on the second side until cooked through, another 5 or 6 minutes. It should be well marked but still juicy.

Transfer to a plate and allow to rest for 10 minutes, or cool to room temperature. Cut the chicken pieces into ½ in [12 mm] strips and arrange on a platter. Arrange the toppings of choice and a small pitcher of dressing around the platter.

Divide the greens or grains (or do as some of our customers do and mix the two) into four shallow bowls. Allow diners to help themselves to chicken strips and toppings, then drizzle on the dressing. Enjoy!

Green Tahini Dressing

1 cup [220 g] tahini

¼ cup [60 ml] fresh lemon juice

1 cup [20 g] mixed herbs, such as parsley, cilantro, chives, or basil

2 garlic cloves, minced

1 tsp fine sea salt

1 tsp Aleppo pepper

Combine all the ingredients in a food processor with ½ cup [120 ml] of water. Purée until smooth and thick, adding more water, 1 Tbsp at a time, until it is as thick as you want. It should be thick enough to coat a spoon but thin enough to drizzle. Taste and add more salt if needed. Store in a tightly covered jar for up to a week; the dressing will thicken as it stands, so thin with additional water as needed.

Date Balsamic Dressing

¼ cup [85 g] date syrup

¼ cup [60 ml] olive oil

2 Tbsp balsamic vinegar

1 Tbsp chopped fresh mint or 1 tsp dried

1 tsp sumac

½ tsp freshly ground black pepper

½ tsp Aleppo pepper

Combine all the ingredients in a sealable jar and shake to blend. Store in the refrigerator for up to a week; the flavor gets even better after a day or two.

TEN MORE WAYS TO USE

MINT

·1·

Fresh Mint Tea

For the simplest of all herbal teas, simply pour hot water over a generous handful of leaves; to serve in the Moroccan style, steep a bag of black tea along with the fresh leaves. Sweeten with honey and serve hot or over ice.

·2·

Simple Tomato Salad

Finely shred 2 or 3 Tbsp of fresh mint and scatter over sliced ripe tomatoes sprinkled with crumbled feta. Dress with a drizzle of olive oil, sea salt, and black or Aleppo pepper.

·3·

No-Cook Summer Pasta Sauce

Combine 2 cups [320 g] of halved grape tomatoes, 1 cup of diced manouri cheese, 3 or 4 chopped scallions, and ½ cup [20 g] of chopped fresh mint in a large bowl. Season with salt and pepper, toss with ½ cup [120 ml] of extra-virgin olive oil, then let the mixture sit at room temperature until it becomes saucy. Toss with 1 lb [455 g] of hot cooked pasta and serve warm or at room temperature.

·4·

Minted Whipped Cream

Heat 1 cup [235 ml] of heavy cream in a medium pan just until a few bubbles start to form around the edges (do not allow to boil) and add a big handful of fresh mint leaves. Remove from the heat and steep until the mint has infused the cream and the cream has cooled. Discard the mint and refrigerate the cream until well chilled, then sweeten lightly with confectioner's sugar and whip to soft peaks. Dollop the cream onto any white or dark chocolate dessert or your favorite mocha coffee drink.

•5•

Savory Marinade

Cut 4 large boneless, skinless chicken breasts into 1½ in [4 cm] chunks. In a blender, grind 1 cup [12 g] of lightly packed fresh mint leaves with 1 medium sweet onion to make a paste. Season well with salt. Set aside 1 or 2 Tbsp of the paste; toss the remainder with the chicken chunks and refrigerate for 30 to 60 minutes. Thread the chunks onto skewers and grill, turning often to prevent burning (a few charred spots are just fine). For a shortcut tzatziki sauce, stir the reserved mint paste into some plain yogurt.

•6•

Peppermint Hot Cocoa

Drop a couple of sprigs into your favorite homemade or prepared hot cocoa mix and steep for 1 to 2 minutes. Discard, top with whipped cream, and garnish with a fresh sprig of mint.

•7•

Mint Chimichurri

Combine 1 packed cup [12 g] of fresh mint leaves, the grated zest of 1 lemon, and 1 garlic clove in a food processor. Pulse four or five times to chop finely but do not purée. Add about ⅓ cup [80 ml] of extra-virgin olive oil or enough to make a loose sauce. Season with salt, pepper, and a few shakes of Aleppo pepper (or a pinch of hot red pepper flakes) and serve over grilled skirt steak, lamb chops, or a meaty fish like halibut or swordfish.

•8•

Minted Strawberry Lemonade

In a bowl, muddle together a few fresh hulled strawberries and a handful of fresh mint leaves. Add about ½ cup [120 ml] of fresh lemon juice (from 6 to 8 lemons) and sweeten with simple syrup. Allow the mixture to steep for a few minutes, then strain into a pitcher filled with ice. Add fresh lemon slices, a few halved berries, and fresh mint sprigs; top off with seltzer. This is also a nice summer cocktail if you add a bit of vodka or limoncello to the muddled mixture.

•9•

Creamy Pepper Sauce

Combine 1 cup [240 g] of sour cream with ½ cup [110 g] of roasted red peppers and ¼ cup [3 g] of fresh mint leaves in a small food processor or blender. Purée until smooth; season with salt and pepper and serve with grilled meats or in a wrap sandwich with leftover roasted veggies.

•10•

Sandwich Stuffer

Substitute fresh mint leaves for lettuce or other greens in a pita sandwich; with bits of meat, fish, or even a scoop of hummus, it's a back-of-house staff favorite lunch on the run.

Bittersweet Chocolate Mint Mousse

Mint is most often used in savory preparations, but I think a whisper of spearmint flavor lightens a rich dessert like this mousse and gives it a festive feel. In the summer I serve this just barely frozen for a refreshing end to a more formal meal; in the winter, I prefer it chilled with a garnish of fresh mint. Either way it's a convenient make-ahead dessert that is always a hit.

SERVES 6 TO 8

2 cups [80 g] coarsely chopped fresh mint leaves, loosely packed (about 1 large store-bought bunch)

2 cups [480 ml] heavy cream

12 oz [340 g] bittersweet chocolate, chopped

¼ cup [55 g] (½ stick) unsalted butter

2 Tbsp granulated sugar

¼ tsp fine sea salt

3 eggs, separated

2 Tbsp confectioner's sugar

1 tsp crème de menthe (optional)

Fresh mint sprigs for garnish

Put the chopped mint in a heatproof bowl. In a saucepan, bring the cream just to a boil and immediately pour it over the mint leaves. Let cool to room temperature, then cover and refrigerate for at least 2 hours or overnight to chill thoroughly.

Put the chocolate in the top of a double boiler and melt over (but not touching) simmering water until smooth, stirring frequently. Add the butter and continue to stir until combined. Let cool for 5 minutes, then add the sugar and salt and mix well.

Add the egg yolks to the chocolate mixture and beat with a wooden spoon until well blended. In a mixer bowl fitted with the whisk attachment, beat the egg whites on high speed just until soft peaks form. Fold the beaten whites into the chocolate mixture.

Strain the flavored cream into a separate mixer bowl, discarding the mint. Beat on medium speed until soft peaks form. Remove the bowl from the mixer and add one-half of the beaten cream to the mousse mixture, folding it in gently until just a few streaks of white remain. Spoon the mousse into individual serving dishes or one large bowl. Add the confectioner's sugar and crème de menthe to the remaining cream and beat until firm peaks form. Cover the bowls of mousse and whipped cream and refrigerate until ready to serve.

To serve, dollop the mousse with whipped cream and garnish with fresh mint leaves.

Blueberry Melon Salsa

In the summertime we serve this as an accompaniment to grilled meats, but it's also a simple, refreshing dish to enjoy at the end of the meal, as a Middle Easterner would, or with yogurt at brunch or breakfast. I find the lime isn't necessary when the fruit is at its peak, but other times of the year it coaxes out a bit more flavor from off-season produce. Extra mint syrup can be stored refrigerated in a covered container for 4 weeks.

SERVES 4

Mint Syrup
1 cup sugar
1 cup tightly packed mint leaves

2 cups [280 g] blueberries
2 cups [310 g] diced honeydew melon
2 Tbsp slivered fresh mint leaves, plus sprigs for garnish
1 Tbsp fresh lime juice

To make the Mint Syrup: Combine the sugar with 1 cup [240 ml] of water in a small saucepan. Bring to a boil, then stir just until the sugar dissolves, about 1 minute. Remove from the heat, add the mint, and stir to combine. Set aside to cool to room temperature. Strain and discard the mint leaves.

Combine the fruit in a large bowl and drizzle with 2 Tbsp of the mint syrup. Add half of the mint leaves and lime juice and toss to combine. Let stand for 30 minutes to combine the flavors, then toss again and add the remaining slivered mint leaves. Serve garnished with the mint sprigs.

3
SPICED

HOT, WARMING, SMOKY

HARISSA

RAS EL HANOUT

BERBERE

SHAWARMA SPICES

ALEPPO PEPPER

URFA PEPPER

Few traditional Middle Eastern dishes scale the fiery heights of Mexican or Szechuan fare, but that hardly means they lack sizzle. Many are served "warm"—that is, with a hint of heat from spices like cumin, ginger, or saffron. A finishing shake or sprinkle of dried chile flakes or ground harissa spices is second nature for many Middle Eastern cooks. And spicy condiments like zhug, a garlicky blend similar to aioli, or pepper paste might be passed at the table so everyone can turn up the temperature to their own preference. In this chapter you'll learn all the ways these warming ingredients can be layered and combined to satisfy the desire for heat in new and exciting ways.

This is also where you'll get better acquainted with versatile Middle Eastern and North African spice blends like berbere, shawarma, and ras el hanout. I think of these mixtures as true convenience foods for their ability to bring a dish together and add layers of flavor to everything I put on the grill or roast in the oven. Pick one or several to keep near the stove; you'll be surprised just how easily a pinch of these warming blends adds the impression of long-cooked flavor to quick meals and sauces without adding overt heat.

That said, there's no denying the appeal of hot, spicy food, and as specialty food merchants, we have seen the humble bottle of Tabasco take a back seat to a more international roster of chile sauces, from sriracha to sambal oelek. Lately, harissa seems to be having a moment, but it's hardly the only Middle Eastern ingredient that can bring the heat. In our household, mellow Aleppo pepper is as ubiquitous as salt, used as both a layering and finishing ingredient that adds just a hint of heat. You won't find many pinkies-up formal dishes in this section, but nearly all are guaranteed to get the party started at your next casual gathering. Don't forget the napkins and the beer!

STARTERS

SOUPS, SALADS, AND SIDES

ENTRÉES

SWEETS

HARISSA
SPICES
LIQUID HARISSA
RAS EL
HANOUT

SHAWARMA
SPICES
ALEPPO
PEPPER
URFA
PEPPER
BERBERE
DRIED
GINGER

Harissa

You are probably most familiar with harissa in its liquid or paste form as a ready-to-use condiment, but we also sell harissa as a dry spice blend. Either of those products is a wonderful way to inject both heat and depth into a dish, and I tend to use them in tandem to create layers of flavor. We toast, mix, and grind our own harissa spices at the warehouse in Brooklyn, and its fans are so devoted, we sell more than a hundred pounds each week. The mixture combines five types of chiles (including guajillo and ancho) and whole caraway, cumin, and coriander seeds, all of which we toast separately and then grind together into a not-too-fine mixture that is finally seasoned with garlic, paprika, and salt and pepper. It's a labor-intensive process, but the resulting spice blend is heady, complex, and just fiery enough.

> WHAT TO LOOK FOR • Choose a spice mixture that is more chunky than fine. You should be able to pick out individual bits of spices and chiles—and pops of different flavors on your tongue. Store harissa spices away from heat, which will dissipate its flavors. Liquid harissa, in paste or sauce form, should be refrigerated after opening.

> SERVE WITH • Harissa has an affinity for fish and seafood. Dry harissa spices need heat and moisture (usually oil) to encourage their flavors to develop and bloom, making them a good choice for marinades and other cooked dishes. Liquid harissa can be used as is, in much the same way you would use any hot sauce, to season dips or dressings or squirt directly onto a burger.

Ras el Hanout

This spice blend comes from North Africa and features many of the warming spices associated with baking: cinnamon, cloves, and allspice. As is typical in spice blends, the mixtures vary from maker to maker, with savory ingredients like cumin, thyme, and even ground rosebuds making an appearance in some versions. The version we sell under our private label includes turmeric but not cumin (which can push the mixture far more to the savory end of the spectrum). Always read the label to see exactly what your blend contains, especially if you will be using it in any of the sweets recipes in this book!

Berbere

This medium-spicy Ethiopian blend has a base of paprika and garam masala, with strong accents of baking spices like ginger and cinnamon. Toasted ground cumin and anise seeds give it an appealing crunchy texture. Although it has many of the same warming notes as ras el hanout, it skews more savory due to notes of onion and garlic. Berbere is the grill master's best friend, as it is the perfect accent for almost anything cooked over an open flame. To make your own, see page 160.

WHAT TO LOOK FOR • A bright, rich red color indicates a blend that will have vibrant flavor; if it's dull or dark, chances are the mixture has been improperly stored or is past its prime. Bits of the ground cumin and coriander seeds should be visible as well. If possible, give the berbere blend a sniff; there should be a faint aroma of toasted chiles.

SERVE WITH • Berbere can be used in dishes that are cooked, as in marinades and sauces, or sprinkled on as a finishing seasoning. It's especially good on grilled meats and poultry, but it also has an affinity for seafood, including shrimp and lobster.

Shawarma Spices

If you've ever had a shawarma sandwich, thin slices of marinated beef or other meat cooked on a vertical rotisserie, then you know how much the seasoning contributes to the end product. Allspice is the dominant note, followed by cumin and coriander, making an intensely fragrant blend that fills your house with enticing aromas as it cooks.

WHAT TO LOOK FOR • We make two blends, one for chicken and another for meat. To make your own, see page 204. Like all ground spice blends, shawarma spices should be stored away from heat and light to preserve their fresh flavors.

SERVE WITH • Shawarma obviously pairs well with any grilled meat, either as part of the marinade or sprinkled on top. Sprinkle it on vegetables before roasting or grilling.

Aleppo Pepper

Even a cursory glance through the recipes in this book will make it obvious how often we reach for the dried pepper shaker at my house, even when making dishes that aren't intended to come across as "spicy." In particular, I use mild Aleppo pepper as a finishing touch on cooked vegetables, dips and spreads, and salad dressings to add a dash of color, a textural note, and a gentle flavor enhancement.

As the name indicates, Aleppo peppers are native to Syria, and they are still widely grown and consumed throughout the region. These days we source ours from Turkey, where we are able to ensure a more consistent supply.

WHAT TO LOOK FOR • The flakes should be pliable but not damp or clumpy and have a good red color, which indicates freshness. Store them away from heat in a tightly covered container.

SERVE WITH • I consider Aleppo a finishing pepper, one that can be sprinkled on foods and eaten as is, as well as cooked into a recipe. I use it as freely as salt because its kick is so mild.

Urfa Pepper

This Turkish chile, also called Urfa biber, has only recently become readily available outside of the Middle East. It has a stronger bite than the milder Aleppo peppers. On the plant it is more burgundy than red in appearance and dries to a rich color indicative of its deeper, winey flavor with smoky notes similar to a chipotle. It is full of flavor, with a nice heat that lingers.

WHAT TO LOOK FOR • Urfa peppers are allowed to dry on the vine before harvest, and like a sun-dried tomato, they remain somewhat soft, with a slightly chewy texture. Look for a deep red-brown hue and a smoky aroma.

SERVE WITH • I love it in braises and stews, where the longer cooking time brings out its complex flavors; 1 Tbsp would elevate a pot roast to something company worthy. Use it to season pulled pork or chicken—it adds complexity along with heat.

Apricot Hot Pepper Jelly

Unlike most hot pepper jellies, this one has a lovely fruitiness that makes it a wonderful addition to a cheese plate alongside some Manchego or Brie. It also makes a great glaze for grilled salmon. If you are new to jelly making, this is the perfect entry-level recipe. There is no fresh fruit to pit, peel, and process, and the dried apricots cook up to a thick, jammy consistency without the addition of pectin. I use the fresh Urfa and Aleppo peppers from my garden, but unless you grow your own they are hard to come by, so in this recipe I've supplemented dried Aleppo pepper with more readily available habaneros. It will be very spicy; substitute milder jalapeños if you want a less incendiary product. Note that this jelly (pictured on page 84) is not fully processed and must be stored in the refrigerator before and after using.

MAKES THREE 8 OZ [230 G] JARS

2 cups [400 g] sugar
1 cup [240 ml] apple cider vinegar
½ cup [80 g] thinly sliced dried apricots
¼ cup [35 g] finely diced red onion
¼ cup [30 g] finely diced red bell pepper
¼ cup [26 g] finely diced fresh habanero peppers
2 Tbsp Aleppo pepper flakes

Put the sugar, vinegar, and apricots in a saucepan and stir to combine. Bring to a boil, then add the onion and fresh and dried peppers. Reduce the heat to medium and simmer until thickened and fragrant, about 20 minutes, stirring occasionally. Don't overcook the jelly—it will continue to thicken as it cools. To check, pour a spoonful onto a chilled saucer and tilt it back and forth to cool. If it is still drippy, simmer the mixture for another 5 minutes and test again.

When it is thickened to your liking, ladle the hot jelly into sterilized jars, cover with the lids, and store in the refrigerator for up to 6 months.

Brooklyn Nachos

If nachos took a spin through the Mediterranean, this might be the result. We swapped out refried beans for favas and feta for the Cheddar, and added a heaping handful of herbs and spices. It's a big, delicious pile of cheesy, beany goodness with the dippers built right in. And like regular nachos, they'll be gone before you know it.

SERVES 4 TO 6

¼ cup [60 ml] extra-virgin olive oil

1 shallot, finely chopped

1 garlic clove, minced

One 15 or 19 oz [430 or 540 g] can fava beans (foul mudammas)

2 tsp Aleppo pepper

1 tsp ground cumin

½ tsp ground allspice

1 tsp fine sea salt

4 cups [180 g] pita chips, homemade from 4 to 6 pitas (page 49) or purchased

1 bunch scallions, both white and green parts, thinly sliced

½ red onion, sliced into thin half moons

1 plum tomato, diced

¼ cup [10 g] chopped fresh parsley

¼ cup [10 g] chopped fresh mint

1 tsp sumac

1 cup [240 g] plain yogurt, stirred until smooth

½ cup [60 g] crumbled feta cheese

¼ cup [35 g] sliced pitted green or black olives

Mint sprigs, for garnish

Heat the oil in a saucepan over medium heat. Add the shallot and garlic and sauté until softened and fragrant, 4 to 5 minutes. Add the beans and their liquid, then stir in 1 tsp of the Aleppo pepper and the cumin, allspice, and ½ tsp of the salt. Reduce the heat to low and simmer, covered, for 10 to 12 minutes, or until thick and fragrant. Keep warm.

To assemble, spread the pita chips on a large platter. In a bowl, toss the scallions, red onion, tomato, parsley, mint, remaining ½ tsp of salt, and sumac together until combined. Spoon the fava beans onto the pita chips and drizzle with the yogurt. Top with the vegetable relish, crumbled feta, and olives. Sprinkle with the remaining Aleppo pepper and garnish with mint sprigs. Serve immediately.

Bold and Spicy Hummus

We go through so much of this hummus in our stores that the kitchen whips up four or five batches *every single day*, ensuring that the dill is always fresh and green. Its herbaceous flavor is a perfect complement to the kick of peppers. I especially like this hummus (pictured on page 108) spread on multigrain toast with some sliced tomato and a sprinkle of sea salt.

MAKES 2 CUPS [440 G]

2 cups [320 g] cooked chickpeas, drained and liquid reserved (see Note, page 40)

¼ cup [55 g] tahini

¼ cup [60 ml] fresh lemon juice

½ tsp fine sea salt

¼ cup [2 g] packed fresh dill, thick stems discarded

1 tsp hot red pepper flakes

¼ tsp cayenne pepper

Put the chickpeas in a blender or food processor with 3 Tbsp of the reserved liquid. Add the tahini, lemon juice, and salt and blend until smooth. Check the consistency and add more of the reserved chickpea liquid by the tsp if it is too thick.

Scrape the hummus into a mixing bowl and stir in the dill, pepper flakes, and cayenne. The hummus can be stored in a covered container in the refrigerator for a day or two, after which the dill will lose its vibrancy. For best flavor, serve at room temperature.

Spiced Salt

At the end of the summer I always have lots of herbs and fresh peppers left in the garden that I don't want to lose to an unexpected frost, so I've gotten in the habit of making huge batches of this (pictured on page 42) each year. We use it as an all-purpose seasoning throughout the winter, spring, and early summer until the new crop is ready, and it is also a nice homemade gift. It will be different every year, depending on which herbs and peppers you use. If you are using fresh chiles and herbs from your garden, tie the stems in bunches and hang the herbs for at least 1 week and the peppers for up to 4 weeks, or until they are very thoroughly dried. I like the texture the chile seeds add, but if you want a more conservative heat, you can remove them.

MAKES ABOUT 3 CUPS [450 G]

3 or 4 dried Thai bird's eye chiles

2 whole dried Aleppo chiles or 1 tsp Aleppo pepper flakes

1 tsp Urfa pepper flakes

1 to 2 cups [20 to 40 g] (whatever you have on hand) mixed fresh herb leaves (or home-dried leaves, stems discarded), such as thyme, oregano, mint, za'atar, or marjoram

1 small bunch chives, chopped (about 1 cup [48 g])

2 garlic cloves, minced

1 lb [455 g] flaky salt, such as Maldon or Fleur de Sel

Line a rimmed baking sheet with parchment paper.

Seed the chiles if you prefer a milder heat; otherwise tear or chop into small pieces and place in a food processor with the pepper flakes. Add the herb leaves to the food processor along with the chives and garlic. Pulse on and off until everything is well combined and the chiles are chopped medium fine but identifiable flecks remain. The mixture will be somewhat damp from the garlic.

Stir the chile-herb mixture into the salt until blended, then spread on the prepared baking sheet, breaking up any clumps with your fingers. Let the mixture stand at room temperature until bone dry, blending with your hands now and then. This can take anywhere from 3 days to 1 week. Alternatively, dry the mixture on your oven's lowest setting for about an hour, checking often.

When fully dried, transfer the mixture to jars and cover tightly with the lids. Use within 1 year.

SAHADI'S SNACK MIX
page 224
ZA'ATAR BREAD
page 98

BROOKLYN NACHOS
page 155
SWEET-AND-SOUR
BEEF HAND PIES
page 76
SAHADI'S HOT WINGS
page 168

Fiery Berbere Shrimp

Easy, easy, easy and truly tasty. Make an extra skewer or two; the leftovers are delicious chopped into a salad, folded into a quesadilla, or stuffed into a pita with veggies and a bit of yogurt. Jumbo shrimp are pricier than smaller shrimp, but they are really the best for grilling because they can develop a bit of that delicious char around the edges without overcooking. This makes about 3 cups [390 g] of spice blend; store the extra in a tightly sealed jar and use within three months for best flavor.

SERVES 6

Berbere Spice Mix

1 Tbsp whole cumin seed
1 tsp whole anise seed
2 cups [160 g] paprika
½ cup [40 g] garam masala
1 Tbsp ground ginger
1 Tbsp hot curry powder
1 Tbsp ground cinnamon
1 Tbsp ground cardamom
1 Tbsp onion powder
1 Tbsp fine sea salt
1 tsp granulated garlic
1 tsp ground allspice
1 tsp cayenne pepper

Shrimp

½ cup [120 ml] extra-virgin olive oil
2 lb [910 g] jumbo shrimp, peeled and deveined
Lemon wedges, for serving

Make the berbere spice mix: In a dry skillet over medium heat, toast the cumin and anise seeds until golden. Transfer to a spice grinder or mortar and crush lightly; you want some texture.

Transfer the toasted seeds to a bowl and add the remaining ingredients. Mix well.

To make the shrimp: Combine ½ cup [65 g] of the berbere spice and the oil in a large bowl. Add the shrimp and use your hands to massage the spice blend into the shrimp. Cover the bowl and refrigerate for 4 to 24 hours.

Preheat a gas or charcoal fire or ridged grill pan until very hot. Oil the grates well using tongs and an oil-saturated paper towel.

Thread the shrimp onto metal skewers, making sure the shrimp are lined up in the same direction for ease of cooking and turning. Place the skewers over the hottest part of the grill and sear for 2 to 3 minutes per side, or until browned at the edges and marked. Don't overcook them; they should be *just* cooked through! Serve hot or at room temperature with lemon wedges on the side.

TEN MORE WAYS TO USE

BERBERE

·1·

Smoky Popcorn

Stir 1 tsp of berbere into 3 to 4 Tbsp of melted butter to pour over a bowl of freshly popped popcorn.

·2·

Spicy Cream Cheese

Blend berbere into softened cream cheese and spread on a toasted bagel, stir into scrambled eggs, or fold into an omelet.

·3·

Roasted Brussels Sprouts

Toss halved sprouts with a few tablespoons of oil and 1 tsp of berbere. Spread on a rimmed baking sheet and bake at 375°F [190°C], stirring once as they roast, for about 30 minutes, or until starting to brown.

·4·

Cocktail Rim

Dip the rim of a glass into orange or lime juice, then coat the rim in berbere. Let dry before filling with your favorite mezcal cocktail to echo the smoky notes of the paprika.

·5·

Potato Chip Seasoning

Toss plain kettle chips with a little bit of good extra-virgin olive oil, then sprinkle with berbere. Warm in a 425°F [220°C] oven for 5 minutes.

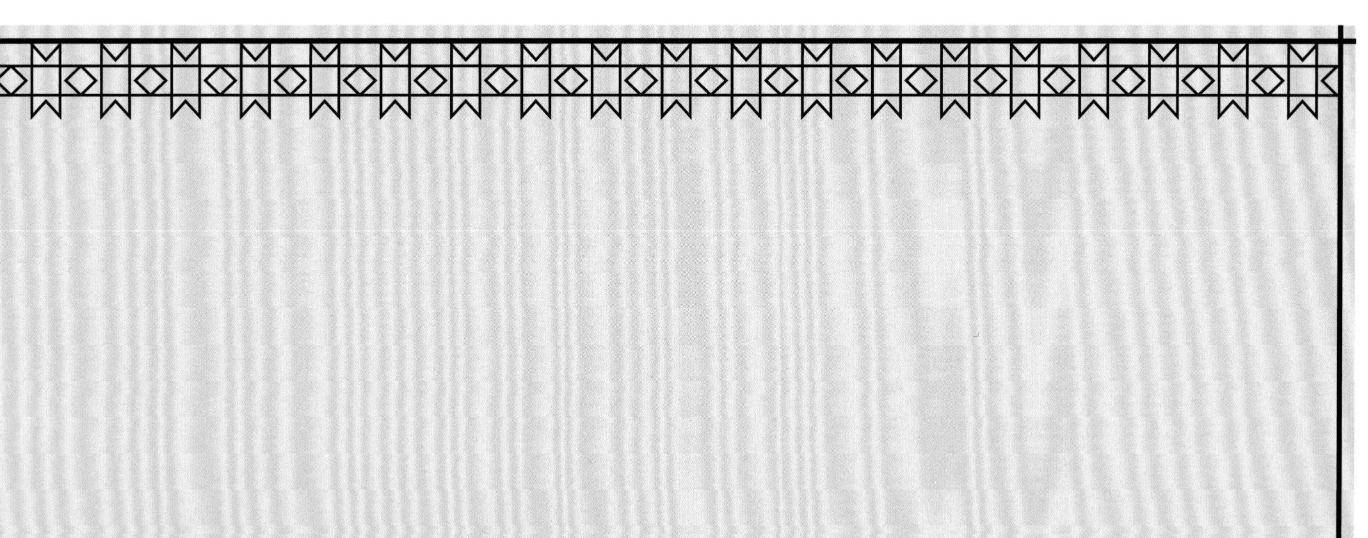

·6·

Simplest Smoky Marinade

Season ½ cup [120 ml] of oil with 2 Tbsp of berbere and ½ tsp of salt, and use to flavor chicken or fish before throwing them on the grill.

·7·

Bean Salad

Spike your favorite vinaigrette with 1 tsp or more of berbere and use to dress a hearty mixture of black or kidney beans, chopped celery, bell pepper, and scallions. Fold in a big handful of chopped fresh parsley.

·8·

Finishing Sprinkle

Add a pinch to buttered corn on the cob, avocado toast, or a baked potato with sour cream.

·9·

Drawn Butter

Stir 1 Tbsp of berbere into ½ cup [115 g] melted, clarified butter to serve with boiled lobster or steamed shrimp.

·10·

Bloody Mary Booster

Season tomato juice with berbere, lemon juice, and a shake of Worcestershire; garnish with a cucumber spear.

Green Zhug

In the store, we sell lots of bottled red zhug, and it's a great year-round hot sauce. But when grilling season rolls around, I like to cook up big batches of this fresher, brighter green version, typical of a sauce served in both Yemen and Israel. It's my go-to in the summer when the peppers in my yard are coming in faster than I can use them, and it's amazing on all kinds of grilled meats and seafood dishes. If you really like it searing hot, double the jalapeños and omit the poblano pepper.

MAKES ABOUT 2 CUPS [500 G]

¾ tsp cumin seeds

½ tsp coriander seeds

2 bunches fresh cilantro (leaves and stems), chopped

2 jalapeños, roughly chopped

1 poblano pepper, cored, seeded, and roughly chopped

3 cloves garlic, peeled

2 tsp fresh lemon juice

1 tsp fine sea salt

¼ tsp ground cardamom

Put the cumin and coriander seeds in a small dry skillet. Toast over medium heat, shaking often, just until they start to pop and are very fragrant. Transfer to a plate to cool, then grind to a powder in a spice grinder or with a mortar and pestle.

Combine the cilantro, jalapeños, poblano pepper, garlic, and lemon juice in a blender and buzz until finely chopped but not fully puréed. Add the ground spices along with the salt and cardamom and whir until blended but still slightly chunky. Add a few tablespoons of water and continue to blend to a thick sauce consistency. Transfer to a tightly covered jar and refrigerate for up to 3 days; for longer storage, top the zhug with a thin layer of extra-virgin olive oil (about 2 Tbsp) to prevent the surface from oxidizing and turning brown.

Green Scallop Ceviche with Zhug

If you have green zhug in the refrigerator and a handful of beautifully fresh scallops, you can make this sophisticated, elegant starter in a matter of minutes. I especially like the way the green zhug works in this recipe; it has more complexity than chopped raw chiles and adds nice color, too. But in a ceviche, anything goes, so make it your own; if you prefer a squirt of liquid harissa, that would also be delicious.

SERVES 4

1 lb [455 g] large sea scallops
3 mini bell peppers, cut into rings
1 Tbsp Green Zhug (page 164)
Zest and juice of 1 lime
1 garlic clove, minced
½ tsp fine sea salt
⅓ cup [15 g] chopped fresh cilantro
4 scallions, both white and green parts, sliced
Pita chips, for serving (page 49)

Use a small, sharp knife to remove the tough muscle from the side of each scallop, then quarter or slice the scallops. Put in a mixing bowl and add the bell peppers.

In a small bowl, whisk together the zhug, lime zest and juice, garlic, and salt. Pour over the scallops and stir to combine. Gently stir in the cilantro and the scallions. Let the ceviche stand for 30 minutes to partially "cook" the scallops, then serve immediately with the chips.

Zesty Calamari Skewers

These tasty little tidbits give fried calamari a real run for its money—and best of all, there's no frying or breading involved, making them a much less guilty pleasure and simplifying cleanup, too. If your crew misses a tomatoey dipping sauce, spice up some prepared marinara sauce with liquid harissa to double down on the fire power.

SERVES 6 TO 8

¼ cup [60 ml] extra-virgin olive oil
Zest and juice of 1 lemon
2 garlic cloves, minced
¼ cup [10 g] chopped fresh parsley
2 tsp Urfa pepper
1 tsp fine sea salt
½ tsp ground cumin
2½ lb [1.2 kg] calamari bodies, cleaned
4 cups [80 g] baby arugula, for serving
Lemon wedges, for serving

In a large bowl, whisk together the oil, lemon zest and juice, garlic, parsley, Urfa pepper, salt, and cumin. Transfer half of the mixture to a small bowl and reserve. Add the calamari to the bowl and toss well to coat in the marinade. Then cover the bowl or transfer to a resealable plastic bag, seal, and refrigerate for at least 4 hours, preferably overnight.

Preheat an outdoor grill or ridged grill pan until very hot. Oil the grates or ridges well. Thread the calamari lengthwise onto metal skewers, making sure they lie flat. Grill until browned on both sides, turning once, 8 to 10 minutes total. Do not overcook, as the calamari can become rubbery and tough quickly.

Spread the arugula on a serving platter and top with the calamari skewers. Drizzle with the reserved parsley mixture and serve with lemon wedges.

Sahadi's Hot Wings

If you are looking for an alternative to buffalo wings that are just as tasty but a bit more unexpected *and* baked rather than fried, look no further. Our wings (pictured on page 159) come out crunchy and tender inside because we bake them at a ferocious 500°F [260°C], which causes the fat to render and crisps the harissa-rubbed skin without overcooking the meat. With both cayenne and harissa spices in the coating, you'll want to make sure you have plenty of the cooling feta and herb sauce on hand, as well as some carrot and celery sticks, if you want to be traditional.

SERVES 4 TO 6

Wings

½ cup [50 g] harissa spices

2 Tbsp extra-virgin olive oil

2 garlic cloves, minced

1 tsp fine sea salt

½ tsp cayenne

2½ lb [1.2 kg] chicken wings, separated at joint, tips discarded

Feta Dipping Sauce

½ cup [120 g] plain yogurt, full or reduced fat

¼ cup [30 g] crumbled feta cheese

2 Tbsp chopped fresh parsley, plus more for garnish

2 Tbsp chopped dill

2 Tbsp minced cucumber

1 garlic clove, minced or grated

1 tsp fresh lemon juice

¾ tsp fine sea salt

½ tsp freshly ground black pepper

Liquid harissa, for serving

To make the wings: In a large bowl, combine the harissa spices with the oil, minced garlic, sea salt, and cayenne, stirring to make a paste. Add the wings and mix with your hands until they are thoroughly coated with the spice mixture. Cover and refrigerate for at least 4 hours, preferably overnight.

Preheat the oven to 500°F [260°C] or as close as your oven goes. Coat a rimmed baking sheet thoroughly with olive oil. Spread the wings in the pan in a single layer. Bake for 45 minutes, moving the pan from the top to the bottom rack and turning the wings every 15 minutes to ensure they brown evenly.

To make the dipping sauce: In a small bowl, mix the yogurt with the feta, parsley, dill, cucumber, garlic, lemon juice, salt, and pepper, and stir thoroughly with a fork.

Arrange the hot wings on a platter and shower with the chopped parsley. Serve with the dipping sauce and liquid harissa for those who like it even spicier.

Red Lentil Soup

Red lentils cook more quickly and become far softer and silkier than their brown, green, or black counterparts. In this bright and soothing vegan soup seasoned with Egyptian spices and cumin, they cook down into what is essentially a purée without the need to blend or process them.

SERVES 6 TO 8

3 Tbsp extra-virgin olive oil
1 red onion, diced
4 garlic cloves, crushed
2 bay leaves
1 small dried hot chile, such as Thai
1 Tbsp ras el hanout
1 tsp fine sea salt
2 cups [400 g] red lentils
8 cups [2 L] vegetable stock or water
Juice of 1 lemon
3 scallions, both white and green parts, sliced
½ cup [20 g] chopped fresh cilantro

Heat the oil in a large soup pot over medium heat. Add the onion and sauté for 5 minutes, or until softened. Add the garlic and cook another minute or so until fragrant and the onion is just starting to turn golden. Add the bay leaves, chile, ras el hanout, and salt. Mix well.

Add the lentils and stock and bring to a boil over high heat. When the soup boils, reduce the heat to low and cover the pot. Simmer for 45 minutes, or until the lentils are extremely tender.

Remove from the heat, and discard the chile and bay leaves. Reheat if necessary just before serving, then stir in the lemon juice, scallions, and cilantro, and taste for seasoning. Serve hot.

Alicia's Saffron Chicken Soup

Talk about comfort food! This is the best kind of peasant dish: a warming, sustaining meal in a bowl that is packed with interesting flavors and textures, from chewy chorizo to silky cabbage. While not overtly spicy, the broth, thickened only with lightly crushed potatoes, delivers a slow burn thanks to a double dose of saffron and picante smoked paprika. It is so easy to make yet so richly flavored, you'll want to serve it for a winter dinner gathering. You can make it a day ahead, but be sure to adjust the seasoning after you reheat it, stirring in a little more paprika or hot sauce as needed, and adding more broth to loosen the consistency if the beans absorb too much of the liquid. To take this over the top, serve with croutons topped with a dab of toum. It goes well with a glass of rustic red wine.

SERVES 8

2 Tbsp olive oil

1 large onion, thinly sliced

2 medium carrots, scrubbed and cut into ½ in [12 mm] chunks

2 celery stalks, finely chopped

3 large garlic cloves, minced

2 bay leaves

1 Tbsp hot (picante) smoked paprika or 1 Tbsp mild smoked paprika mixed with ½ tsp cayenne

1 Tbsp chopped fresh oregano leaves

½ tsp saffron threads

1 lb [455 g] dried chickpeas

4 oz [115 g] serrano ham or prosciutto, cut into ½ in [12 mm] cubes

4 oz [115 g] Spanish-style cured chorizo, cut into ½ in [12 mm] rounds

8 small red potatoes, scrubbed and halved

8 cups [2 L] low-sodium chicken broth or stock

6 chicken drumsticks

½ medium green cabbage (about 1 lb [455 g]), cored and cut into 8 wedges

Fine sea salt and fresh black pepper

½ cup [20 g] chopped fresh parsley

Heat the oil in a large pot over medium-high heat. Add the onions and sauté until starting to soften. Add the carrots, celery, garlic, and bay leaves and cook and stir for another 3 to 4 minutes, until fragrant and the onions are very soft. Stir in the paprika, oregano, and saffron.

Add the chickpeas, ham, chorizo, and potatoes to the pot and stir to coat with the seasonings. Pour in the broth and bring to a boil over medium-high heat. Reduce the heat to a simmer; cover the pot, leaving the lid just slightly askew to allow steam to escape, and cook until the chickpeas are tender, about 1 hour. Stir to break up the potatoes a bit.

Add the chicken and cabbage to the pot and simmer until the chicken is cooked through and the cabbage is tender, about 20 more minutes. Transfer the chicken to a plate and when cool enough to handle, pull off the meat, discarding the skin and bones. Return the meat to the soup and season with salt and pepper.

To serve, place 1 cabbage wedge in each wide, shallow bowl and ladle the soup, meat, and chickpeas around it. Sprinkle with parsley and serve hot.

TEN MORE WAYS TO USE

ALEPPO AND URFA PEPPERS

•1•

Kicked-up Egg Salad

Flavor ½ cup [120 g] of mayo with 1 tsp of Urfa pepper, 2 minced scallions, and a bit of diced red bell pepper. Let the mayo stand for 20 minutes or so to blend the flavors, then add 6 chopped hard-cooked eggs and ¾ cup [115 g] of diced unpeeled Persian cucumbers. Season with salt, lemon juice, and a bit more Urfa pepper if desired.

•2•

Boosted Broth

Add 1 tsp of Aleppo pepper to any broth-based vegetable or chicken soup. It will add flavor without additional sodium, and the heat will be very subtle.

•3•

Kebab Topper

Add 1 tsp of pepper flakes to a sliced sweet onion with a few tablespoons of chopped parsley to make a quick topping for grilled chicken, lamb, or pork skewers.

•4•

Peppery Dip

Grate a small garlic clove into 2 cups [480 g] of Greek yogurt or labneh and add chopped fresh mint, minced scallion, and 1 tsp of Urfa pepper. Serve topped with flecks of freshly ground black pepper, with fresh veggies or pita chips for dipping.

•5•

Easy Pilaf

Sauté 1 minced shallot, 1 tsp of Urfa pepper, and ½ tsp of salt in 2 Tbsp of oil or butter. Add 1 cup [200 g] of rice and toast in the seasoned oil for 3 to 4 minutes. Add 2 cups [480 ml] of broth or water and simmer over low heat for 18 minutes, or until the rice is tender. Remove from the heat, allow the rice to steam for 10 minutes, then fluff with a fork and serve.

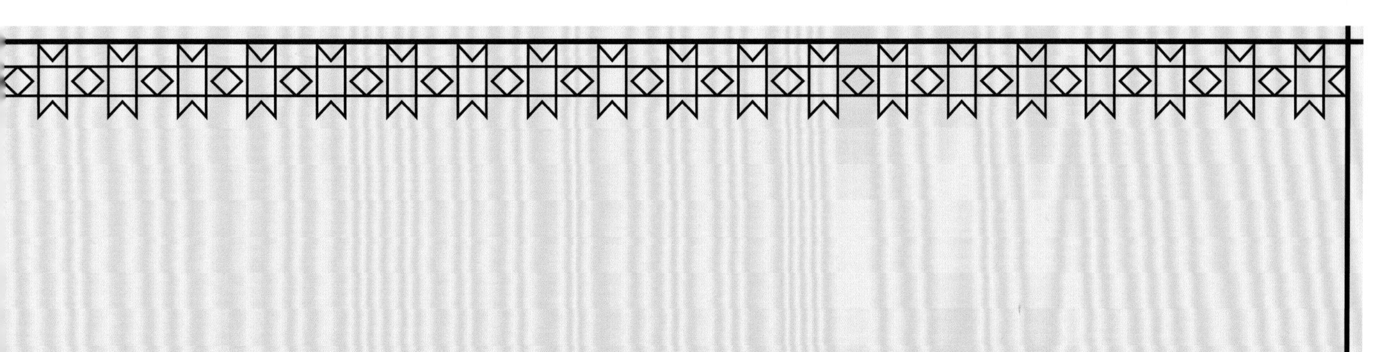

·6·

Spicy Peanut Butter

Grind 1 lb [455 g] of roasted unsalted peanuts in a food processor with 2 Tbsp of honey, 2 tsp of Aleppo pepper, ¼ tsp of ground cayenne pepper, and ¼ tsp of fine sea salt until the mixture is as smooth or chunky as you prefer. Taste and add more honey if you like a sweeter spread. The heat will increase after a day or two, but if you want it really spicy, use Urfa pepper instead of the Aleppo pepper.

·7·

Zesty Dressing

Stir 1 tsp of Aleppo pepper into your vinaigrette to serve with pasta salads or broccoli salad, or to moisten a sandwich. I mix it up in a large batch to use throughout the week. You'll get pockets of spice in each bite when it's freshly made, but after a few days the heat will be more dispersed as the pepper melds with the other flavors.

·8·

Peppery Potatoes

Boil red new potatoes until just tender, about 15 minutes, then drain and quarter. Toss the hot potatoes with 1 to 2 Tbsp of Greek yogurt, the grated zest of one lemon, sea salt, and as many pepper flakes as you like.

·9·

Spiced Fruit

Sprinkle Aleppo pepper and a squeeze of lime on fresh summer fruit, like watermelon or mango spears.

·10·

Hot Vinegar

Steep a few tablespoons each of Aleppo and Urfa pepper in 2 cups [480 ml] of apple cider vinegar at room temperature for at least 2 weeks. When it's good and spicy, drizzle over anything that needs a bit of punch for heat and texture.

Sizzled Zucchini with Pepper Relish

This is the recipe to make converts of all those zucchini skeptics who consider it bland and boring. Marinated, grilled, then hit with a dose of crunchy pepper relish, the squash is a lively side dish for any grilled entrée. The mix of fresh and dried, sweet and spicy peppers makes it explode with flavor. Leftovers are so good in sandwiches or grain salads that I always make enough for six even though we are only four. In fact, my family gets cranky if I don't plan accordingly!

SERVES 6

¼ cup [60 ml] plus 1 Tbsp extra-virgin olive oil
1 tsp Aleppo pepper
1 tsp Urfa pepper
1½ tsp fine sea salt
1 tsp freshly ground black pepper
1¾ lb [800 g] zucchini or yellow summer squash, cut into diagonal slices
1 bunch scallions, white and green parts separated, sliced
¼ cup [30 g] chopped red bell pepper
¼ cup [30 g] chopped yellow or orange bell pepper
¼ cup [10 g] chopped fresh parsley
1 Tbsp seeded and chopped jalapeño pepper
1 tsp chopped garlic

Preheat the broiler and line a broiler pan or baking sheet with foil.

In a large bowl, stir together the ¼ cup [60 ml] of oil and the Aleppo and Urfa peppers, 1 tsp of the salt, and the black pepper. Add the zucchini and stir to coat with the mixture, then stir in the white parts of the sliced scallions.

Spread the zucchini slices on the prepared pan in a single layer and broil, turning them once, for about 5 minutes per side or until just browned and tender.

While the zucchini cooks, combine the bell peppers, parsley, jalapeño, garlic, and scallion greens. Season with the remaining ½ tsp of salt. Spoon the relish over the hot zucchini and serve warm or at room temperature.

Winter Squash with Roasted Pumpkin Seeds

Delicata is a mild-flavored squash with attractive striped skin that is completely edible when cooked. Because it is on the bland side all on its own, I like to turn up the volume a bit by seasoning it aggressively and roasting it to concentrate the flavors. Pumpkin seeds add some welcome crunch, and a drizzle of roasted squash seed oil (try the one made by Stony Brook WholeHeartedFoods) really seals the deal but is entirely optional.

SERVES 4

2½ lb [1.2 kg] winter squash such as delicata (see Note)
¼ cup [60 ml] extra-virgin olive oil
2 tsp ras el hanout
1 tsp fine sea salt
1 tsp Aleppo pepper
3 Tbsp chopped fresh parsley
1 Tbsp roasted pumpkin seed or squash oil, or extra-virgin olive oil
1 Tbsp unsalted roasted pumpkin seeds

Preheat the oven to 450°F [230°C].

Halve the squashes and scrape out the seeds. Cut the halves crosswise into ½ in [12 mm] slices and place in a large bowl. Add the oil, ras el hanout, salt, and Aleppo pepper, and toss to combine. Add 2 Tbsp of the parsley and toss again.

Spread the squash on a rimmed baking sheet in a single layer. Roast until tender and just browned, about 30 minutes. Place in a large serving dish and drizzle with roasted pumpkin seed oil. Sprinkle with the pumpkin seeds and remaining 1 Tbsp of parsley.

NOTE

You can substitute slices of peeled butternut squash, kabocha, or acorn squash for the delicata, but you'll want to slice these denser squashes more thinly, about ⅓ in [8 mm] thick.

Spicy Escarole and Beans

This combination of beans and greens will be familiar to Italian cooks, but I think the addition of spices and hot chiles makes it even more enticing. It works equally well as an accompaniment to simple entrées or as a meatless entrée because the beans give it a satisfying heft. To make this an especially satisfying one-dish meal or brunch dish, crack 4 eggs on top of the mixture as it simmers with the beans (cover the pan to help the eggs set) and dust with a bit more Aleppo pepper. Wash the escarole well—the leaves can harbor lots of gritty soil.

SERVES 4

¼ cup [60 ml] extra-virgin olive oil
1 Spanish onion, sliced
4 garlic cloves, sliced
1 large head escarole or 2 smaller ones, chopped
1 tsp fine sea salt
1 tsp Aleppo pepper
½ tsp Urfa pepper (or an additional tsp of Aleppo pepper)
½ tsp ground cumin
½ tsp ground coriander
½ tsp ground black pepper
½ cup [60 ml] vegetable stock or water
One 15 oz [430 g] can cannellini or cranberry beans, drained

In a large skillet with a lid, heat the oil over medium heat. Add the onion and sauté until tender but not browned, about 5 minutes, then add the garlic and sauté for another minute. Add the escarole and cook gently, turning with tongs, until all the leaves are wilted. Add the salt, Aleppo and Urfa peppers, cumin, coriander, and black pepper, and sauté for another 5 minutes.

Add the stock and bring to a boil, then lower the heat, cover the pan, and cook until just tender, about 15 minutes. Gently fold in the beans and simmer on low heat for 5 minutes to blend the flavors. Adjust the seasonings and serve hot or at room temperature.

Spring Vegetable Salad with Mustard Seed Dressing

Each year I host a gigantic Easter brunch buffet. If the weather is good, we spill out into the yard; either way, I always serve some type of spring vegetable salad to welcome the return of warmer days and lighten up the meal. I am partial to this combination of asparagus, snap peas, and English peas, but I'll use whatever is freshest and available at the market. The mustard seeds add a pleasant crunch and bite to the crisp veggies.

SERVES 4

1½ lb [680 g] assorted green spring vegetables, such as asparagus, snap peas, and frozen baby peas, in equal quantities

1 Tbsp herbes de Provence

1½ tsp fine sea salt

2 spring onions, sliced

1 Tbsp yellow mustard seeds

½ cup [120 ml] extra-virgin olive oil

½ cup [120 ml] champagne or prosecco or white wine vinegar

1 tsp Dijon mustard

½ tsp freshly ground black pepper

½ tsp Aleppo pepper

For asparagus, trim off the tough ends and cut the spears into 2 in [5 cm] pieces. For snap peas, remove the strings. For frozen green peas, place in a strainer and run under cool water to thaw; drain well. Fill a large bowl with ice and water and place in the sink.

Bring 1 cup [240 ml] of water to a boil in a small saucepan. Add the herbes de Provence and 1 tsp of the salt and reduce the heat to low. Blanch the vegetables separately in the herb water until crisp-tender, 4 to 5 minutes for the asparagus, 2 to 3 minutes for snap peas or frozen peas. Use a slotted spoon or a wire skimmer to transfer each batch to the ice-water bath to cool and set their color before adding the next batch to the herb water.

Drain the blanched veggies well and put them in a mixing bowl with the spring onions. Put the yellow mustard seeds in a small dry skillet and heat over medium-low heat just until they begin to pop, 2 to 3 minutes. Transfer to a plate to cool. Whisk together the oil, vinegar, and mustard and the remaining ½ tsp salt, black pepper, and Aleppo pepper until emulsified, then whisk in the mustard seeds. Pour half the dressing over the vegetables and toss to coat. If they look dry, add more dressing and toss again (you may have dressing left over). Serve chilled or at room temperature.

OODS
SAHADI IMPORTING CO.
MID
SAHADI'S
718.624.4550
SAHADIS.COM
SAHAD

Harissa Mac and Cheese

Like most families, mine loves macaroni and cheese, and I love to give traditional dishes an update, so this makes everyone happy. Harissa helps lighten the richness of a cheesy béchamel sauce and adds a welcome kick as well as some dimension to a dish that can be rather one-note. You can use any cheese or a mixture of cheeses here, from the traditional Cheddar or Gruyère to a Middle Eastern kasseri—just make sure they are sharp and rich. Radiatore pasta is my preferred shape for mac and cheese because the ridges really hold a lot of cheesy sauce, but elbows or penne are fine choices, too. Don't skip the buttery crumbs—the golden crust is the best part!

SERVES 6 TO 8

½ cup [110 g] plus 2 Tbsp (1¼ sticks total) unsalted butter

¼ cup [15 g] panko bread crumbs

6 cups [1.4 L] whole milk

½ cup [70 g] unbleached all-purpose flour

1 lb [455 g] radiatore pasta

2 Tbsp harissa spices or ¼ cup [60 ml] liquid harissa

2 tsp fine sea salt

1 tsp freshly ground black pepper

1 egg yolk

4 cups [320 g] grated sharp cheese such as Cheddar or asiago, or a combination

Preheat the oven to 375°F [190°C]. Butter a 9 by 13 in [23 by 33 cm] casserole dish. Bring a large pot of salted water to a boil.

In a high-sided skillet, melt 2 Tbsp of the butter over medium heat. Add the panko and toast over medium heat, flipping and shaking the pan frequently, until it just starts to brown. Transfer the crumbs to a plate to cool, and wipe out the skillet.

Heat the milk in a saucepan over medium heat until almost simmering; do not let it boil. In a separate skillet, melt the remaining ½ cup [110 g] of butter over medium heat. When the butter bubbles, add the flour all at once and cook for 1 minute, stirring to break up any lumps. Whisk in the hot milk, a little at a time, stirring constantly to keep the mixture smooth. Continue whisking until the mixture bubbles and thickens, 8 to 12 minutes.

While the sauce cooks, add the pasta to the boiling water and cook *just* to al dente, about a minute less than what the package directs. Don't overcook, as the pasta will cook further in the oven. Drain and set aside.

Remove the skillet from the heat and stir in the harissa, salt, and pepper. Place the egg yolk in a small bowl and whisk in 1 Tbsp of the milk mixture to temper it, then stir it into the skillet. Combine thoroughly, then stir in the cheese.

Add the pasta to the cheese mixture and combine very well. Spread in the prepared baking dish and top with the toasted bread crumbs. Bake until golden brown and bubbling, about 30 minutes. Serve hot.

Cardamom-Spiced Chicken Kebabs

Cardamom is a lovely spice that is primarily appreciated for its use in baking and sweets. In the Middle East it is often used as an accent in savory blends. Here, just a touch of cardamom helps bring together the flavors of cumin, coriander, and garlic. The Green Zhug echoes the same flavor notes and brings the heat in a serious way! This recipe is made on a grill pan, but it could easily be made on a barbecue grill instead.

SERVES 6 TO 8

½ cup [120 ml] extra-virgin olive oil

1 tsp ground coriander

1 tsp ground cumin

½ tsp ground cardamom

1 tsp fine sea salt

2 garlic cloves, minced

1 jalapeño, minced

¼ cup [10 g] chopped fresh parsley

2 lb [910 g] boneless, skinless chicken breast, cut into chunks

Pita breads, for serving

Green Zhug (page 164)

In a large bowl, whisk the oil with the coriander, cumin, cardamom, and salt until well blended. Add the garlic, jalapeño, and parsley and blend well. Add the chicken, turn to coat thoroughly, then cover and refrigerate overnight.

Preheat the broiler and line a broiler pan with foil. Oil the foil lightly.

Thread the chicken chunks onto skewers and arrange on the broiler pan. Broil, turning once, until well browned on all sides, 5 to 7 minutes per side. Let the skewers cool slightly, then pile them on a platter and serve with warm pitas and Green Zhug.

Berbere-Spiced Chicken Thighs

For a simple weeknight dinner with unexpected punch, you can't do much better than this. The chicken marinates overnight, so all you need to do is fire up the oven and arrange the pieces in a baking dish on the day you serve it. The berbere gives the chicken wonderful color as well as flavor with next to no effort. And if you are looking for a new idea to update your Thanksgiving spread, try marinating the whole bird before roasting it as usual. You will need to multiply the marinade ingredients by three or four, depending on the size of your turkey; a triple batch should be enough for a 12 to 15 lb [5 to 7 kg] bird. Scatter the aromatics in the pan then set the bird on a roasting rack on top. Let the turkey rest for at least 20 minutes before carving.

SERVES 4

¼ cup [60 ml] extra-virgin olive oil
3 Tbsp berbere, store-bought or homemade (page 160)
1 tsp cayenne
1 tsp minced garlic
½ tsp fine sea salt
4 large bone-in chicken thighs
1 bunch fresh thyme
2 fresh hot red peppers, such as Fresno or red jalapeños
½ large red onion, sliced
4 garlic cloves, sliced
Chopped fresh parsley, for garnish

In a small bowl, mix the oil with the berbere, cayenne, minced garlic, and sea salt, stirring well to combine thoroughly. Put the chicken thighs in a shallow bowl and pour the marinade over them, turning to coat all over. Cover and refrigerate for at least 4 hours or overnight.

When ready to cook, preheat the oven to 425°F [220°C]. Toss the thyme together with the whole peppers, onions, and garlic. Spread these aromatics in a baking dish large enough to hold the chicken thighs in a single layer. Roast, basting with the pan juices every 15 minutes or so, for 40 minutes, or until an instant-read thermometer inserted in the thickest part of a thigh registers 165°F [75°C] and the skin is browned and crisp.

Garnish with the chopped parsley and serve with some of the pan juices spooned over all.

Jambalaya, Sahadi's Way

Hearty rice dishes like this one are beloved throughout the Middle East, so recasting an iconic southern dish with some of Sahadi's classic ingredients isn't really a huge stretch. We start with a base of jasmine rice, then add a flurry of Middle Eastern spices, bits of merguez sausage and preserved lemon, and chicken chunks for a fabulous one-dish meal that appeals to everyone.

SERVES 6 TO 8

1½ tsp fine sea salt

1 tsp Aleppo pepper

1 tsp freshly ground black pepper

1 tsp ground allspice

1 tsp dried oregano

1 tsp dried thyme

½ tsp ground nutmeg

¼ cup [60 ml] olive oil

1 lb [455 g] boneless, skinless chicken breast, cut into 1 in [2.5 cm] pieces

1 lb [455 g] merguez, sliced into coins

1 cup [140 g] chopped onion

1 cup [120 g] chopped celery

1 cup [100 g] diced fennel

1 cup [120 g] diced red and yellow bell peppers

¼ cup [65 g] minced preserved lemon rind, store-bought or homemade (page 43)

2 bay leaves

1 cinnamon stick

3 garlic cloves, minced

2 plum tomatoes, diced

¼ cup [60 ml] liquid harissa

4 cups [960 ml] chicken stock or water

2 cups [400 g] raw jasmine rice

1 cup [48 g] sliced scallions, both white and green parts

1 cup [160 g] cooked chickpeas

1 cup [40 g] chopped fresh parsley

Combine the salt, Aleppo and black peppers, allspice, oregano, thyme, and nutmeg in a small bowl and set aside.

In a heavy pot or Dutch oven, heat the oil over medium-high heat. Add the chicken and sausage and sauté for 5 to 6 minutes, or until just browned. Add the onion, celery, fennel, and bell peppers and sauté for 5 minutes, or until softened. Stir in the spice mixture, preserved lemon rind, bay leaves, cinnamon stick, and garlic and sauté until the mixture is very fragrant, about 5 minutes. Reduce the heat to low, add the tomatoes and harissa, cover the pan, and cook for 15 minutes, stirring now and then to keep the mixture from scorching or sticking.

Uncover the pan and stir in the stock. Bring to a boil over medium-high heat. Add the rice, scallions, and chickpeas, cover, and cook for 25 minutes, or until the rice is tender. Just before serving, stir in the parsley.

Moroccan Marinated Chicken Breasts

This recipe is yet another example of how the rich blend of spices in ras el hanout can give a simple preparation depth and nuance with very little effort. Marinating chicken in yogurt tenderizes the meat and keeps it juicy as it grills. Serve this with a room-temperature grain dish, like the Millet Pilaf with Almonds and Feta on page 115, and a cooling salad of Persian cucumbers.

SERVES 4

½ cup [120 g] plain Greek yogurt, full or reduced fat
1 Tbsp ras el hanout
1 tsp fine sea salt
1 tsp hot paprika
1 tsp hot red pepper flakes
4 large bone-in, skin-on chicken breast halves
Chopped fresh cilantro, for garnish

In a medium bowl, stir together the yogurt, ras el hanout, salt, paprika, and red pepper flakes. Add the chicken and turn to coat thoroughly with the seasonings. Cover the bowl and marinate for 2 hours in the refrigerator.

Prepare a gas or charcoal grill. When hot, mound most of the coals to one side. Place the chicken breasts over the hottest part of the fire, skin side down, and cook until the skin has developed a bit of char and the fat has rendered. Turn the breasts skin-side up, move to the cooler side of the grill, and cover the grill. Cook the chicken, turning once or twice, until cooked through, 25 to 30 minutes.

Alternatively, you can prepare this in the oven. Preheat the oven to 350°F [180°C] and arrange the chicken in a baking dish large enough to hold them without touching. Cover and bake for 30 minutes, then uncover and bake for an additional 15 minutes.

Garnish with the chopped cilantro. Serve hot or at room temperature.

TEN MORE WAYS TO USE

RAS EL HANOUT

·1·

Butternut Squash Soup

Augment the seasonings in your favorite squash soup recipe with 1 tsp of ras el hanout before simmering, then sprinkle a pinch on each serving.

·2·

Sweet Potato Purée

Mash roasted or boiled sweet potatoes with a bit of butter and a pinch of ras el hanout. Spread on toast or serve as an accompaniment to pork, duck, or lamb.

·3·

Savory Dip

Stir caramelized red onions and ras el hanout into softened cream cheese mixed with yogurt or sour cream to serve with chips or vegetable sticks.

·4·

Dry Rub for Lamb

Rub ras el hanout directly onto a leg of lamb before roasting, or sprinkle onto lamb shanks before browning and braising.

·5·

Zippy Tomato Sauce

Season a few tablespoons of oil with ras el hanout, then add a can of chopped plum tomatoes and their liquid. Simmer until thickened, then serve over couscous or orzo, or add canned chickpeas for an instant vegetarian entrée.

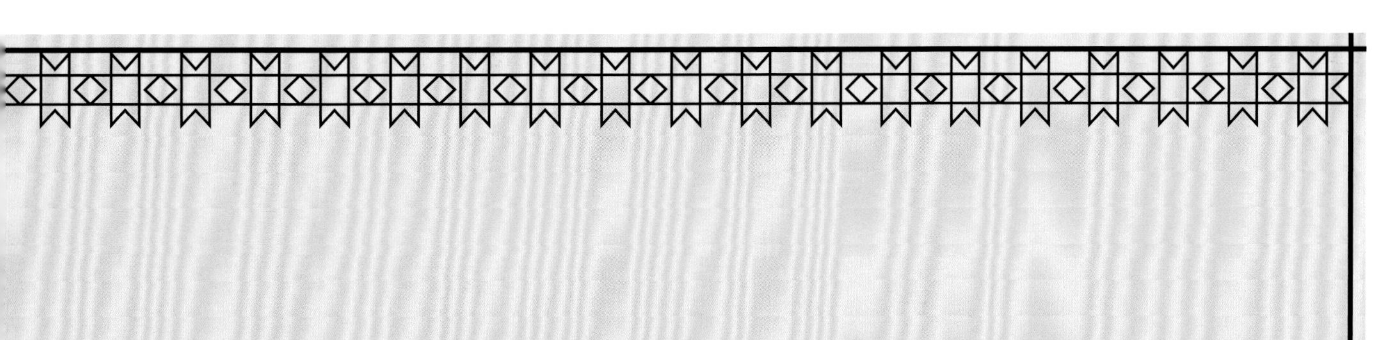

•6•

Compound Butter

Stir 1 tsp of ras el hanout into a softened stick of butter, then refrigerate until firm. Melt 1 to 2 tsp onto cooked salmon or tuna steaks.

•7•

Better Baking

Replace your usual pumpkin pie spices with ras el hanout for a surprise twist on a standard spice bread or squash pie recipe.

•8•

Roast Veggies

Warm 1 tsp of ras el hanout in olive oil to bloom the spices, then toss with fall vegetables like Brussels sprouts, parsnips, carrots, or fingerling potatoes before roasting.

•9•

Spiced Vanilla Pudding

Warm up a packaged or home-made pudding recipe with a generous pinch of ras el hanout to give it a holiday taste and aroma.

•10•

Richer Rice

Toast rice in oil seasoned with ras el hanout before adding liquid, then bake in a covered casserole or Dutch oven.

Slow-Roasted Harissa Salmon

You get a double dose of harissa spices in this super-easy party dish, which uses both ground harissa spices and liquid harissa. Despite all that bold seasoning, this isn't overwhelmingly fiery, as the fatty fish has a mellowing effect. It makes a striking centerpiece for a buffet table and is a lot more interesting than the typical poached salmon with dill sauce. Watch it win over those who claim they don't like fish! Should there be leftovers, they are excellent in a grain bowl, which is how we serve it at our Industry City café.

SERVES 8 TO 10 GENEROUSLY

⅔ cup [160 ml] extra-virgin olive oil
⅓ cup [35 g] harissa spices
¼ cup [60 ml] liquid harissa
2 garlic cloves, grated
1 skinless side of salmon, about 4 lb [1.8 kg]
2 lemons, thinly sliced
Fresh herb sprigs, such as dill, parsley, or mint, for garnish

Stir together the oil, harissa spices, liquid harissa, and garlic in a small bowl. Cover and set aside at room temperature for at least 1 hour and up to 24 hours to allow the flavors to develop.

Preheat the oven to 275°F [140°C].

Put the salmon in a roasting pan or baking dish just large enough to hold it. Pour the harissa mixture over the fillet, rubbing it onto the flesh to coat it completely with the spices and oil. Arrange the lemon slices on top, reserving a couple for garnish.

Roast the salmon until it is just short of cooked through, basting it with the pan juices every 15 minutes. After 30 minutes, take a peek inside to see if it is beginning to flake; there should still be a bit of a deep red core. If it's not quite there, cook a bit longer, checking every 5 minutes.

Let the fish cool in the roasting pan. Transfer it to a serving platter and break it into irregular chunks. Serve at room temperature, drizzled with the pan juices and garnished with the remaining lemon slices and the herb sprigs.

Couscous Bowl with Spiced Lamb Strips

This is another lunchtime bestseller at our Industry City store, where we offer this tender, well-seasoned lamb stuffed into a fresh pita, atop a salad, or on a bed of couscous, as it is presented here. A lively herb sauce brings together all the elements of this hearty, healthy, flavor-packed bowl. Double up on the sauce if you like—you'll want to serve it with eggs, fish, and grilled meats all year long. You can prepare the couscous ahead of time if it's easier, but toasting the grain in the same pan the lamb was seared in really gives it a lot more flavor. This is delicious served hot or at room temperature.

SERVES 6

Spiced Lamb

3 Tbsp extra-virgin olive oil

1½ tsp fine sea salt

1 tsp ground ginger

1 tsp ground cumin

½ tsp ground coriander

½ tsp ground allspice

1 lb [455 g] boneless leg of lamb, cut into 3 in [8 cm] strips

1 red onion, diced

2 garlic cloves, minced

2 tsp minced fresh ginger

2 cups [280 g] Israeli couscous (see Note)

5 cups [1.2 L] chicken stock or water

½ tsp freshly ground black pepper

Herb Sauce

1 cup [40 g] chopped fresh parsley

¼ cup [10 g] chopped fresh mint

1 Tbsp chopped fresh dill

1 anchovy fillet

1 Tbsp drained capers

2 tsp fresh lemon juice

1 small garlic clove

½ tsp fine sea salt

½ cup [120 ml] extra-virgin olive oil

1 cup [160 g] cooked chickpeas, Persian cucumber slices, grape tomatoes, and 1 tsp Aleppo pepper, for serving

To prepare the spiced lamb: Combine 1 Tbsp of the oil, 1 tsp of the salt, the ginger, cumin, coriander, and allspice in a sealable plastic bag. Add the lamb, seal the bag, and massage the marinade into the meat. Refrigerate for at least 4 hours and up to overnight.

When ready to serve, heat the remaining 2 Tbsp of oil in a 4 qt [3.8 L] saucepan over medium-high heat until sizzling. Add the marinated lamb and sauté just until browned on all sides; you don't want it to cook through. You may need to cook the meat in batches to ensure the pan stays hot enough to sear the meat without overcooking. Transfer the meat to a bowl, leaving any oil in the pan, and cover to keep warm.

In the same pan, sauté the onion, garlic, and ginger until they are aromatic and the onion softens. Add the couscous and stir to coat the grains lightly with oil. Add the stock, the remaining ½ tsp of salt, and the black pepper and bring to a boil. Stir, cover the

pan, and lower the heat to a simmer. Cook for about 25 minutes, or until the grains are tender and most of the liquid has been absorbed.

To make the herb sauce: While the couscous is cooking, combine the parsley, mint, dill, anchovy, capers, lemon juice, garlic, and salt in a food processor. Pulse until all are uniformly chopped and mixed. Add the oil and blend well. (The sauce can be refrigerated in a tightly covered jar for up to 5 days.)

To serve, divide the couscous among six bowls. Top each serving with some of the lamb strips and any juices that have accumulated in the bowl. Add the chickpeas and drizzle with the herb sauce. Garnish with cucumber slices and grape tomatoes and sprinkle a bit of Aleppo pepper over all.

NOTE

Israeli couscous is sometimes labeled Mediterranean couscous or pearl couscous, depending on the brand. Either way, make sure you are using the large, buckshot-size couscous, not the fine grains.

Kibbeh Pan Pie

Kibbeh might be the best-known and best-loved Lebanese dish, but there is no way around the fact that forming and stuffing the football-shaped croquets is a labor of love that takes plenty of time. Instead, we bake the spiced ground beef mixture on an industrial-size baking sheet topped with a layer of pine nuts, then serve it cut into diamond shapes. It hits all the right flavor notes but is so much easier to assemble, especially when you are feeding a large group. It has become a Saturday tradition in our store, where we go through as many pans as the kitchen has time to prepare. Serve it at room temperature as part of a meze spread.

SERVES 8

2½ cups [400 g] fine bulgur

2½ lb [1.2 kg] finely ground lean lamb or beef, or a combination

1 large onion, finely minced

1 Tbsp fine sea salt

2 tsp ground allspice

1 tsp freshly ground black pepper

2 Tbsp pine nuts

1 Tbsp extra-virgin olive oil

Put the bulgur in a mixing bowl and cover with 2½ cups [600 ml] of cold water. Set aside for 30 minutes.

Drain the bulgur in a fine sieve. Use your hands or the back of a spatula to squeeze as much water as possible from the grains. Return the bulgur to the bowl and add the meat, onions, salt, allspice, and pepper. Use your hands to mix very thoroughly, kneading the ingredients into a smooth paste.

Preheat the oven to 425°F [220°C].

Oil a 9 by 13 in [23 by 33 cm] baking pan and pat the meat mixture into the pan in an even layer. Scatter the pine nuts evenly over the meat and lightly press into the surface. With the tip of a sharp knife, make 4 or 5 cuts down the length of the pan, then make crosswise cuts on the diagonal to create diamond shapes about 1 by 2 in [2.5 by 5 cm]. Drizzle the top with the oil.

Bake the kibbeh for 30 minutes, or until browned and just cooked through. Drain off the oil that has accumulated in the pan and let rest for 10 minutes before serving. Serve hot or at room temperature.

Spicy Beef Kebabs with Tzatziki

These may look unassuming, but make no mistake, these kefte-style meat skewers are generously seasoned with both fresh and dried chiles. Throw a few on the grill at your next barbecue and watch them disappear long before the burgers and dogs. We like to make hefty, quarter-pound patties, but smaller meatball-size kebabs are great for parties and game nights. You can make the tzatziki 1 or 2 days ahead of time, but it may separate as it stands. Either drain off any liquid that accumulates on the surface or stir it back in, depending on your preferred thickness.

SERVES 4

Beef Kebabs

1 lb [455 g] ground beef or lamb, or a mixture

1 small onion, minced

2 garlic cloves, minced

1 jalapeño pepper, seeded and minced

¼ cup [10 g] chopped fresh parsley

¼ cup [10 g] chopped fresh cilantro

¼ cup [2 g] chopped fresh dill

1 tsp paprika

1 tsp kosher salt

1 tsp freshly ground black pepper

1 tsp Urfa pepper

1 egg, lightly beaten

2 Tbsp bread crumbs

Tzatziki

1 cucumber, unpeeled

1 cup [240 g] plain Greek yogurt, full or reduced fat

2 scallions, both white and green parts, thinly sliced

1 garlic clove, minced

2 Tbsp chopped fresh parsley

2 Tbsp chopped fresh dill

½ tsp fine sea salt

½ tsp ground white pepper

Juice of ½ lemon or more

Warm pitas for serving

To make the beef kebabs: Put the meat in a large bowl and break up with your fingertips. Add the onion, garlic, jalapeño, parsley, cilantro, and dill and mix well with your hands. Sprinkle the paprika, salt, black pepper, and Urfa pepper evenly over the mixture and mix again. Add the egg and bread crumbs and mix one more time, being careful not to overwork the mixture. Cover the bowl with plastic wrap and refrigerate for 30 minutes to firm it up a bit.

Continued

Divide the mixture evenly into four portions. Press a metal skewer onto the top of one portion and form the meat around the skewer into a flattened football shape. Repeat with the three remaining portions of meat. Refrigerate for at least 15 minutes and up to 4 hours, covered with plastic. They should be chilled and firm when they go on the grill.

To make the tzatziki: Grate the cucumber using the coarse holes on a box grater. Wrap the shredded cucumber in a kitchen towel and twist to release the liquid. Scrape the shreds into a mixing bowl and add the yogurt, scallions, garlic, parsley, dill, salt, white pepper, and lemon juice. Mix with a fork until well blended. Taste and add more lemon juice or salt as needed.

Make a hot fire in a grill or preheat a ridged grill pan over high heat. Grill the kebabs until well browned on one side, about 3 minutes, then carefully turn to grill the other side. Continue cooking until browned on the second side and cooked to your preference, about 4 or 5 minutes for medium. Transfer to a platter and serve with warm pitas and the tzatziki.

Easy Meat Filling

When the only thing lurking in the recesses of your freezer is a package of ground meat, try this well-spiced and crowd-pleasing sauté. You can stuff the mixture into taco shells, spoon it into cored bell peppers and bake for stuffed peppers, or serve it on slider buns like a sloppy Joe. Depending on how you serve it up, add a complementary topping of shredded lettuce, asiago cheese, sliced scallions, or olives.

SERVES 4

2 Tbsp extra-virgin olive oil
1½ lb [680 g] ground beef, turkey, or lamb
1 medium onion, chopped
2 garlic cloves, chopped
1 tsp Urfa pepper
1 tsp Aleppo pepper
1 tsp ground cumin
½ tsp coriander
Fine sea salt and ground black pepper
½ cup [120 ml] chicken or vegetable broth
½ tsp liquid harissa

Heat the oil in a large skillet. When hot, add the ground meat. Cook the meat over medium-high heat, breaking it up with a spoon, until it starts to brown and is no longer pink, 6 to 8 minutes. Transfer the meat to a plate and pour off all but 1 or 2 Tbsp of the fat from the pan.

Add the onion and garlic to the fat remaining in the skillet and sauté over medium heat, stirring often, until softened, about 5 minutes. Add the Urfa and Aleppo peppers, cumin, and coriander, season with salt and black pepper, and stir for 1 to 2 minutes, or until well combined and fragrant.

Stir in the broth and harissa and mix well, then stir in the browned meat. Bring to a simmer and cook over low heat until the flavors are combined and the mixture is thickened, about 30 minutes.

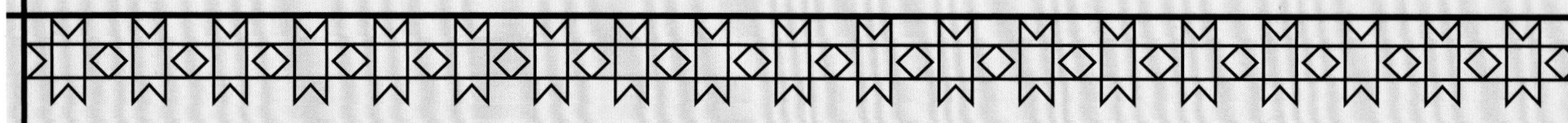

TEN MORE WAYS TO USE

HARISSA SPICES AND LIQUID HARISSA

·1·

Broiled Asparagus

Spread asparagus on a rimmed baking sheet and drizzle with olive oil. Sprinkle with 1 Tbsp of harissa spices and toss to distribute. Broil the asparagus until just starting to blister, turning once, 8 to 10 minutes.

·2·

Whole Harissa Cauliflower

Core a head of cauliflower and place it in a heavy Dutch oven with about ½ in [12 mm] of water. Drizzle the cauliflower with extra-virgin olive oil and sprinkle with harissa spices. Cover and roast in a 475°F [240°C] oven for 25 minutes, then uncover the pan, baste with the pan juices, and continue to roast until the cauliflower is tender, with a few browned spots.

·3·

Harissa Eggs

Warm 1 tsp of harissa spices in 2 tsp of olive oil until fragrant in a nonstick skillet. Add 1 or 2 eggs and cook in the bright red seasoned oil to your preference, sunny-side up or over easy.

·4·

Clams with Harissa

For a spicier take on Clams Steamed with Za'atar and Herbs (page 127), substitute 1 Tbsp of harissa spices for the za'atar and add ½ cup [100 g] of diced tomatoes and ½ cup [80 g] of chopped chorizo. Garnish with chopped fresh cilantro.

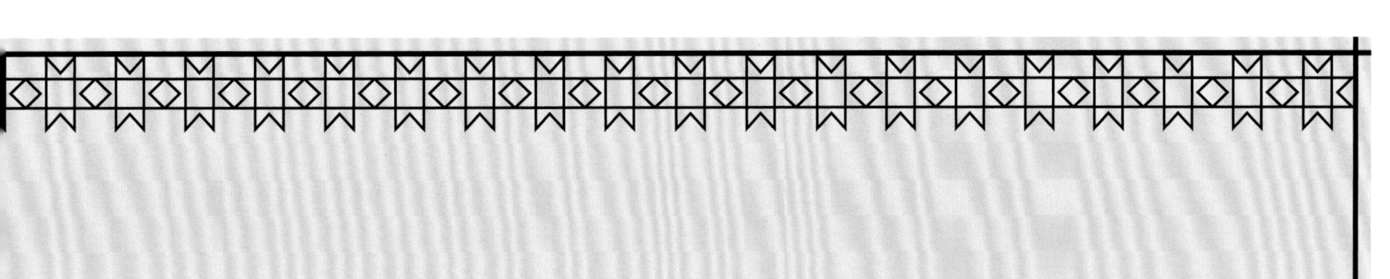

·5·

Seafood Marinade

One-quarter cup [115 ml] of extra-virgin olive oil mixed with 1 Tbsp of dry harissa spices makes a gorgeous marinade for a mixed seafood grill of shrimp, scallops, and squid.

·6·

Roasted Potatoes

Rub baby Yukon golds with melted butter seasoned with harissa spices, spread them on a baking sheet, and roast until tender.

·7·

Burger Topper

Season thickly sliced sweet onions with dry harissa spices and sauté slowly in olive oil until soft. Pile onto a beef, turkey, or black bean burger.

·8·

Taco Filling

Add liquid harissa to well-browned beef or turkey, then spoon into a taco shell or flatbread. Serve sprinkled with sliced scallions and crumbled feta cheese.

·9·

Bloody Maria

Season tomato juice with a healthy squirt of liquid harissa and spike with tequila.

·10·

Harissa Hot Wings

Combine equal parts melted butter and liquid harissa as a dip for fried or roasted chicken wings.

Shawarma-Crusted Roast Beef Tenderloin

A whole filet of beef is an easy way to make an occasion seem special without a lot of work. The secret is the shawarma spices, which create a crusty, flavorful exterior. Here the meat is roasted at high temperature for a rosy, rare interior, just as we serve it at the store. Need I say that leftovers make a great sandwich?

SERVES 8 TO 10

Shawarma Spice Blend

1 Tbsp ground allspice

1 tsp cayenne

1 tsp ground cumin

1 tsp ground coriander

1 tsp granulated garlic

½ tsp ground cloves

½ tsp paprika

½ tsp ground ginger

½ tsp ground cardamom

½ tsp freshly ground black pepper

½ tsp ground cinnamon

¼ tsp ground turmeric

Tenderloin

5 lb [2.3 kg] beef tenderloin (filet mignon), silver skin removed

¼ cup [60 ml] extra-virgin olive oil, plus more for the pan

To make the shawarma spice blend: Combine all the ingredients in a bowl and mix well.

To make the tenderloin: Put the beef in a large bowl. In a small bowl, combine the oil with 2 Tbsp of the shawarma spices until well blended. (Reserve the remaining shawarma spices for another use.) Rub the spice mixture all over the beef, coating it thoroughly. Cover the bowl and refrigerate for at least 4 hours, or preferably overnight.

Preheat the oven to broil. Coat a large, foil-lined baking sheet lightly with oil.

Put the filet mignon in the center of the sheet, tucking the thin tail portion underneath to make the entire filet a uniform thickness (if you have kitchen string, you can tie the tail end to keep it in place). This ensures the meat will cook evenly. Place the pan under the broiler and sear on all sides, turning to brown evenly, for 10 to 15 minutes. Lower the oven temperature to 475°F [240°C] and continue to roast the meat for 15 minutes, or until an instant-read thermometer registers 115°F [45°C] for rare. If you prefer your meat more well done, adjust the time accordingly, roasting another 3 to 4 minutes for medium-rare (120 to 125°F [50 to 55°C]). Transfer the beef to a cutting board, cover loosely with foil, and let rest for at least 20 minutes. Serve warm or at room temperature.

Sweet and Spicy Nut Brittle

One of the best parts of working in this business is that I always have top-quality nuts available for snacking or baking. This is a fun way I like to use them that also doubles as a nice holiday gift.

MAKES ABOUT 4 CUPS [560 G]

2 cups roasted unsalted mixed nuts (about ½ lb [230 g]), coarsely chopped

1½ cups [300 g] sugar

1 cup [240 ml] Amaretto or bourbon

2 Tbsp honey

2 Tbsp unsalted butter

¾ tsp Aleppo pepper

1 tsp flaky sea salt

Preheat the oven to 300°F [150°C]. Spray a rimmed baking sheet with nonstick spray.

On a separate rimmed baking sheet, spread the nuts in a single layer and toast in the oven for 5 minutes. Transfer the nuts to a large bowl and cover to keep warm. (Warming the nuts helps the caramel flow over them more readily.)

In a 1 qt [960 ml] saucepan, combine the sugar, amaretto, honey, and butter. Attach a candy thermometer to the side of the pan. Heat over medium heat until the butter melts and the sugar dissolves, then continue to boil until the mixture reaches 300°F [150°C] (hard crack stage).

Carefully pour the sugar mixture over the nuts and mix quickly with a silicone spatula or wooden spoon, coating all the nuts. Immediately pour onto the prepared baking sheet and spread in a thin layer. Sprinkle with the Aleppo pepper and salt. Let cool completely, then break into pieces and store in an airtight container.

Chewy Ginger Spice Cookies

I can't think of a better way to illustrate the convenience of Middle Eastern spice blends than with these very adult ginger cookies. Ras el hanout, bolstered by some additional ground ginger, does the job of a half dozen individual spices, making for an incredibly complex—and not too snappy—gingersnap with far less fuss. Small nuggets of candied ginger and a crust of raw sugar add wonderful texture.

MAKES 3 DOZEN COOKIES

1½ cups [210 g] all-purpose flour
1½ tsp ras el hanout
1½ tsp ground ginger
1 tsp baking soda
¼ tsp salt
½ cup [110 g] (1 stick) unsalted butter, at room temperature
½ cup [100 g] light brown sugar, packed
⅓ cup [65 g] granulated sugar
1 large egg
¼ cup [80 g] unsulfured molasses
½ cup [90 g] finely diced candied ginger, plus more cut into thin strips, for garnish
½ cup [100 g] raw or demerara sugar

Preheat the oven to 350°F [180°C] and line two rimmed baking sheets with parchment paper.

Sift together the flour, ras el hanout, ground ginger, baking soda, and salt and set aside.

In the bowl of a stand mixer, beat together the butter, brown sugar, and granulated sugar on medium speed until light. Beat in the egg, then add the molasses and mix well. Scrape down the sides of the bowl with a rubber spatula and mix again briefly.

With the mixer on low, add the flour mixture and combine just until the flour is incorporated. Scrape down the sides of the bowl and the beaters and use the spatula to mix in the diced candied ginger. Chill the dough for 1 hour or up to overnight.

Pour the raw sugar into a shallow bowl. Roll generous tabelspoons of the dough into 1 in [2.5 cm] balls, then roll the balls in the sugar. Arrange the balls on the prepared baking sheets, allowing 2 in [5 cm] between them, as they will spread quite a bit as they bake. Top each cookie with 2 strips of candied ginger. Bake for 10 to 12 minutes, or until the cookies are just firm on top when touched with a fingertip and light golden brown.

Allow the cookies to cool on the baking sheets for 10 minutes, then transfer to a wire rack to cool completely.

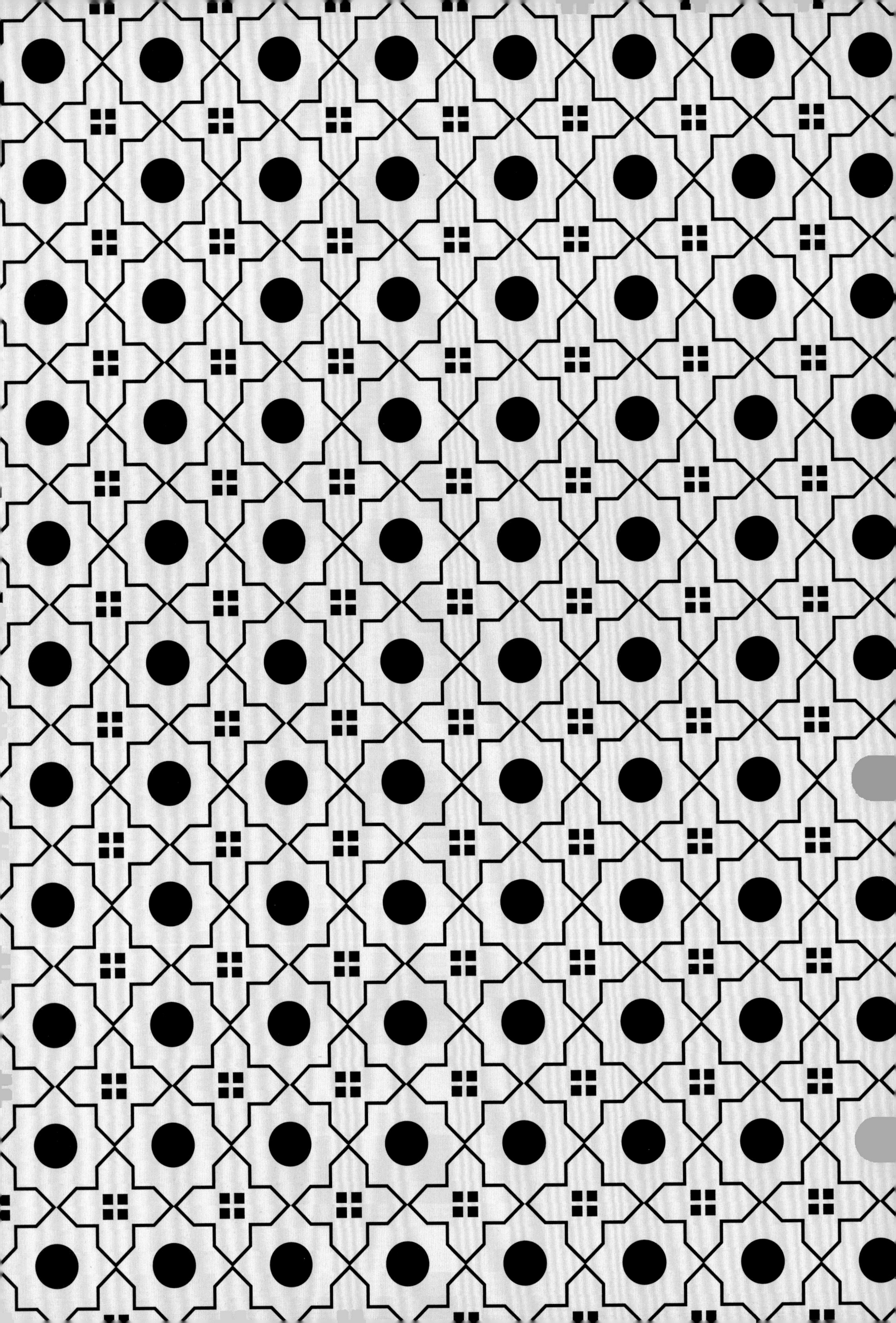

4
NUTTY

RICH, MEATY, SATISFYING

PISTACHIOS

TAHINI

BASMATI RICE

MASTIC

DRIED BEANS

PINE NUTS

DUKKAH

It is not an overstatement to say that for Middle Easterners, nuts are synonymous with hospitality, and they have been the backbone of our business since my great-great uncle Abrahim opened the first Sahadi's store in 1895. You'd be hard-pressed to find a Middle Eastern home that doesn't have a small bowl of meshakkal, a mixture of seeds and nuts, set out on a table as a sign of welcome. The blend might include peanuts coated in sesame seeds and several types of shelled nuts, such as almonds, cashews, or hazelnuts, but it would also definitely contain pistachios in the shell as well as some kind of seed, most likely from a pumpkin or squash, also in the shell. The ritual of cracking the shells and extracting the tender contents is considered a convivial pastime to share with friends and family.

Sourcing our nuts directly from growers is the only way we've found that ensures we are offering the very highest quality: we buy only the biggest, most intact nuts from each crop, the whitest cashews and brightest pistachios, leaving the smaller specimens and broken nuts to be sold to supermarkets and discounters. In the early '90s, when the local business that had done our roasting for decades decided to close, we bought their facility and began roasting our nuts too, because we didn't trust anyone else to meet our exacting standards. That's how essential nuts are to our business, and to Middle Eastern cuisine.

Not surprisingly, nuts, seeds, and the ingredients made from them—especially tahini—find their way into all manner of dishes throughout the Middle East, contributing crunch, toasty flavor, and an unctuous richness and body to desserts, salads, pilafs, and dressings. Lately staple nuts like pistachios, walnuts, and cashews have been joined by chestnuts and hazelnuts as customer favorites, but as is so often the case, these recipes can be adapted to your own nutty pleasure. Whichever nuts you choose, you'll find these are some of the most indulgently satisfying recipes in the book—recipes that seem a little bit elevated and special, even when simply prepared. Like that inviting bowl of meshakkal, these recipes are the ones you'll reach for when you want your family or guests to know they are appreciated.

SNACKS, STARTERS, AND BREAKFASTS

SOUPS, SALADS, AND SIDES

ENTRÉES

SWEETS

BASMATI RICE
TAHINI
DRIED SMALL FAVAS
(FOUL MUDAMMAS)

DUKKAH
PISTACHIOS
MASTIC
PINE NUTS

Pistachios

For flavor, texture, and perhaps most of all color, nothing else in the nut world can equal the pistachio. It is without doubt the nut most associated with Middle Eastern and Mediterranean cuisine, where the ancient trees are a part of the culture. The nuts are used as a finishing touch for desserts, as a textural counterpoint for grain and vegetable dishes, and as a snack eaten out of hand.

Pistachios grow all over the Middle East, from Greece to Lebanon, and really anywhere with hot summer days and cool (but not freezing) winter nights, including California and even Sicily, which produces bright green nuts that are especially pretty in desserts and salads. To our palates, Iran grows the world's best-tasting pistachios, but the tariffs on imported Persian goods make them prohibitively expensive for American consumers. (That said, if you happen to be traveling in Europe and come across Iranian pistachios, snap them up!)

There are a dizzying number of factors to consider when buying pistachios, including the variety, color, and roasting method. Middle Easterners prize bright green color over size, so don't assume bigger is better. Botanically, there are two kinds of pistachios: Persian and Turkish. The Turkish nuts are longer and skinnier, with very hard shells that are difficult to open. The Persian variety has a stubbier, more rounded shell that tends to pop open more readily. California growers produce pistachios in the Persian style, but they are lighter colored and less vibrant than those grown elsewhere. At Sahadi's, we import our pistachios from Turkey and dry roast them as they do in Lebanon. To ensure they roast evenly, we buy only the top of the crop, because they are more consistently sized.

WHAT TO LOOK FOR • Always buy whole nuts, not chopped or ground, because you never know what condition the nuts were in before they were chopped. If your recipe calls for chopped pistachios, it is best to chop them by hand; if you grind them in a food processor they will become mealy. When you shop for pistachios, you are most likely to find either nuts in the shell that have been roasted and salted, or raw shelled nuts, which are usually unsalted. For most of the recipes in this book you want the latter, which allow you to control the amount of salt going into your dish. Toasting intensifies the nut's flavor—giving you more bang for your buck, taste-wise—so, depending on the recipe, you may be directed to give your raw, shelled nuts a quick roast in the oven or a skillet. If you come across shelled nuts that have been roasted you can skip that step, but generally shelled pistachios are sold raw, and buying them that way gives you more options. Store your pistachios, both in and out of the shells, in the freezer to keep them fresh.

SERVE WITH • Pistachios' neutral flavor goes with many things, but the taste is delicate, so don't pair them with bold ingredients that might overshadow them—you will just be wasting your money. They go with almost any fruit, fresh or dried, and in baked goods the combination of pistachios and honey is hard to beat. And remember, it's simply not done to serve them out of the shell as a snack—it's part of the social ritual to extract the nutmeats from the shells one at a time while chatting and drinking coffee, with the added benefit that it prevents you from downing hundreds of calories at a time. Sometimes the old way is the best way!

Tahini

Tahini, a paste made from sesame seeds that have been hulled and pulverized, is the peanut butter of the Middle East and just about as ubiquitous as PB is in the United States. It is, of course, the essential ingredient in hummus; it's actually this sesame paste that defines a dip or spread as a hummus (not the chickpeas, as many people assume), but that's just the tip of the iceberg. Its fluid texture makes it easier to incorporate into recipes than stiffer, thicker nut butters, and it gives sauces and dressings a satisfying density.

Tahini can also serve as a fat. For instance, we use it in place of oil in many of our granolas because it adds flavor while binding the ingredients and keeping them from burning.

Tahini is just about the only product in this section that we never attempt to make ourselves at Sahadi's, because getting the completely smooth texture we prefer requires specialized equipment to pulverize the seeds completely; it's definitely not something you can make at home, simple though it may seem.

Tahini will last a good long time in the pantry, but it needs to be stirred regularly to keep the oil from separating from the ground seeds. Once it is truly separated, which will be clearly visible, it becomes oily and gritty, and stir as you might, you can never really get it to emulsify again. To remind myself to keep it combined, I store my tahini next to my olive oil, and every time I reach for the oil I flip the jar of tahini over to stop the contents from settling.

WHAT TO LOOK FOR • Most people are very brand loyal when it comes to their tahini of choice, and there are considerable differences from company to company, so you may want to try a few before you settle on a favorite. Chalk this up to cultural preferences. US-made tahini is ground from toasted sesame seeds and have a more pronounced flavor than imported tahini. Middle Easterners tend to use tahini as a binder and flavor carrier rather than as a primary flavor, and they prize a pure white color, so their tahini of choice is made from raw seeds. Textures vary from country to country, too, with Lebanese products being a bit thicker than those coming from Turkey. While Lebanese tahini is more expensive, ounce for ounce, you end up using less because for most applications you will want to thin it out. In the end, it's usually a wash, so buy the brand you like best, or consider your planned use and choose accordingly.

SERVE WITH • Tahini is especially versatile because it can swing sweet or savory. It has an affinity for chocolate, but it also rounds the sharp edges of bitter greens like kale. Thinned with lemon juice, water, and herbs, it's used to sauce everything from kebabs to chopped salads. Because it is so much more fluid than peanut butter, you can also use it in a salad dressing instead of oil or with just a tad of oil.

Basmati Rice

We sell many types of rice at Sahadi's, but we sell more basmati than any other variety. Its delicate aroma makes it unique among grains, and the fluffy, separate texture of cooked basmati is especially well-suited to many of the rice dishes and pilafs favored throughout the Middle East. On its own, even without seasonings, it has a nutty flavor that can carry a dish.

WHAT TO LOOK FOR • One thing that sets basmati rice apart from other varieties is that its flavor intensifies over time. So while with most types of rice you would seek out the freshest, youngest grains, aficionados prize older, more aged basmati for its depth of flavor. It is not necessary to rinse basmati rice before cooking, though many have adopted this practice in response to concerns about possible contaminants. We source our rice from a trusted supplier and therefore dispense with that step, but if you have any doubts or questions about your rice, go ahead and rinse the grains under running water in a mesh strainer.

SERVE WITH • Basmati is a neutral canvas for just about anything you like to eat and can be served hot or at room temperature, but you should take care not to overwhelm its inherent nuttiness. Warm, it is lovely combined with spices, nuts, and/or dried fruit; in a salad preparation I tend to pair it with a more delicate dressing that won't overwhelm its perfumed aroma, and I add vegetables for crunch.

Mastic

You won't find this resinous product on the spice shelf of your local market, but its flavor, aroma, and thickening properties are so unique it's worth seeking out from a specialty store or online, as it has no true substitute. Also known as mastika, the hardened gummy resin of the mastic tree is sold in small translucent droplets called "pearls" or "tears," and these must be ground to a powder before using. Countries all across the Middle East use mastic to flavor everything from chewing gum to liqueurs to preserves with an astringent piney tang.

WHAT TO LOOK FOR • Even though you will need to grind it at home, it's always best to buy mastic in its whole, unground form so you can be sure it is of good quality. Look for distinct whole "pearls" with a clear aroma and dry texture that allows them to move freely in the container, not sticking together.

SERVE WITH • Use mastic to enrich and lightly thicken soups, and to provide body and a stretchy quality to Middle Eastern ice cream. Its distinctive flavor enhances a variety of breads and baked goods, including many served at holiday celebrations, such the Greek Easter sweet bread known as tsoureki.

Dried Beans

Chickpeas get all the press these days, as much for the recently discovered properties of their cooking liquid, aquafaba, as an egg-white substitute, as for their mild, nutty flavor and versatility outside the hummus bowl. But they are hardly the only legume prized in the Middle East. Fava beans (foul mudammas) are everywhere in the Middle East. These are not the seasonal broad beans found in Italian cooking; favas are small, dark red beans the size and shape of a navy bean. Many Middle Easterners eat them daily for breakfast; they are also used in dips, and soups, and paired with other local ingredients in hearty stews.

WHAT TO LOOK FOR • Both favas and chickpeas are available dried and cooked (in cans). When buying dried legumes, look for whole beans without a lot of broken or crushed bits (which indicates poor storage and handling) and with a clean aroma.

SERVE WITH • Favas pair amazingly well with fresh pita bread, extra-virgin olive oil, labneh, tomatoes, and cucumbers, as either a traditional Middle Eastern breakfast or an easy lunch bowl. Pair them with chickpeas as the base for a delicious and flavorful falafel.

Pine Nuts

Pound for pound, pine nuts, also known as pignolis, are just about the most expensive nuts you can buy. These pale, tear-shaped nuts are best known to most cooks as the nutty component in pesto, but they are widely appreciated in the Middle East, too. They have been used in cooking (and as a symbol of affluence) since ancient times. Found nestled inside the cones produced by certain pine trees around the world, these oily little nuggets are not cultivated commercially in the United States because the trees take years to reach a productive stage, and harvesting is extremely labor intensive. Most of the world's commercial crop comes from Spain, Italy, or the Middle East. A similar nut from China is also marketed as pignolis and can be used interchangeably with them, although their flavor is not as delicate and refined.

WHAT TO LOOK FOR · With the exception of Chinese pine nuts, you should choose nuts with a pure creamy, off-white color. A brown tip is a dead giveaway that the pine nuts are the less-prized Chinese type. Wherever their origin, they should have a clean, nutty aroma with no rancid notes and should snap when you bite into them. Spanish pine nuts are the most expensive, costing at least twice as much as the Chinese equivalent. My rule of thumb is to use pricey Spanish pine nuts for cookies (or my mother's famous salad) where their flavor is dominant and opt for the more affordable Chinese nuts if they will be crushed or blended into a sauce or stew.

SERVE WITH · Pine nuts are amazing in cookies and cakes, are wonderful tossed into green salads, and add flavor and texture to chicken soup and pilafs.

Dukkah

When you see how many ingredients are involved in making our dukkah—fifteen in all, most of them individually roasted and chopped—you will understand why it is one of the costlier products we offer. Midway between a seasoning and a condiment, dukkah is a multipurpose blend of finely chopped nuts, seeds, and spices that originated in Egypt. While there is no standardized recipe for dukkah, most blends do include cumin and coriander. Beyond that, the cook has plenty of leeway to use whatever nuts and seeds are on hand, and to season the mixture with dried herbs like za'atar or mint, and dried pepper flakes. We use almonds and pistachios as the foundation, adding nigella, sesame seeds, and thyme, but hazelnuts, sunflower seeds, and pine nuts are also popular additions. If you want to try making your own, you'll find a simplified recipe on page 229.

WHAT TO LOOK FOR · At the store we make our dukkah almost entirely by hand, grinding each type of nut separately to control the size of the pieces. When buying dukkah, you should be able to identify individual elements; if it is too finely ground, the flavors will blend together rather than excite the palate with contrasting tastes and textures. For that reason, you should always be sure to give your jar a shake before you use your dukkah, as the finer pieces may settle to the bottom, and you want each bite to contain a little bit of each ingredient. Store dukkah in the fridge and use it up within a few months for the freshest flavor.

SERVE WITH · The mealy, bread crumb–like texture of dukkah makes it excellent for crusted or breaded dishes, and it pairs especially nicely with fish and poultry. It also has an affinity for vegetables and grain dishes.

ALMOND
NATURAL
$7.50 / LB
[4045]
ALMONDS
ROASTED UNSALTED
$8.50 / LB
[4055]

Lebanese Breakfast

We offer this stick-to-your-ribs stew of small beans on our weekend brunch menu, and served with other savory toppings like labneh, olives, and cucumbers, it is very typical of how many in the Middle East start their days. However, if you were to serve it as a quick and healthy supper, or a pack-along lunch, accompanied by some bread for scooping up the lemony, cumin-scented mixture, I think you would find it to be a perfect anytime meal.

SERVES 6

¼ cup [60 ml] extra-virgin olive oil, plus more for drizzling

1 onion, finely diced

2 large garlic cloves, minced

Two 15 or 19 oz [430 or 540 g] cans fava beans (foul mudammas)

2 tsp ground cumin

1 tsp fine sea salt

1 tsp freshly ground black pepper

1 tsp Aleppo pepper

½ cup [20 g] chopped fresh parsley

1 lemon, halved

¼ cup [45 g] Kalamata olives, whole

Fresh sliced tomatoes, sliced cucumbers, labneh, and warm Za'atar Bread (page 98) or pitas, for serving

Heat the oil in a large saucepan over medium-high heat. Add the onion and garlic and sauté just until tender, about 5 minutes. Drain the beans, reserving ½ cup [120 ml] of the liquid. Add the beans and ¼ cup [60 ml] of the reserved liquid to the pot, crushing some of the beans a bit with a wooden spoon to make a thick sauce. Add the cumin, salt, and black and Aleppo peppers, and mix well. Lower the heat and simmer for 10 minutes, or until the beans are very tender and the flavors have blended. If it looks too dry, stir in as much of the remaining ¼ cup [60 ml] cooking liquid as needed to make a fluid, chunky mixture.

Transfer the bean mixture to a shallow bowl and sprinkle with the parsley. Squeeze some lemon juice over the dish and drizzle with more olive oil. Garnish with the olives. Serve the beans with a platter of sliced tomatoes and cucumbers, labneh drizzled with extra-virgin olive oil, and bread for dipping.

Sahadi's Snack Mix

Think of this snack mix (pictured on page 158) as the loosest of all possible recipes, and use whichever nuts you have and like best. The most important thing is to include at least one nut or seed in the shell; it makes eating the mixture a more interactive, less mindless activity and prevents you from wolfing down a whole bowlful at once. I like the kick the spicy coated peanuts add, and if I am feeling really fancy, I mix in some dark chocolate toffee pistachios.

MAKES ABOUT 2 CUPS [200 G]

¼ cup [35 g] pistachios in the shell
¼ cup [35 g] roasted, salted cashews
¼ cup [33 g] roasted, salted macadamia nuts
¼ cup [35 g] roasted, salted almonds
¼ cup [35 g] wasabi-coated peanuts
¼ cup [35 g] sesame-coated peanuts

Combine all the ingredients in a bowl and mix well to distribute the wasabi nuts evenly. Store in an airtight container and use within 2 weeks.

Fava Dip

Like chickpeas, canned fava beans (also labeled "foul mudammas") are a convenient and flavorful staple to keep on hand, and the quality is generally nearly as good as freshly cooked dried beans. When I use canned, I don't drain them, as I think the liquid adds body to the mixture, but if you have concerns about sodium, you maybe prefer to rinse them under running water.

MAKES 4 CUPS [1 KG]

One 15 or 19 oz [430 or 540 g] can fava beans (foul mudammas)

1 small tomato, diced

1 small onion, diced

2 garlic cloves, minced

1 small hot red chile, seeded and minced

2 Tbsp fresh lemon juice

2 Tbsp extra-virgin olive oil

1 Tbsp finely chopped fresh parsley

1 tsp ground cumin

1 tsp fine sea salt

1 ripe tomato, diced, for garnish

½ cup [20 g] chopped fresh parsley, for garnish

Aleppo pepper, for garnish

Sliced Persian cucumbers or seasoned pita chips, for serving

Put the fava beans in the bowl of a food processor. Add the tomato, onion, garlic, chile, lemon juice, olive oil, and parsley and process. Season with the cumin and salt and continue to blend until smooth. (The dip can be refrigerated for up to 5 days at this point; bring back to room temperature to serve.)

Transfer the dip to a bowl or plate. Top with the tomato and parsley. Sprinkle generously with Aleppo pepper. Serve with the cucumber slices or chips.

Red Pepper Walnut Spread (Mohammara)

My grandmother made this frequently, and I absolutely love it. Drying the peppers takes some forethought but virtually no effort, and it results in a wonderfully hearty dip that also happens to be vegan, so it's a nice alternative to cheese- or dairy-based dips. I like to keep it on the rustic, chunky side to eat with crudités, like endive spears.

MAKES ABOUT 2 CUPS [400 G]

2½ lb [1.2 kg] red bell peppers, cored, seeded, each cut into 8 pieces
½ cup [20 g] white bread crumbs
½ cup [120 ml] extra-virgin olive oil
3 Tbsp pomegranate molasses
1 Tbsp fresh lemon juice
1½ tsp fine sea salt
1 tsp sugar
1 tsp Aleppo pepper
½ cup [60 g] chopped walnuts

Line a rimmed baking sheet with paper towels and arrange the pepper pieces in a single layer, skin-side up. Cover with another layer of towels. Leave the pepper pieces in a cool, well-ventilated spot for 1 or 2 days; they should still be crisp, but a little of their moisture should have drained off.

Put the peppers in a food processor with the bread crumbs, oil, pomegranate molasses, lemon juice, salt, sugar, and Aleppo pepper and pulse until coarsely chopped. Adjust for salt. Add the walnuts and continue to pulse until the mixture is uniformly chopped and as smooth or chunky as you prefer.

Deviled Eggs with Dukkah

Much more than just a garnish, the dukkah in this updated classic adds crunchy texture as well as body to the smooth yolk filling. If you're not looking for the spicy kick of Aleppo pepper to top things off, substitute a sprinkle of sumac. The dukkah recipe itself is flexible; if you are missing one or two ingredients, just leave them out. You'll get about 1½ cups [200 g]; store extra in a tightly sealed jar.

SERVES 4 TO 6

Dukkah

2 Tbsp poppy seeds
1 Tbsp coriander seeds
1 Tbsp cumin seeds
1 Tbsp fennel seeds
2 tsp black peppercorns
½ cup [70 g] roasted unsalted almonds
½ cup [70 g] shelled pistachios, roasted
2 Tbsp toasted sesame seeds
2 tsp Aleppo pepper
2 tsp sumac
2 tsp dried thyme
1 tsp fine sea salt

Deviled Eggs

6 large eggs
2 Tbsp mayonnaise
2 Tbsp plain Greek yogurt, low or full fat
2 Tbsp dukkah, plus more for garnish
1½ tsp Dijon mustard
Fine sea salt and freshly ground black pepper
Aleppo pepper, for garnish

To make the dukkah: Preheat the oven to 425°F [220°C]. On a small rimmed baking sheet or large baking pan, stir together the poppy seeds, coriander seeds, cumin seeds, fennel seeds, and peppercorns. Toast in the oven until the spices are fragrant and you can just hear them beginning to pop, 2 to 3 minutes. Transfer to a bowl and cool thoroughly.

In a food processor, process the almonds until they are the size of the pistachios, then add the pistachios, toasted seeds, sesame seeds, Aleppo pepper, sumac, thyme, and salt. Pulse on and off until the nuts are chopped quite fine and the ingredients are combined but not evenly ground; you want to leave some bigger bits of nuts for texture. Add salt if needed.

To make the deviled eggs: Put the eggs in a saucepan with water to cover and place over high heat. When the water just reaches a boil, remove from the heat and cover the pan. Let the eggs stand in the hot water for 15 minutes, then drain and cover with cold water. When cool enough to handle, peel the eggs, keeping them as intact as possible.

Halve the eggs lengthwise and scoop the yolks into a bowl. Add the mayonnaise, yogurt, dukkah, mustard, and salt and black pepper, and mash with a fork until smooth. Using a small spoon or a pastry bag, fill the egg whites, mounding the filling slightly. Garnish with extra dukkah and a sprinkle of Aleppo pepper. Refrigerate until ready to serve.

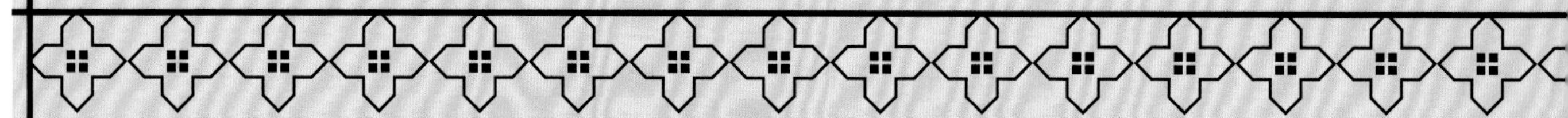

TEN MORE WAYS TO USE

DUKKAH

·1·

Dukkah Dogs

Brush prepared triangles of crescent dough on one side with beaten egg and press dukkah onto the eggy surface. Roll them around mini franks as for pigs in a blanket and bake as directed on the dough package.

·2·

Easy Dip

Blend dukkah with olive oil until it is a relatively pourable paste. Add salt, a bit of chopped fresh parsley, and a squeeze of lemon juice. Serve with endive spears, celery stalks, or crackers for scooping.

·3·

Everything Spread

Stir 1 to 2 Tbsp of dukkah into labneh, Greek yogurt, or cream cheese, then schmear onto a toasted bagel. Top with smoked salmon and a bit of thinly sliced red onion if desired.

·4·

Gluten-Free Breading Mixture

Rub boneless pork chops, chicken pieces, or sturdy fish fillets lightly in oil or beaten egg, then dredge in dukkah. Shallow fry or bake until the breading is golden and the protein is cooked through.

·5·

Enriched Eggs

Stir 1 to 2 tsp of dukkah and 1 Tbsp of cream cheese, cut into bits, into nearly set scrambled eggs.

·6·

Cheese Straws

Combine ¾ cup [25 g] of grated asiago cheese with 3 Tbsp of dukkah. Sprinkle half the mixture on a sheet of prepared puff pastry, and use a rolling pin to press the cheese and dukkah lightly into the surface of the dough. Turn the dough over, sprinkle with the remaining dukkah mixture, and roll again. Using a pastry wheel or a sharp knife, cut the dough crosswise into strips about ¾ in [2 cm] wide and transfer to a parchment paper–lined baking sheet. Press one end of each strip onto the parchment paper and twist the strip four or five times. Chill the strips for 15 minutes, then bake at 375°F [190°C] until browned and crisp. Serve warm.

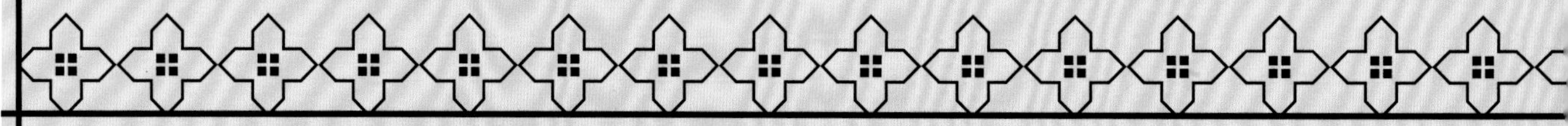

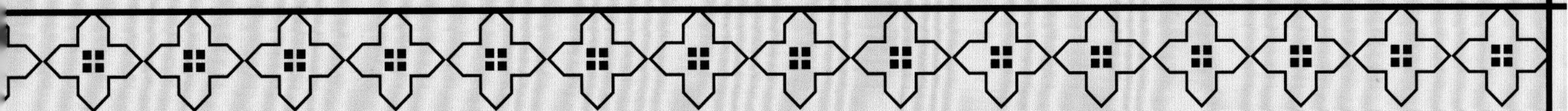

·7·

Brown Butter Noodles

Heat ¼ cup [55 g] (½ stick) of unsalted butter in a skillet until the foam subsides. Continue to cook the butter over low heat until it begins to darken slightly and smells nutty. Add 2 Tbsp of dukkah and 1 garlic clove, minced, and stir for 30 seconds to release the oils and fragrance of the dukkah. Add 8 oz [230 g] of cooked egg noodles and toss to warm through and coat with the mixture. Serve hot.

·8·

Goat Cheese Salad

Roll a small log of soft goat cheese in dukkah, pressing the bits onto the surface to coat very well. Chill the cheese for at least 30 minutes. Before serving, slice the cheese into ½ in [12 mm] rounds and warm in a toaster oven or 300°F [150°C] oven to heat through but not melt. Carefully slide one or two slices onto each serving of green salad dressed with a simple vinaigrette.

·9·

Dukkah Lunch Bowl

Blend 1 Tbsp of dukkah into a serving of cooked grains such as barley, quinoa, or brown rice. Scoop into a bowl and add a handful of arugula. Top with a 6-minute egg, a few slices of Persian cucumber, and a few grape tomatoes, then drizzle all with a bit of harissa mayo. Serve at room temperature.

·10·

Finishing Sauce

Thin dukkah with fruity olive oil and add a big handful of mixed, chopped fresh herbs to spoon onto grilled swordfish.

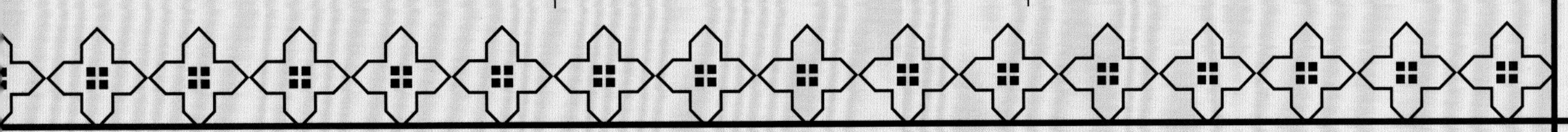

Individual Spinach-Walnut Pies

Always a great favorite at Lent, when my family goes meatless, these hand pies have become a year-round go-to now that so many of our customers and friends are eating less meat. I find they fly off of a holiday buffet table, and they work well for picnics, too, as they can be served at room temperature. The ground nuts make them a bit heartier than the usual spinach pie.

MAKES 8

¾ cup [90 g] walnut pieces
1½ lb [680 g] fresh spinach, tough stems discarded
⅓ cup [80 ml] extra-virgin olive oil
1 cup [140 g] minced onion
2 Tbsp fresh lemon juice
1 tsp sumac
1 tsp fine sea salt
½ tsp freshly ground black pepper
1 recipe Basic Bread Dough (page 98)

Preheat the oven to 350°F [180°C]. Line two rimmed baking sheets with parchment paper.

Spread the walnuts in a pie pan and toast in the oven until lightly browned, about 5 minutes. Allow the nuts to cool a bit, then chop finely by hand or pulse in a food processor.

Wash the spinach well and put it in a saucepan with the water that clings to the leaves. Cover the pan and cook the spinach over high heat until fully wilted, about 4 minutes, turning the leaves to cook evenly. Place the spinach in a strainer and press with the bottom of a ladle until no more liquid can be released. Chop the spinach fairly finely.

Heat 1 Tbsp of the oil in a large skillet over medium-high heat. Add the onions and cook, stirring, until soft and translucent, about 5 minutes. Remove from the heat and add the spinach, walnuts, remaining olive oil, lemon juice, sumac, and salt and pepper and combine thoroughly. Set aside for 15 minutes or so to cool.

Divide the dough into eight equal portions. On a lightly floured surface, roll each dough ball into a circle about 8 in [20 cm] in diameter. Place about 2 Tbsp of the spinach mixture in the center of each. Bring the sides over the filling from three points, pinching the three seams firmly to seal and forming a triangular pastry. Transfer the pie to the prepared baking sheet. Repeat with the remaining dough circles and filling.

Bake for 15 minutes, or until slightly puffed and golden brown. Let stand for 10 minutes before serving hot, or let cool to room temperature. These are best eaten the day they are made, but if you have leftovers, wrap them in plastic while still warm and store at room temperature for up to 2 days or freeze for up to 3 months.

Beef and Pine Nut Flatbread Pizzas

With hints of sweet, spicy, and nutty flavors, these appealing flatbreads hit all the right notes, and they always disappear as fast as I can form them. I like to make this with the extra spicy pepper paste that I make from the peppers grown in my backyard, but dried pepper flakes will do the trick, too.

MAKES 10

1 Tbsp extra-virgin olive oil

½ cup [70 g] chopped onion

12 oz [340 g] lean ground beef or lamb, or a combination

2 Tbsp pomegranate molasses

1 tsp ground sumac

½ tsp ground allspice

½ tsp ground cinnamon

½ tsp fine sea salt

¼ tsp freshly ground black pepper

2 tsp Turkish Pepper Paste (recipe follows), or Aleppo pepper or Urfa pepper

2 Tbsp pine nuts

1 recipe Basic Bread Dough (page 98)

Heat the oil in a medium skillet. Add the onion and cook, stirring often, until soft and translucent, 3 to 4 minutes. Scrape the onions into a mixing bowl and let cool for 10 minutes.

Add the meat to the bowl and add the pomegranate molasses, sumac, allspice, cinnamon, salt, black pepper, and pepper paste. Mix well to form a paste. Add the pine nuts, mixing gently to keep them whole.

Preheat the oven to 525°F [275°C] or as high as your oven goes. Line two rimmed baking sheets with parchment paper.

Divide the dough into ten equal portions, about 1½ oz [40 g] each. Flour a work surface. Roll out one dough ball into a thin 8 in [20 cm] disk. Transfer to one of the prepared baking sheets. Top the dough with 2 Tbsp of the meat mixture, spreading it thinly from edge to edge. Repeat with three more dough balls to make four flatbreads, two per baking sheet.

Bake the flatbreads, rotating them on the pans after 45 seconds to ensure they brown evenly, for 1 to 2 minutes, or until the meat is sizzling and the edges and bottom of the dough are lightly browned. There will be some bubbles in the dough; pierce with a fork to release or leave as is, your call. Serve hot or at room temperature. These are best eaten the day they are made, but if you have leftovers, wrap them in plastic while still warm and refrigerate for up to 3 days or freeze for 1 to 2 months.

Turkish Pepper Paste

Some people cultivate roses; I raise chiles. Every summer our small Brooklyn backyard is crowded with planters (mostly empty olive buckets from the store) hosting as many varieties as I can get my hands on, from tiny Thai bird's eye chiles to Fresnos, jalapeños, and, of course, Aleppo and Urfa peppers. Some I dry, but I also like to preserve them in the form of this spicy condiment that we use all year long. If you don't have access to fresh Urfa peppers, you can use any combination of sweet and hot red peppers. This is meant to be quite hot, but you can easily tone down the flames by moderating the type and quantity of red peppers you use. Covered with a layer of oil, it will keep for months in the refrigerator. Use it as you would Calabrian chile paste or Tabasco sauce.

3 lb [1.4 kg] mixed red bell peppers and fresh hot red peppers, such as Urfa, Thai, red jalapeño, serrano, Fresno, or Hatch chiles

1 tsp sea salt

2 to 3 Tbsp extra-virgin olive oil

Line two rimmed baking sheets with paper towels. Halve the peppers and remove the cores and seeds. Cut the bell peppers into 2 in [5 cm] pieces. Place the pieces inner-side down on the paper towels and set aside overnight to dry out a bit.

Preheat the oven to 250°F [120°C] and line a clean rimmed baking sheet with parchment paper. Transfer the pepper and chile pieces to a food processor and add the salt. Purée to a smooth paste.

Dump the paste onto the prepared baking sheet and spread fairly thinly. Place in the oven for 2 hours, stirring frequently, until the texture has become quite thick and dry. Let the paste cool completely, then scrape it into a sterilized jar and cover with the oil. Refrigerated, the paste will keep for 1 month.

Savory Winter Wheat Soup with Herbs

Shelled wheat and winter vegetables are the backbone of this unusual, toothsome, and hearty soup. Wheat berries are a perfect cold-weather food because they are nutritious and filling, but they can be a bit mild-flavored, so to wake up the flavor, I like to stir in something green and vegetal at the end—in this case, a dollop of pesto and a heap of fresh herbs. It's a trick I use a lot when making grain dishes, especially in the winter. You can add the pesto to the pot of soup before you serve it, or spoon a bit onto each serving for a pretty presentation. This is a great option for vegan entertaining or times when you want to eat healthier, and you won't miss the meat or dairy here because it's so full of flavor.

SERVES 6

½ cup [120 ml] extra-virgin olive oil

1 cup [120 g] sliced celery

1 cup [140 g] chopped onion

1 cup [140 g] chopped carrot

4 garlic cloves, minced

1 tsp berbere, store-bought or homemade, page 160 (you could also substitute your favorite mixed herb seasoning, like Greek, Italian, or herbes de Provence)

1 tsp fine sea salt

1 tsp freshly ground black pepper

½ cup [25 g] sun-dried tomatoes (not oil-packed), chopped or snipped with kitchen shears

1 whole dried red chile

1 tsp Aleppo pepper or ½ tsp hot red pepper flakes

½ tsp smoked paprika

1 cup [200 g] hulled wheat berries

4 cups [80 g] fresh baby spinach

½ cup [20 g] chopped fresh parsley

¼ cup [45 g] prepared pesto

¼ cup [10 g] chopped fresh cilantro

Heat the oil in a large pot over moderately high heat. Add the celery, onions, carrot, and garlic and cook, stirring now and then, until softened, about 5 minutes. Add the berbere, salt, and black pepper and stir to coat the vegetables. Add the sun-dried tomatoes, dried chile, Aleppo pepper, and paprika. Cook, stirring frequently, until softened and fragrant, about 5 minutes. Add the wheat berries and stir for 30 seconds or until the grains are coated with oil and shiny.

Add 8 cups [2 L] of water to the pot and bring to a boil over high heat. Reduce the heat to a simmer, cover, and cook over low heat for 45 to 50 minutes, or until the wheat berries are tender but not mushy.

Add the spinach to the wheat berries and stir to combine. Cover the pot again and cook for 5 minutes, or until the spinach is wilted. Add the parsley, pesto, and cilantro, stir to combine, and serve hot.

Chicken Soup with Pine Nuts

I think most of us have an emotional attachment to chicken soup, for its mystical healing qualities and its grounding, familiar flavors. I was introduced to this version by one of our longtime employees thirty years ago, and we have been serving it in the store ever since. The secret ingredient here is mastic gum, or mastika. You won't notice the piney flavor, but you will appreciate the body it lends to the soup, so do seek it out, even if it means a bit of online searching. Enriched with pine nuts and a drizzle of pine nut–infused oil, this soup is light and comforting, and it looks as good as it tastes.

SERVES 8 TO 10

2 lb [910 g] bone-in chicken thighs
12 cups [2.8 L] low-sodium chicken stock or water
½ tsp mastic
1 cup [140 g] chopped onions
1 cup [120 g] chopped celery
½ cup [100 g] basmati rice
1 tsp fine sea salt
1 tsp freshly ground black pepper
1 tsp Aleppo pepper
2 Tbsp extra-virgin olive oil
¼ cup [30 g] pine nuts
1 cup [12 g] chopped fresh parsley

Put the chicken in a large soup pot and add the broth. Bring to a boil, skimming off any foam that rises to the surface. Reduce the heat to low, stir in the mastic, and simmer, covered, for 45 minutes, skimming off the foam once or twice more.

Use a slotted spoon to transfer the chicken pieces to a plate. With a large spoon, skim off as much fat from the surface of the broth as possible and discard. Add the onions, celery, rice, sea salt, black pepper, and Aleppo pepper. Simmer for 15 minutes, or until the rice is tender but not mushy.

When the chicken is cool enough to handle, shred the meat and discard the skin and bones. Heat the oil in a small skillet. Add the pine nuts and toast over medium heat, stirring constantly, until just lightly colored, about 3 minutes. Use a slotted spoon to transfer the pine nuts to paper towels to drain, reserving the oil in the pan.

Return the shredded chicken to the soup pot and stir in the parsley and pine nuts. Adjust the seasoning if needed. Serve drizzled with some of the reserved pine nut oil.

Basmati Rice Salad with Broccoli, Bacon, and Sunflower Seeds

Midway between a pilaf and a salad—or maybe the best of both worlds?—this dish is packed with textures and flavors. Serve it warm as an accompaniment to the protein of your choice, or make it up to a day ahead and serve at room temperature as a substantial grain salad. Basmati rice is the best choice for dishes that will be served at room temperature, because the grains stay separate and hold their shape without clumping or becoming mushy. An orangey dressing and tart dried cranberries keep things lively.

SERVES 4

1 cup [200 g] basmati rice
1 cup (about 6 oz [175 g]) small broccoli florets
3 bacon strips
½ cup [120 ml] almond or sunflower oil
¼ cup [60 ml] white wine vinegar
¼ cup [60 ml] fresh orange juice
1 tsp Dijon mustard
½ tsp fine sea salt
½ tsp freshly ground black pepper
½ cup [24 g] sliced scallions, both white and green parts
¼ cup [10 g] chopped fresh parsley
¼ cup [35 g] roasted unsalted sunflower seeds
¼ cup [35 g] dried cranberries

Combine the rice with 2 cups [480 ml] of water in a saucepan and bring to a boil over high heat. Cover, reduce the heat to low, and simmer for 15 minutes, or until the rice is just tender. Fluff the rice with a fork, add the broccoli to the pan, then replace the lid and set aside to steam for 5 minutes. Transfer the rice and broccoli to a bowl, fluff with a fork, and let cool for a few minutes.

While the rice cools, cook the bacon in a small skillet until crisp. Drain on paper towels and chop or tear into small pieces. Whisk together the oil, vinegar, orange juice, mustard, salt, and pepper in a small bowl. Add the scallions, parsley, bacon, sunflower seeds, and dried cranberries to the rice and toss to combine. Drizzle with the dressing and toss again.

Mom's Million-Dollar Salad

My mother is famous for this salad, which she makes year-round for parties. The name is a cheeky reference to the pricey ingredients—especially the pine nuts, since we use only those imported from Spain for this special dish. It is the centerpiece of our annual Memorial Day picnic, which often has one hundred and twenty or more in attendance, so you can imagine how many pounds of pine nuts we go through. But it's such a winning recipe that I think you'll agree it is worth every cent. Use the best-quality Parmigiano-Reggiano you can find—it's worth it.

SERVES 6

¼ cup [60 ml] plus 2 Tbsp extra-virgin olive oil

½ cup [60 g] pine nuts, preferably Spanish

¼ cup [60 ml] white wine vinegar (such as prosecco or champagne)

1 garlic clove, minced

½ tsp fine sea salt

½ tsp Aleppo pepper

¼ tsp freshly ground black pepper

8 oz [230 g] mixed baby greens

4 baby red bell peppers, sliced into rings, or 1 large red bell pepper, cored, seeded, and thinly sliced

1 small fennel bulb, halved lengthwise then sliced thinly crosswise

½ small red onion, sliced into half moons

½ cup [80 g] diced Turkish dried apricots or cranberries

4 oz [115 g] chunk Parmigiano-Reggiano, the best quality you can find

In a sauté pan, warm the ¼ cup [60 ml] olive oil over medium-low heat. Add the pine nuts and sauté until browned, about 4 minutes, stirring often. Strain the oil into a small bowl, then spread the pine nuts on paper towels to drain. Let the nuts and oil cool completely.

Add the remaining 2 Tbsp of olive oil to the cooled pine nut oil. Whisk in the vinegar, garlic, salt, and Aleppo and black peppers.

Put the greens in a large bowl. Add the bell peppers, fennel, onion, and dried fruit and toss to combine. Use a vegetable peeler to shave the cheese over the salad in large curls. Just before serving, drizzle with the dressing and toss well. Sprinkle with the pine nuts and serve immediately.

Kale Slaw with Grapes and Pistachios

I never get tired of thinking up new ways to use kale, which is fortunate, because there seems to be some in my CSA box every week during the summer! Happily, our customers have benefited from all my experimentation and seem to enjoy these substantial salads as much as I do. This sweet-tangy version with lots of snap and crunch has become one of our best sellers, year-round.

SERVES 4

1 bunch kale
1 tsp fine sea salt
½ tsp freshly ground black pepper
½ cup [80 g] halved seedless red grapes
1 red bell pepper, stemmed, seeded, and diced
½ celery stalk, sliced thinly crosswise
¼ cup [35 g] toasted unsalted pistachios (see Note)
¼ cup [60 ml] extra-virgin olive oil
¼ cup [60 ml] cider vinegar
2 tsp Dijon mustard

Strip the kale leaves from the tough stems and discard the stems. Slice the leaves into ribbons and sprinkle with the salt and pepper. With your hands, roughly massage the leaves to break down the membranes and soften them up a bit.

Put the kale in a large bowl and add the grapes, red pepper, celery, and pistachios. Toss well. Whisk the oil with the vinegar and mustard in a small bowl until creamy. Pour over the salad and toss to coat the ingredients thoroughly. The salad will hold for 1 to 2 hours, but after that the color will be less vibrant. Serve within 24 hours.

NOTE

If you can only find salted toasted nuts, reduce the salt in the dressing accordingly.

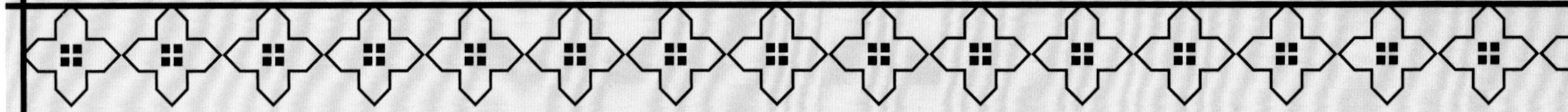

TEN MORE WAYS TO USE PISTACHIOS

·1·
Pistachio Pesto

Give your pesto a new twist by substituting an equal quantity of pistachios for the pine nuts in your favorite recipe. Basil is a classic, but when it's not in season I've used everything from carrot tops to fresh za'atar to make pesto, so get creative. You can use either raw or roasted nuts in a pesto; you'll have a stronger pistachio taste with the roasted nuts, but raw nuts will give you a more vibrant green color—your choice!

·2·
Top a Salad

A handful of lightly toasted pistachios and dried cranberries is an easy way to dress up a kale salad or a winter salad of bitter greens and citrus.

·3·
Party Log

A log of goat cheese rolled in chopped toasted nuts is a pretty and tasty centerpiece for a cheese tray. For an especially Christmasy look, mix the pistachios with some dried sour cherries or cranberries.

·4·
Nutty Bruschetta

Smear toasted baguette slices with fresh ricotta, then sprinkle with toasted pistachios and a few flakes of a sea salt like Maldon.

·5·
Boost Your Butter Cookies

Toasted, chopped pistachios can be substituted in just about any cookie recipe that calls for chopped walnut or pecan pieces, and the resulting cookie will be less rich and oily, with lovely green accents to boot.

·6·
Pistachio Butter

In a food processor, blend raw pistachios with a bit of neutral oil (or pistachio oil if you happen to have some) until spreadable. Spread on toasted whole-grain toast and drizzle with honey or date molasses for a nice change of pace in the morning.

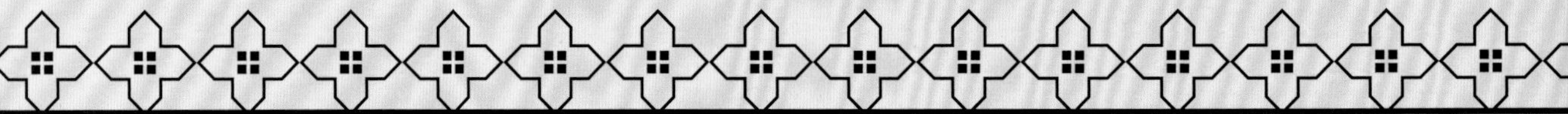

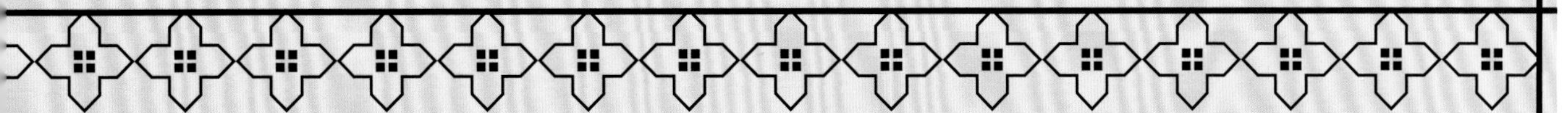

·7·

Pistachio Paste

Combine 1 cup [140 g] of pistachios with ¼ cup [50 g] of sugar in a food processor. Pulse on and off just until finely ground and combined (don't overprocess or the nuts will become mealy). Use the paste as you would marzipan to fill croissants, holiday cookies, or coffee cakes.

·8·

Nutty Asparagus

For a less predictable alternative to asparagus with slivered almonds, toss 1 lb [455 g] of trimmed asparagus with 1 to 2 Tbsp of olive oil, ½ cup [70 g] of raw pistachios, salt, and pepper. Spread on a baking sheet and broil until lightly browned, about 10 minutes. (If you only have roasted nuts, sprinkle them on once the asparagus is done.)

·9·

Green, Green Salsa

Coarsely chop fresh mint, toasted pistachios, and the zest and flesh of a small lemon. Moisten with some good olive oil, season with salt, and spoon onto a roasted whole fish or broiled fish fillet.

·10·

Cheese Topper

Roast a handful of shelled raw pistachios for 5 to 6 minutes in a 350°F [180°C] oven. When cool, transfer to a small bowl and mix with a handful of dried cranberries. Add just enough honey to bind the fruit and nuts (it shouldn't be too loose) and spoon over a whole Brie or Camembert. Serve with crackers.

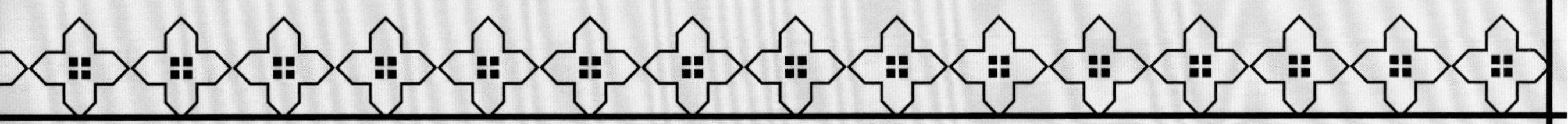

Pan-Roasted Broccoli and Chestnuts

Chestnuts aren't used much in American kitchens, probably because it's a chore to extract the roasted nutmeats from their tough, leathery shells. Fortunately, packages of cooked chestnuts are now available in most markets, and these creamy nuts add a festive fall flavor and meaty heft to lots of dishes, including this easy preparation. It's a crowd-pleasing holiday or cold-weather side with an unexpected twist.

SERVES 6

3 anchovy fillets, rinsed and finely chopped, or 2 tsp anchovy paste
1 tsp fine sea salt
1 tsp Urfa pepper
1 tsp freshly ground black pepper
¼ cup [60 ml] extra-virgin olive oil
2 heads broccoli (about 3 lb [1.4 kg] total), cut into florets
1 cup [130 g] cooked chestnuts, cut into quarters
½ cup [20 g] chopped fresh flat-leaf parsley
2 garlic cloves, finely chopped
Zest and juice of one Meyer or regular lemon

Preheat the oven to 400°F [200°C].

Combine the anchovy fillets, salt, Urfa pepper, and black pepper in a mixing bowl and mash into a paste with a wooden spoon. (If using anchovy paste, just mix well.) Add the oil and blend thoroughly, then add the broccoli to the bowl. Toss to coat with the mixture.

Turn out the broccoli onto a rimmed baking sheet, spreading it in a single layer. Sprinkle the chestnuts evenly over the broccoli. Roast, stirring once, just until the broccoli is crisp-tender and has a few browned edges, about 20 minutes.

While the broccoli is roasting, combine the parsley, garlic, and lemon zest and juice in a small bowl. Stir the parsley mixture into the broccoli as soon as it comes out of the oven. Transfer to a serving dish and serve hot.

Warm Roasted Cauliflower with Tahini-Yogurt Dressing

We are always happy to share recipes with customers who want to try their hand at our family favorites at home, but we love it even more when customers return the favor! This recipe is a variation on one that came to us from longtime patron Steve Marcus, who devised a hearty cauliflower side dish incorporating all his preferred Sahadi's staples. It's well-spiced and tangy, with a hint of sweetness from dried apricots, and a nice cold-weather option when there aren't a lot of fresh green veggies to choose from.

SERVES 6 TO 8

1 head cauliflower
½ cup [120 ml] extra-virgin olive oil
2 Tbsp za'atar
1 tsp fine sea salt
1 tsp Aleppo pepper
¼ cup [55 g] tahini
¼ cup [60 g] plain Greek yogurt, full or low fat
2 Tbsp fresh lemon juice
½ tsp ground white pepper
¼ cup [10 g] chopped fresh parsley
¼ cup [40 g] chopped Turkish apricots

Preheat the oven to 425°F [220°C].

Cut the cauliflower into 2 in [5 cm] florets and mound on a large rimmed baking sheet. Toss with ¼ cup [60 ml] of the oil and the za'atar, ½ tsp of the salt, and the Aleppo pepper. Spread the cauliflower in a single layer and roast, turning once or twice as it cooks, until golden brown, 25 to 30 minutes.

While the cauliflower is roasting, whisk together the tahini, yogurt, remaining ¼ cup [60 ml] of olive oil, and the lemon juice in a large bowl. Season with the remaining ½ tsp of salt and the white pepper. Add 2 Tbsp of water to thin to drizzling consistency, adding more by the tsp as needed.

Add the warm cauliflower and toss to coat with the dressing. Gently stir in the parsley and apricots to distribute evenly. Serve warm.

Roasted Asparagus with Toasted Walnuts and Goat Cheese

When the season's first spears appear in the markets, I often turn to this easy but elegant dish. I like the way the nutty flavors of walnuts and walnut oil temper the astringent green bite of the asparagus, and the colors are just so appealing after the long months of root vegetables and potatoes. Serve it with baby lamb chops and a millet or freekeh pilaf.

SERVES 4 TO 6

1 lb [455 g] asparagus, tough ends trimmed
2 Tbsp plus 1 tsp walnut oil
½ tsp paprika
½ tsp fine sea salt
½ tsp freshly ground black pepper
2 Tbsp soft fresh goat cheese
2 Tbsp toasted walnuts

Preheat the broiler.

Spread the asparagus on a rimmed baking sheet and drizzle with the 2 Tbsp of walnut oil. Toss the spears to coat with the oil, then sprinkle with paprika, salt, and pepper and toss again. Spread the spears in a single layer. Broil, shaking the pan once or twice to cook the spears evenly, until just browned and tender, 5 to 6 minutes.

Transfer the asparagus to a serving bowl and sprinkle with the goat cheese and nuts. Drizzle with the remaining 1 tsp of walnut oil and serve warm or at room temperature.

Pistachio Pilaf

This is the kind of homespun dish that every Middle Eastern grandmother can make in her sleep but that rarely appears in restaurants. It combines rice with pasta for a side dish with a silkier texture than the usual baked rice or grain pilaf. Pistachios both flavor the oil the rice is cooked in and add texture to the finished dish.

SERVES 4

3 Tbsp grapeseed or canola oil
½ cup [70 g] raw pistachios
½ cup [50 g] fideo (short vermicelli noodles) or orzo
1 cup [200 g] basmati rice
½ tsp fine sea salt
¼ tsp freshly ground black pepper
Pinch of grated nutmeg
Pinch of ground allspice
2 cups [480 ml] chicken stock or water

Preheat the oven to 350°F [180°C].

Heat the oil in a heavy, ovenproof casserole with a lid over medium-high heat. Add the pistachios and cook until fragrant and lightly browned, 3 to 4 minutes. Use a slotted spoon to transfer the nuts to a plate and set aside.

Add the pasta to the flavored oil and sauté, stirring frequently, until toasted and slightly golden, 4 to 5 minutes. Add the rice, salt, pepper, nutmeg, and allspice and stir to coat the pasta and rice with the seasonings. Cook until the spices become fragrant, about 1 minute.

Add the stock and bring to a boil. Cover the pot and place it in the oven for 18 minutes, or until the rice is nearly tender. Remove from the oven, stir in the reserved pistachios, and let stand, covered, for 10 minutes or until ready to serve.

Freekeh with Toasted Nuts

Freekeh is a very traditional Middle Eastern grain of the wheat family that looks similar to farro. The grains are "burnt" or toasted for a subtly smoky flavor that is very appealing. Once relatively unusual outside of Middle Eastern groceries, freekeh has become much more mainstream in the last few years. Toasty and nutty yet not too heavy, it is perfect for anyone looking for ways to incorporate more whole grains into their diet.

SERVES 4

2 Tbsp extra-virgin olive oil
1 onion, chopped
2 garlic cloves, minced
½ tsp sea salt
½ tsp freshly ground black pepper
½ tsp ground allspice
1 cup [200 g] freekeh
2 cup [480 ml] chicken or vegetable stock or water
½ cup [70 g] toasted sliced almonds (see Note)
2 Tbsp toasted pine nuts (see Note)
Chopped fresh dill, for garnish (optional)

Heat the oil in a saucepan over medium heat until it begins to shimmer. Add the onion and garlic and sauté for 5 minutes, or until it starts to soften. Season the onions with the salt, pepper, and allspice and continue to cook, stirring frequently, until fragrant, about 5 minutes. Add the freekeh to the pan and stir for 1 minute to coat with the seasonings and toast slightly. Stir in the stock and bring to a boil over high heat.

Cover the pan, reduce the heat to low, and simmer the freekeh for 25 to 30 minutes, or until tender and the liquid has been absorbed.

Fluff the freekeh with a fork and transfer to a serving bowl. Sprinkle with the toasted nuts and dill (if using), and serve hot.

NOTE

To toast nuts, preheat the oven to 350°F [180°C]. Spread the almonds and pine nuts on separate baking sheets or pie pans and toast until fragrant and just starting to color, 5 to 7 minutes for the almonds, 3 to 5 minutes for the pine nuts. Shake the pans frequently and watch the nuts closely, as they can go from golden to blackened in an instant. Transfer to a room-temperature plate or bowl as soon as you remove them from the oven to prevent them from coloring further.

Farfalle with Almond-Arugula Pesto

More robust than a traditional Genovese pesto, this version has the additional advantage of being easy to make in the months when fresh basil is hard to come by and can be lacking in flavor. Because the toasted almonds are more assertive than pine nuts, I've substituted grated Pecorino for the usual Parmesan, making this a gutsy but still subtle combination. I like to pair it with a shaped pasta so the herbaceous, nutty sauce clings better, but by all means, use whatever you have on hand. This is, after all, pantry cooking at its best. The pesto can be stored in the refrigerator for a few days in a tightly covered jar topped with a bit of oil, but the color is best when used immediately.

SERVES 4 TO 6

4 cups [80 g] baby arugula
½ cup [120 ml] almond oil
3 garlic cloves, crushed
¾ tsp fine sea salt
¼ cup [35 g] roasted unsalted almonds
¼ cup [15 g] grated Pecorino-Romano cheese
1 tsp Aleppo pepper
1 lb [455 g] farfalle pasta

Bring a large pot of water to a boil for the pasta.

While the water heats, combine the arugula, ¼ cup [60 ml] of the oil, garlic, and salt in a food processor or a blender. Pulse just until finely chopped. Add the almonds, cheese, Aleppo pepper, and remaining ¼ cup [60 ml] of oil and pulse until well combined.

When the pasta water has come to a boil, salt it generously and add the pasta. Cook according to the package directions, or until just al dente. Set aside 1 cup [240 ml] of the pasta cooking water, then drain the pasta well and return to the pot.

Add the pesto to the pot with the pasta and add 1 or 2 splashes of the cooking water to loosen it. Toss the pasta with the pesto until well coated, adding a bit more pasta water if needed to make a creamy, thick sauce. Serve warm or at room temperature.

Portobellos Stuffed with Herbed White Beans

Over the years I've accumulated a fairly extensive repertoire of vegetarian entrées, and we get more requests for them at the store every week. This is one of our favorites, and it works as a substantial side dish for a simple lamb or beef roast as well. I prefer to use Roman beans because they hold their shape well, but cannellini, cranberry, or even black beans would be good here, too.

SERVES 6

1 Tbsp plus 2 tsp extra-virgin olive oil

2 tsp balsamic vinegar

½ tsp fine sea salt

½ tsp freshly ground black pepper

6 large portobello mushrooms, stems and gills removed

½ cup [70 g] finely chopped onions

2 garlic cloves, minced

1 Tbsp chopped fresh rosemary

One 15 or 19 oz [430 or 540 g] can Roman or cranberry beans, drained, reserving ¼ cup [60 ml] of the liquid

2 cups [40 g] baby spinach or chard

¼ cup [10 g] finely chopped fresh parsley

¼ cup [15 g] grated fresh asiago cheese

2 Tbsp panko bread crumbs

Heat the oven to 450°F [230°C]. Line a rimmed baking sheet with foil or parchment paper.

In a bowl, whisk together the 2 tsp of oil and the vinegar and season with salt and pepper. Arrange the mushroom caps, stem-side up, on the baking sheet and drizzle with the seasoned oil. Bake until tender, 8 to 10 minutes.

While the mushrooms cook, make the filling. Heat the remaining 1 Tbsp of oil in a skillet over medium heat. Add the onion and sauté until soft, 2 to 3 minutes. Add the garlic and rosemary and cook for 1 minute, or until fragrant. Stir in the beans, the reserved liquid, and the spinach, combining well. Continue to cook over medium heat until the beans are hot and the spinach has wilted, about 5 minutes. Remove from the heat and transfer to a bowl.

Add the parsley, cheese, and panko to the bean mixture and mix well. Adjust the salt and pepper if necessary. Divide the bean filling among the hot mushroom caps and drizzle with the remaining olive oil and balsamic mixture. Return to the oven and bake for an additional 5 minutes, or until the filling is hot and the mushrooms are just beginning to brown. Serve warm or at room temperature.

Seared Tuna Loin with a Sesame Mustard Seed Crust

A piece of tuna loin this big is without question an extravagance, but as the centerpiece of a party spread, it has few equals. It's meaty enough for those who are not avowed fish lovers and light enough for those who, like me, love fish of all kinds! The combination of seeds and peppers make a fantastic crust that really sets off the rare-cooked fish beautifully. Best of all, it's fast to assemble, works hot or cold, and feeds a crowd. No wonder it's my tried-and-true when we have a houseful. Should there be any leftovers, a few slices atop a green salad make an excellent lunch.

SERVES 10 TO 12

½ cup [60 g] black mustard seeds
½ cup [70 g] toasted sesame seeds
2 Tbsp Aleppo pepper
2 Tbsp large flaky salt, such as Maldon
One 4 lb [1.8 kg] piece of tuna loin
2 Tbsp extra-virgin olive oil

On a rimmed baking sheet, stir together the mustard seeds, sesame seeds, Aleppo pepper, and salt until well combined. Roll the tuna loin in the mixture to coat completely, pressing the seed mixture into all sides.

Heat the oil in a large, heavy skillet over high heat until hot. Very carefully lower the tuna into the skillet and sear for 2 minutes, or until well browned. Turn the tuna and continue to sear until brown and crusty on all sides, including the ends. This should take no more than 10 to 12 minutes total. The tuna interior will be cooked rare.

Let the tuna rest for 10 minutes before serving hot or at room temperature, or wrap well and refrigerate overnight and serve cold on a buffet.

Christmas Rice

Every Christmas Eve, my cousin Sonia makes an absolutely gorgeous buffet, and her rice, with bits of lamb, chicken, and nuts, is the star of the show. This simplified version captures the heady flavors and aroma with a lot less effort. Mastic, while not strictly essential, adds a distinctive quality that I think really makes the dish.

SERVES 8 GENEROUSLY

One 3½ lb [1.6 kg] chicken, cut into serving pieces

1 Tbsp coarsely ground black pepper

1 Tbsp fine sea salt

2 tsp ground allspice

1 whole nutmeg, grated, or 1 tsp ground

2 bay leaves

2 mastic "tears"

¼ tsp ground cardamom

½ cup [120 ml] extra-virgin olive oil

⅓ cup [40 g] pine nuts

⅓ cup [45 g] whole blanched almonds

⅓ cup [45 g] raw shelled pistachios

2 cups [260 g] roasted and shelled chestnuts

1½ lb [680 g] diced boneless leg of lamb or beef stew meat

2½ cups [500 g] white rice

Chopped parsley, for garnish

Plain yogurt, for serving (optional)

Put the chicken in a large soup pot with 6 cups [1.4 L] of water and the pepper, salt, allspice, nutmeg, bay leaves, mastic, and cardamom. Bring to a boil over high heat, then reduce the heat to low, cover, and simmer for 45 minutes, or until the broth is fragrant and the chicken is cooked through. Use a slotted spoon to transfer the chicken to a plate, reserving the stock.

When the chicken is cool enough to handle, shred the meat and discard the skin and bones. Cover and keep warm. Use a large spoon or a ladle to skim off as much fat as possible from the broth.

Heat the oil in a large pot over medium heat and line a plate with paper towels. Add the pine nuts and cook in the oil until golden, about 2 minutes, then use a slotted spoon to transfer the nuts to the paper towels to drain. Repeat with the almonds, pistachios, and chestnuts (the almonds and chestnuts may take 1 or 2 minutes longer to brown), leaving the oil in the pot.

Raise the heat to medium-high and when hot, add the lamb all at once. Cook the meat, stirring occasionally, until it releases its juices, about 10 minutes, then continue to cook until the liquid evaporates, another 10 minutes. Add 1½ cups [360 ml] of the reserved chicken stock, cover the pot, and cook the meat slowly over low heat until very tender, 30 to 45 minutes. The meat should be almost falling apart.

Add 3½ cups [840 ml] of the remaining chicken stock to the pot and bring to a boil. Add the rice, return to a boil, then reduce the heat to low, cover, and simmer for 20 minutes. Remove from the heat and arrange the shredded chicken on top. Cover the pot again and let stand for 30 minutes.

To serve, mix the rice well to distribute the meat throughout. Mound the rice mixture onto a platter and scatter the toasted nuts over all. Sprinkle with the parsley. Pass the yogurt at the table.

Dukkah-Crusted Pork Cutlets

Thin-cut pork chops with a bread crumb coating are just fine, but the same chops with a dose of dukkah are an entirely different story—warm from the cumin seeds, crunchy with bits of seeds and nuts, much more interesting to eat—and all with the shake of a jar. Serve this over a bed of lightly dressed, lemony arugula, or with an easy fruity dipping sauce.

SERVES 4

Apricot Dipping Sauce

¼ cup [45 g] Turkish apricots, coarsely chopped

2 tsp extra-virgin olive oil

¼ cup [35 g] chopped onions

¾ tsp ras el hanout

¼ tsp fine sea salt

Pork Cutlets

4 thin-cut pork cutlets or chops

1 cup [60 g] panko bread crumbs

2 Tbsp dukkah, store-bought or homemade (page 229)

1 large egg

½ cup [120 ml] extra-virgin olive oil, plus more as needed

¼ cup [55 g] (½ stick) unsalted butter, plus more as needed

3 cups [60 g] baby arugula

Juice of 1 lemon

½ tsp fine sea salt

½ tsp freshly ground black pepper

Lemon wedges, for serving (optional)

To make the dipping sauce: Soak the apricots in 1 cup [240 ml] of hot tap water for 20 minutes to soften.

Heat the oil in a small skillet until hot, then add the onions. Sauté until golden, 2 to 3 minutes, then add the ras el hanout and stir for another minute, until fragrant. Add the apricots and soaking water and simmer for 5 minutes, or until very soft.

Purée the mixture in a blender until smooth. Season with salt.

To make the pork cutlets: If necessary, pound the pork cutlets to an even ¼ in [6 mm] thickness between two pieces of plastic wrap. Mix the panko and dukkah in a shallow dish. Break the egg into a second shallow dish and beat lightly with a fork to break it up. One at a time, dredge the cutlets first in the egg and then in the panko mixture, coating them thoroughly. Set aside on a plate.

Heat ¼ cup [60 ml] of the oil and the butter together in a large skillet over medium-high heat until quite hot. Carefully place two of the breaded cutlets in the skillet. Sauté without moving until browned on the bottom, about 5 minutes, adjusting the heat slightly if they are getting too dark too quickly. Turn the cutlets and brown on the other side for 3 to 4 minutes longer, just until cooked through. Don't overcook or the pork will become tough.

Transfer the cooked cutlets to a plate and keep them warm. Cook the remaining cutlets, adding more oil or butter as necessary.

To serve, toss the arugula with the lemon juice, the remaining ¼ cup [60 ml] of oil, and the salt and pepper. Serve the pork, warm or at room temperature, over the arugula salad, with the dipping sauce and garnished with the lemon wedges, if using.

Beef and Lentil Bowl with Tahini Dressing

At our café, we add strips of beef cooked with heady shawarma spices to a traditionally vegetarian dish of rice and lentils. The deeply browned, crispy onions are the heart of the dish, so don't rush that step or they will burn and make the oil bitter. Toasting the lentils and rice in the onion-flavored oil gives the dish a richness and depth of flavor you don't often find in a simple bowl of lentils. Use any leftover flavored oil for pilafs and dressings or to sauté meat.

SERVES 6

1 lb [455 g] beef top round, cut into thin strips

½ cup [120 ml] extra-virgin olive oil

1 Tbsp shawarma spices (see page 204)

1 Tbsp dry red wine

1 large onion, cut into thin slices and separated into rings

2 cups [400 g] French lentils

1 cup [200 g] jasmine rice

2 tsp fine sea salt

2 tsp freshly ground black pepper

1 tsp ground allspice

½ cup [110 g] tahini

¼ cup [60 ml] fresh lemon juice

1 Tbsp chopped fresh parsley

1 tsp minced garlic

Persian cucumbers, sliced, pickled vegetables, and grape tomatoes, for serving

Put the beef in a bowl or sealable plastic bag. Add 1 Tbsp of the oil, the shawarma spices, and the red wine and turn the meat to coat it with the mixture. Cover the bowl or seal the bag and refrigerate for at least 4 hours or overnight.

Heat the remaining oil in a skillet over medium heat. When it is shimmering but not smoking, add the onions. Fry the onions, stirring frequently, until browned and crispy, 10 to 12 minutes. With a slotted spoon, transfer the onions to paper towels to drain in a single layer. Reserve the oil.

Put 2 Tbsp of the flavored oil in a 4 qt [3.8 L] pot and heat over medium-low heat. Add the lentils and rice and stir to coat with the oil. Season with the salt, pepper, and allspice, and mix well. Add 8½ cups [2 L] of water, bring to a boil, cover, and reduce the heat to low. Simmer for 25 minutes, or until the water is absorbed and the rice and lentils are tender.

Whisk the tahini with the lemon juice, parsley, and garlic until combined. If the sauce is too thick to drizzle, add water, 1 Tbsp at a time, until smooth and pourable. Season with salt.

Heat 1 Tbsp of the reserved oil in the skillet over medium-high heat until just smoking. Add half the beef strips and cook quickly until just browned, turning once. Transfer the beef to a plate and repeat with the remaining beef strips, adding more oil to the pan if needed.

To build the bowls, scoop the lentil and rice mixture into serving bowls. Top with beef strips and scatter crispy onions over all. Drizzle with some of the tahini dressing. Serve with the cucumbers, pickles, and grape tomatoes.

Tahini Swirl Brownies

Though the flavor is subtle, date syrup gives these brownies exceptional depth of flavor without a lot of extra sweetness for a best-of-class version. These are as rich as they come, so I cut them into very small pieces, but that's your call!

MAKES TWENTY-FIVE 1½ IN [4 CM] BROWNIES

1 cup [220 g] (2 sticks) plus 2 Tbsp unsalted butter
6 oz [170 g] unsweetened chocolate
1 cup [140 g] all-purpose flour
¼ tsp sea salt
4 large eggs
1½ cups [300 g] granulated sugar
½ cup [100 g] light brown sugar
2 Tbsp date syrup or date molasses
2½ tsp vanilla extract
¾ cup [165 g] well-stirred tahini
½ cup [60 g] confectioner's sugar
1 tsp orange blossom water

Preheat the oven to 350°F [180°C]. Grease a 9 in [23 cm] square baking pan, then line it with a strip of parchment paper, allowing two long ends to drape over the sides of the pan (this will help you lift out the brownies when they are done).

Combine the 1 cup [220 g] of butter and the chocolate in a saucepan. Place over low heat, stirring just until melted and combined. Let cool completely.

While the chocolate cools, stir the flour and salt together in a bowl. In the bowl of an electric mixer, combine the eggs, granulated and brown sugars, date syrup, and 2 tsp of the vanilla and beat on medium speed until just blended. Add the cooled chocolate mixture and combine briefly. Fold in the flour mixture by hand, blending just until no streaks of flour are visible. Set aside.

Melt the remaining 2 Tbsp of butter and scrape it into a mixing bowl. Add the tahini, confectioner's sugar, remaining ½ tsp vanilla, and the orange blossom water and mix well. Spread all but 1 cup [240 g] of the chocolate mixture in the prepared pan and smooth the top. Drop spoonfuls of the tahini mixture over the surface, then top with spoonfuls of the reserved brownie batter. Drag the tip of a wooden skewer or paring knife through the tahini mixture and batter to make swirls.

Bake for 30 minutes, or until a toothpick inserted in the middle comes out almost clean with a few very moist crumbs attached. Set the pan on a wire rack to cool completely before transferring the parchment paper and brownies to a cutting board. Cut into 25 small squares.

Store the brownies in an airtight container for up to 5 days or freeze for up to 1 month.

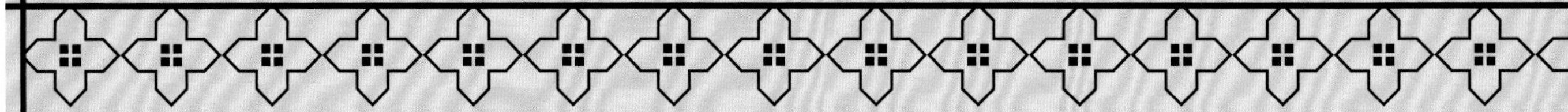

TEN MORE WAYS TO USE

TAHINI

·1·

Creamy Tahini Dressing

Swirl a few tablespoons of tahini into ½ cup [120 g] of yogurt. Season with salt and add a squirt of lemon and, if you like, a burst of herbal flavor from finely chopped parsley or cilantro to lighten it. Drizzle over sturdy greens or roasted cauliflower, sweet potatoes, or chickpeas.

·2·

Tahini Vinaigrette

For a more hearty, creamy take on a mixed green salad, whisk a few tablespoons of tahini into the vinaigrette.

·3·

Lebanese Baked Fish

Variations of this very traditional recipe are served throughout the Middle East; all are based on an oven-baked fillet of white fish, cooked simply with just a bit of olive oil and seasoning until flaky, topped with a lemony tahini sauce. While the fish bakes, blend 1 cup [220 g] of tahini with ¼ cup [60 ml] of hot water in a blender until fluffy. Add 1 or 2 minced garlic cloves, 2 Tbsp of fresh lemon juice, ½ tsp of salt, and a generous handful of cilantro, fresh za'atar, marjoram, or parsley and blend until smooth. Taste for seasoning and add more lemon or salt. Dollop onto the hot fish fillets and serve immediately. Garnish with toasted pine nuts and/or caramelized onions if desired.

·4·

Sesame Noodles

Loosen ⅓ cup [75 g] of tahini with soy sauce, a dash of mirin, and a small drizzle of toasted sesame oil. Toss with hot cooked rice noodles or pasta and serve topped with sliced scallions, toasted sesame seeds, and another tiny drizzle of sesame oil if desired.

·5·

Dipping Sauce

Thin out ½ cup [110 g] of tahini with ¼ cup [60 ml] of coconut milk. Add 1 Tbsp of red curry paste and serve with baked chicken tenders, battered and fried cauliflower or broccoli, or with crudité.

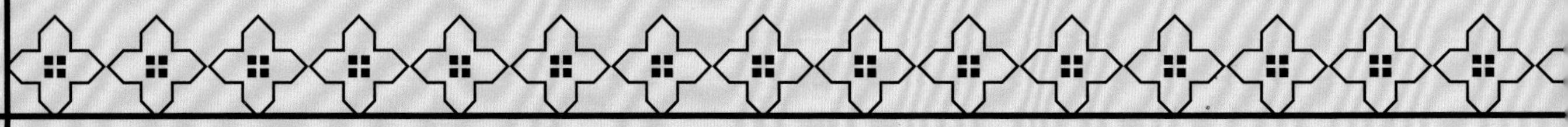

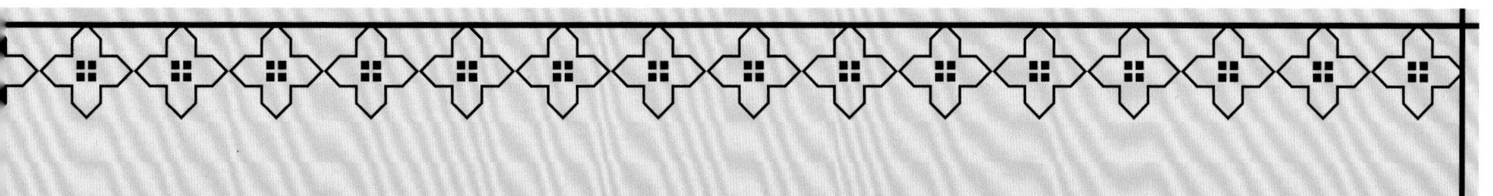

· 6 ·

Toasty Cocoa

In a mug, stir together 1 Tbsp of tahini and ¼ cup [60 ml] of milk (dairy or nondairy). Microwave until very hot but not boiling (about 1 minute), then stir to combine. Add 2 oz [55 g] of finely chopped bittersweet or semisweet chocolate and stir to melt. Top off the mug with more milk and microwave for another minute or so, until the chocolate is completely melted and the cocoa is hot. Top with a pinch of cinnamon or grated nutmeg.

· 7 ·

Peanut Butter Cookies 2.0

Tahini can stand in for peanut or almond butter in just about any cookie recipe if you adjust its consistency. Just stir in confectioner's sugar by the Tbsp until the mixture is spreadable but not flowing, then substitute it 1-for-1 for the nut butter. Sprinkle the tops of the cookies with sesame seeds to underscore the sesame flavor if you like.

· 8 ·

Fudgy Smoothie

Put a frozen banana in a blender with 2 Tbsp of cocoa powder, 2 Tbsp of tahini, a pinch of cinnamon, and 1 dried pitted date. Add 1 cup [240 ml] of milk (dairy or nondairy) and blend until smooth, adding more milk if you prefer a thinner shake.

· 9 ·

Sandwich Spread

Stir tahini together with date syrup and spread on toast or crackers. It's like PB&J without the refined sugar.

· 10 ·

Ice Cream Topping

Thin tahini with a few tablespoons of honey or date molasses and warm gently; spoon over vanilla or dulce de leche ice cream.

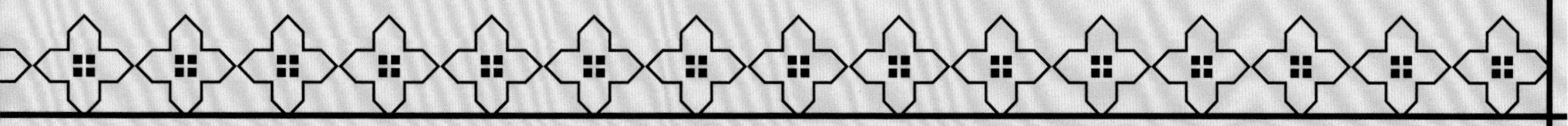

Sesame Cookies (Barazek)

Barazek are very traditional cookies, simple and homey, and although they may not be the showiest item in our pastry case, they shine with pure sesame flavor. The surprise crunch of the chopped pistachio hidden underneath always delights me. My dad loves these cookies, so we both enjoyed the process of developing this recipe!

MAKES 15 COOKIES

1 cup [220 g] (2 sticks) unsalted butter, at room temperature

½ cup [100 g] sugar

1 large egg

3 cups [420 g] unbleached all-purpose flour

¼ cup [85 g] honey

½ cup [70 g] toasted sesame seeds

2 Tbsp chopped unsalted raw pistachios

Put the butter in the bowl of an electric mixer and beat on high speed until fluffy, 2 to 3 minutes. Add the sugar and beat well, scraping down the bowl once or twice, until completely blended. Add the egg and beat until combined.

With the mixer on low, add the flour in three batches, waiting for each addition to be completely incorporated before adding more. Mix until a soft dough forms. Turn out the dough onto a work surface and form into a flattened disk. Wrap in plastic and refrigerate until slightly firm, about 1 hour.

Preheat the oven to 350°F [180°C]. Place the open jar of honey in a saucepan of water and warm over low heat until it is very fluid, or heat briefly in the microwave.

Put the dough on a sheet of parchment paper and cover with a second sheet. Roll out the dough very thin, about ⅛ in [4 mm] thick. Use a 3 in [7.5 cm] round cutter to cut circles, lifting off the scraps. (You can reroll the scraps after chilling them until firmed up a bit, about 15 minutes.) With a pastry brush, brush the cookies gently with the honey and completely coat the tops with the sesame seeds.

Use a thin spatula to transfer the cookies to an ungreased baking sheet. As you place each cookie, slip ½ tsp of the chopped pistachios under its center. Bake for about 25 minutes, or until browned and crisp. Let the cookies cool completely on the baking sheets. Store in an airtight container for up to a week.

Lebanese Sweet Pudding

Farina is served around the world as a breakfast food (you may know it best as the hot cereal called Cream of Wheat). Here it is cooked on the stovetop, then poured into a baking pan to set for a simple, homespun treat. A drizzle of honey keeps the dusting of chopped nuts in place. Cut the pudding into small squares to serve with coffee or tea for an afternoon pick-me-up. It keeps very well in the refrigerator.

SERVES 12 TO 16

1½ tsp mastic "tears"
6 cups [1.4 L] whole milk
2 cups [400 g] sugar
2 cups [350 g] farina
¼ cup [60 ml] rose water
3 to 4 tsp honey
½ cup [60 g] finely chopped pistachios
½ cup [60 g] finely chopped walnuts

Using a small spice grinder or a mortar and pestle, crush the mastic to a fine powder. Combine the milk, sugar, farina, rose water, and mastic powder in a large saucepan. Bring just to a boil over medium heat, stirring constantly to prevent it from scorching or becoming lumpy. Immediately lower the heat to a simmer and continue to cook until the mixture thickens, about 5 minutes.

Pour the pudding into a 9 by 13 in [23 by 33 cm] baking dish and cool to room temperature; it will thicken up and set as it cools.

Place the open jar of honey in a saucepan of water and warm over low heat until it is very fluid, or heat briefly in the microwave. Drizzle the honey over the surface and sprinkle with the pistachios and walnuts. Cut into squares to serve.

SYRIAN ICE CREAM
WITH PISTACHIOS
page 273

CHOCOLATE TAHINI
ICE CREAM
page 272

Chocolate Tahini Ice Cream

Tahini is used in myriad ways in Middle Eastern cooking, but there is so much more that can be done with it beyond sauces and hummus. Here, tahini and date syrup (traditionally used as a breakfast spread) combine for a decadent, dairy-free dessert with a deep, dark chocolate flavor. Use the best-quality, thickest nut milk you can find; it will make a much richer finished product.

MAKES 1 QT [960 ML]

2 cup [480 ml] unsweetened almond or cashew milk or macadamia milk

¼ cup [30 g] almond flour

½ cup [40 g] unsweetened cocoa powder

½ cup [110 g] well-stirred tahini

¾ cup [255 g] date syrup or date molasses

1 Tbsp pure vanilla extract

Combine the nut milk and almond flour in a blender and set aside for 15 minutes to hydrate the flour. Add the cocoa, tahini, date syrup, and vanilla and blend until completely smooth and uniform in color.

Pour the mixture into the canister of an ice cream maker and freeze according to manufacturer's directions until firm. Transfer the ice cream to covered freezer containers and place in the freezer until completely hardened. Keep frozen until ready to serve.

Syrian Ice Cream with Pistachios

Pistachio is perhaps the Middle East's most iconic ice cream flavor and certainly the most popular, but this stretchy, fragrant ice cream has little in common with the bright green stuff you'll find in the supermarket. The taste is subtle and sophisticated, and the sticky mastic gives it a texture that is just plain fun to eat.

MAKES 2 QT [1.9 L]

1 cup [140 g] raw pistachios
4 cups [960 ml] whole milk, preferably organic
2½ tsp sahlab powder (see Note)
1 cup [200 g] sugar
1½ tsp mastic "tears"
2 cups [480 ml] heavy cream, preferably organic
1 to 2 Tbsp rose water, or to taste

Preheat the oven to 350°F [180°C].

Spread the pistachios on a rimmed baking sheet and toast until lightly colored and fragrant, about 5 minutes. Transfer to a bowl to cool.

Pour all but ¼ cup [60 ml] of the milk into a large saucepan. In a small bowl, stir the sahlab into the reserved ¼ cup [60 ml] milk until dissolved. Stir the sahlab slurry into the saucepan of milk and bring to a boil over medium-low heat, stirring frequently to prevent it from scorching. As soon as the mixture reaches a boil, add the sugar and lower the heat to medium-low. Cook the mixture, uncovered, stirring frequently, for 25 minutes, or until slightly thickened.

Using a small spice grinder or a mortar and pestle, grind or pulverize the mastic to a very fine powder. Transfer the powder to a small bowl and blend with 1 Tbsp of the heavy cream. Add to the milk mixture and cook for 5 more minutes, or until it starts to resemble a custard; it will thicken more when you freeze it. Remove from the heat and cool to room temperature. (You can set the saucepan in a bowl of ice water to speed the process.)

Strain the cooled milk mixture into a clean bowl. Add the rose water and the remaining heavy cream, then chill thoroughly for at least 2 hours or overnight.

When you are ready to freeze the ice cream, stir in the pistachios. Pour the ice cream mixture into the canister of an ice cream maker and freeze according to the manufacturer's instructions until it starts to become firm. Transfer the ice cream into freezer containers and place in the freezer for at least 2 hours or until completely hardened. Keep frozen until ready to serve.

NOTE

Sahlab (also called sahlep or salep) is a packaged product similar to pudding mix. It is available in any Middle Eastern grocery store or online.

Pistachio Cheesecake with Kataifi Crust

A very special dessert for a special occasion, this is fragrant, crunchy, and creamy all at once. Traditional cheesecake is indulgent but *so* heavy and rich. Blending the cream cheese filling with labneh, a super-thick yogurt product, lightens the batter and gives it a nice tang without losing any of that creamy decadence. The pistachio-studded kataifi crust bakes up extra crisp, almost like shredded wheat but a lot more buttery and delicious. You'll find kataifi dough in the freezer case next to the phyllo.

SERVES 12

1 cup [220 g] (2 sticks) unsalted butter
8 oz [225 g] kataifi dough
3½ cups [490 g] raw shelled pistachios
7 Tbsp [150 g] honey
1 lb [455 g] labneh
1 lb [455 g] cream cheese, at room temperature
1 cup [200 g] sugar
1 Tbsp orange blossom water
4 eggs
2 egg yolks

Preheat the oven to 375°F [190°C]. Coat a 10 in [25 cm] springform pan with cooking spray.

Melt the butter in a glass measuring cup or small saucepan and set aside to cool slightly. Place the kataifi in a bowl and fluff with your fingers to separate the shreds. Chop 1 cup [140 g] of the pistachios and add to the bowl. Drizzle the butter over the mixture, leaving any white solids behind, and toss to combine thoroughly.

Press the crust mixture into the springform pan, making a compact layer on the bottom and about ¼ in [6 mm] up the sides. Drizzle with 3 Tbsp of the honey. Bake the crust until crisp and well browned, 30 to 40 minutes. Let the crust cool a bit on a wire rack and lower the oven heat to 325°F [160°C].

While the crust is baking, spread the remaining 2½ cups [350 g] of pistachios on a rimmed baking sheet and toast in the same oven, shaking the pan once or twice, until they are golden and fragrant, about 5 minutes. Let cool.

Combine the labneh and cream cheese in the bowl of a stand mixer and beat until smooth. Beat in the sugar and orange blossom water, then add the eggs and egg yolks, one at a time, beating until smooth after each addition. Scrape down the sides of the bowl frequently with a rubber spatula to prevent lumps. Add 1½ cups [210 g] of the roasted pistachios and mix by hand with the spatula until well combined.

Pour the filling into the baked crust, level the top, and bake for 1 hour or until the filling is firm and just beginning to brown at the edges. Transfer to a wire rack and cool completely in the pan.

To serve, release and remove the sides of the springform pan and transfer the cheesecake to a serving plate. Mix the remaining cup [140 g] of toasted pistachios with the remaining 4 Tbsp [85 g] of honey and spoon the mixture onto the cake. Serve chilled or at room temperature.

5
SWEET

LIGHT, FLORAL, DELICATE

NATURAL FLOWER WATERS

DRIED FRUIT

DATE SYRUP

HONEY

HALVAH

MAHLAB

In the Middle East, sweets are regarded as a category unto themselves, not simply the culmination of a full meal. Few restaurants even offer a dessert course, deferring that honor to sweet shops specializing in pastries and ice cream. Instead, restaurant diners punctuate their dinner by choosing from a big bowl of fruit that is brought to the table, or a small serving of something cleansing and refreshing, like watermelon, that serves to counterbalance a rich meal. In fact, just about the only time a Middle Easterner will serve a prepared dessert is at the end of a holiday meal, as a signal that it's time to go home!

This is not to say that we don't love our sweets. As in Europe, there is a strong coffee culture throughout the Middle East, and sweets like cookies, halvah, and baklava are served throughout the day with a cup of strong Turkish coffee. Sweets are also offered in the home whenever a visitor drops by, a tradition so deeply ingrained that it would be considered almost offensive not to welcome a guest with sweets—and equally impolite not to accept the offer.

Sweets can be as simple as a dried apricot dipped in chocolate or as elaborate as homemade phyllo pastry stuffed with pistachios; halvah can be eaten in a sandwich, à la PB&J, and dates might be stuffed with nuts or sliced and tossed into a rice pilaf to impart their mellow sweetness. Sweet spices like cardamom and mahlab (made from the pits of a specific variety of cherry) impart both subtle flavor and a distinctive sweet aroma to coffee, confections, and dairy. At our stores we make trays of cookies, pastries, and sweet puddings using these ingredients every day, and you will find many of them in this chapter, as well as a few recipes I've created along the way to showcase them in a more conventionally Western style.

ROSE
WATER
8.45 fl oz / 250 ml
MAHLAB
DATES AND
APRICOTS
HONEY

DATE SYRUP
ORANGE BLOSSOM
SIMPLE SYRUP
DRIED CHERRIES
HALVAH

Natural Flower Waters

These colorless scented liquids, infused with the essence of orange or rose blossoms, are used throughout the Middle East, from Syria to Morocco. They are made by distilling the petals of damask roses or the blossoms of the Seville orange tree in water until highly fragrant. When added sparingly to sweets or beverages, they impart an elusive background flavor and an alluring aroma, but don't be tempted to go overboard. Too much of the rose, in particular, can cause food to taste soapy, like drinking perfume!

WHAT TO LOOK FOR • There is a huge difference in quality from brand to brand, and in this particular case it pays to spend for quality. If the label lists anything other than flower petals and distilled water, I guarantee you will be getting an inferior product. (Pure flower essences are suspended in oil and intended for medicinal, not culinary use; do not substitute them in these recipes.) You want flower waters that are so fragrant you can almost smell them before you open the bottle; otherwise you will need to use three times as much to achieve the same effect. I prefer those that come from Lebanon, where they have been making and using them for generations, but good ones come from France, as well.

SERVE WITH • In many situations you can use orange blossom and rose waters interchangeably, but orange blossom has a particular affinity for chocolate, while rose is a good companion for dairy. Orange adds a pleasant bitter note to foods; rose contributes floral notes. Middle Easterners dilute orange blossom water with water as a tonic to settle an upset stomach and relieve bloat. When my children were little, I sometimes gave them a bit to soothe colic.

Dried Fruit

In the Middle East, dried fruits such as dates, figs, and stone fruits are both eaten out of hand as a snack and used as a colorful, lightly sweet accent in salads, sauces, and desserts. Apricots in particular are a very typical Middle Eastern and Mediterranean flavoring; many of the treats I remember best from childhood were flavored with apricots, from candy to fruit rolls to my favorite ice cream.

WHAT TO LOOK FOR • When it comes to apricots, color is not always the best indicator of flavor. A bright orange hue indicates fruit that has been treated with sulfur dioxide, which, though not necessarily a bad thing, is undesirable to those looking for an unprocessed, natural product. The organic apricots we import from Turkey are entirely sun dried and unsulfured, with a dark brown color, but they are among the most vividly flavored you will find. In general, try to choose moist, separate fruits without blemishes and with minimal external sugar, which indicates they have not been stored properly. My preferred dates for snacking or smoothies are Medjools from California, which have soft, dense, almost fudgy flesh. They don't stand up well to long cooking, though; for those uses, choose a dried, imported variety. Dried fruit will keep almost indefinitely in an airtight container but will become harder over time.

SERVE WITH • All dried fruits have an affinity for nuts, grains, and full-flavored meats, and I love to pair them with warm spices, like curry powder or ras el hanout. To update cookie and pudding recipes, substitute dried cherries or chopped dates for the more expected raisins or dried cranberries; add interest to rice pilafs by stirring in a handful of slivered apricots just before serving.

Date Syrup

Syrups made from the extracts of boiled fruits, including dates, grapes, and carob, are widely used in the Middle East and North Africa, where refined sugar products are less common. Of these, date molasses—also known as date nectar, date syrup, and date honey—has recently gained favor as an alternative sweetener, making it easier to find than it once was. The thick brown liquid is similar to molasses in color and texture but much sweeter and with a less bitter edge. It can be used in baking as a substitute for granular sweeteners, but you will need to adjust the amount of liquid in your recipe to compensate.

WHAT TO LOOK FOR • As with pomegranate molasses, you should look for a date syrup that is 100-percent fruit, with no added sugars or extenders. I am partial to the pure fruit syrups we import from Lebanon.

SERVE WITH • Date syrup is primarily served as a breakfast spread in the Middle East, although a date syrup and tahini sandwich is the region's answer to a PB&J, and a very typical after-school snack. Because it is very intense, a little drizzle goes a long way over pancakes, oatmeal, yogurt, or cheese, and in beverages and dessert recipes.

Honey

These natural sweeteners are as much a pure expression of their terroir as wine is, taking on the distinctive characteristics of the flowers from which the bees collected pollen. So although honey is used all over the Middle East and Mediterranean for baking and as an all-purpose sweetener, little of it is produced locally. For Middle Easterners, the quality of a honey trumps its provenance, and honeys imported from Germany in particular are known to be of excellent quality. In our stores we carry German honey plus a few domestically produced honeys from small producers. Check your farmers market for honey produced in your area; it's said that eating honey made from local pollen can even help mitigate seasonal allergies.

WHAT TO LOOK FOR · Honey can vary from deep dark buckwheat to pale straw yellow, but the color isn't necessarily indicative of flavor. Check the label, which should tell you what flowers the bees were visiting. They are all delicious but distinctive, and it's worth trying a few to get a better sense of which flavoring you like best. Honey crystallizes when exposed to air; if yours becomes hard or gritty before you use it up, just heat it briefly in the microwave and use immediately.

SERVE WITH · Honey can be drizzled on pancakes, used to sweeten tea, or used as an alternative to refined sugars in baking. I love a lavender honey in fresh lemonade with a splash of orange blossom water. A bit of chestnut honey rubbed on the skin of a roasting turkey helps to create a nice bronze color and adds a bit of flavor.

Halvah

This simple confection is basically just sesame seeds and sugar: the sugar is boiled to a syrup and then mixed with tahini paste until it has a fudge-like texture. In Middle Eastern homes, halvah is eaten with coffee as an afternoon treat. Nuts, especially pistachios, and chocolate are the most typical flavorings; Israel produces layered halvahs with layers of coating chocolate sandwiched between slabs of marbled, plain, or flavored halvah.

You will likely find two types of halvah when you go to purchase: imported, from the Middle East—Lebanon, Syria, Israel—and domestic halvah. Imported halvah is sticky and crumbly, with underlying tones of flower water. Because it is made from Middle Eastern tahini, which is whiter than American tahini, the halvah is paler than American-made, which has a more caramel color. Domestic halvah also has a lighter, more crumbly texture and is generally not made with flower water, for a purer sesame flavor. Most of what we sell is domestic unless it's labeled imported or "imported style," and we have our house-label halvah made locally, using our own pistachios, because, as in all things, we want what we want!

WHAT TO LOOK FOR · Choose halvah based on how you plan to use it. For cooking, I prefer the way American halvah incorporates itself into a dish. Imported halvah becomes chewy when cooked rather than blending in. Store either kind of halvah at room temperature, away from moisture.

SERVE WITH · Halvah has an affinity for chocolate. It can be served on its own as a sweet bite or incorporated into cookies and other baked goods, or crumbled onto hot cereals or yogurt as a nutty sweetener.

Mahlab

Of all the ingredients in this book, mahlab may be the least familiar to you, but I hope I can make the case for adding it to your sweets and baking pantry. It has a delicate cherry flavor with notes of bitter almond—not surprising, since it is made from the tiny dried kernel of the St. Lucie cherry, a fruit variety that grows around the Mediterranean. To get at the kernels, the cherry pits must be cracked open, and the moist kernels are then dried to a buckshot hardness. When ground, the kernels become very powdery and easy to incorporate into any number of recipes. In Greece, mahlab is an essential ingredient for tsoureki, the Easter sweet bread, and Lebanese families give out little yeast-raised donuts made with mahlab for the holiday; my cousin still makes hundreds every year! And it is what gives stretchy Syrian ice cream its distinctive flavor.

WHAT TO LOOK FOR • Mahlab is used only in ground form, and though it can be purchased both whole and preground, like most spices it is most flavorful when freshly ground. When we import mahlab, generally from Turkey, we buy whole dried kernels and grind them as needed in small batches to ensure that the resulting powder will have maximum punch. If you buy yours whole, grind it extremely fine in a clean coffee grinder or spice mill; otherwise buy ground mahlab in small quantities and aim to use it within 3 to 6 months.

SERVE WITH • Add a bit of mahlab to doughs for scones, yeasted breads, muffins, and cakes when you want to add an elusive hint of cherry flavor. It pairs well with other mild-flavored foods like dairy and cheese and has an affinity for almonds. When we make Syrian twisted cheese at home, we sometimes use mahlab in combination with nigella seeds. It's a nice way to infuse foods with a fruity essence without introducing additional liquid.

Date Pecan Coconut Granola

A generous helping of dates, pecans, and coconut makes this our best-selling granola. It is sweetened with date syrup, which gives it a deep, earthy flavor that is more subtle than sugar or honey. I serve this granola in small parfait glasses layered with plain Greek yogurt and a bit of naturally sweetened preserves. Use kitchen shears to cut the sticky dates into pieces.

MAKES ABOUT 6½ CUPS [650 G]

2¾ cups [275 g] old-fashioned rolled oats (not quick oats)
¾ cup [90 g] pecan halves
⅓ cup [25 g] unsweetened flaked or shredded coconut
2 Tbsp chia seeds
1 tsp ground cinnamon
¼ tsp fine sea salt
½ cup [170 g] date syrup
⅓ cup [75 g] unrefined coconut oil, warmed to a pourable consistency
2 tsp vanilla extract
1 cup [225 g] diced pitted dates

Preheat the oven to 350°F [180°C] and line a rimmed baking sheet with parchment paper.

In a large bowl, mix the oats with the pecans, coconut, chia seeds, cinnamon, and salt. In a smaller bowl, whisk together the date syrup, coconut oil, and vanilla. Pour this liquid over the oat mixture and mix well to coat all the dry ingredients.

Turn out the granola onto the baking sheet and spread as thinly as possible. Bake for 10 minutes, then remove from the oven and stir and turn with a metal spatula. Spread out the granola again and return to the oven for 10 to 12 minutes longer, or until browned. Set aside to cool on the baking sheet until crisp. Mix in the dates and toss to distribute.

Transfer the granola to airtight containers and store at room temperature for up to 3 months.

Syrian Sweet Cheese Pastries

You will find a more straightforward version of these phyllo-based pastries in any traditional Syrian bakery, but I have tweaked the classic recipe to be a little less sweet and a little more flavorful. If you want to serve them as they would be in a Syrian home, use the full 2 cups [480 ml] of sugar syrup. I use about half that amount to help the pistachios adhere without overwhelming the delicate ricotta filling.

MAKES 12

Orange Syrup
2 cups [400 g] sugar
1 tsp orange blossom water

Pastry
1½ cups [330 g] (3 sticks) unsalted butter
1 cup [240 g] full-fat ricotta
1 tsp mahlab
1 tsp sugar
12 sheets (about 1 lb [455 g]) phyllo dough, thawed
½ cup [60 g] finely chopped raw (not roasted) pistachios

To make the orange syrup: Combine the sugar with 2 cups [480 ml] of water in a saucepan and bring to a boil over high heat. When the mixture boils, reduce the heat to low and continue to cook, stirring, until the sugar dissolves and the liquid becomes syrupy, about 10 minutes. Let the sugar syrup cool completely, then stir in the orange blossom water.

To make the pastry: Clarify the butter by melting it in a large saucepan over medium-low heat. When the foam subsides, remove from the heat and allow the butter to stand until the milk solids have settled to the bottom. Carefully pour off the clear liquid butter into a measuring cup, leaving the milky residue behind.

Preheat the oven to 375°F [190°C]. Brush a 9 by 12 in [23 by 30 cm] baking pan with some of the clarified butter.

Combine the ricotta, mahlab, and sugar in a bowl, mixing until smooth and spreadable.

Lay one sheet of phyllo dough on a work surface and brush completely with clarified butter. Fold in half lengthwise and then in half again, creating a long strip. Place a generous tablespoon of ricotta mixture at the end of the rectangle. Fold one corner of the phyllo strip over the filling, forming a triangular point, then continue to fold the phyllo from left to right, and right to left, to make a tight triangular package. Repeat with the remaining phyllo and filling.

Place the triangles in the prepared baking pan, arranging the pastries in pairs, long edges together so they form a square. Brush the triangles with the remaining clarified butter and bake for 10 minutes.

Remove the pan from the oven and pour the orange blossom syrup over the entire tray, starting with 1 cup [240 ml] and adding more if needed. Sprinkle the triangles with the pistachios. Serve warm or at room temperature; leftover pastries can be stored, well covered, in the refrigerator, for up to a day, although they will not be as crisp and flaky as when freshly made.

TEN MORE WAYS TO USE

FLOWER WATERS

·1·

White Coffee

This caffeine-free (and coffee-free!) beverage made of water flavored with orange blossom water and sweetened with honey is popular throughout the Middle East. It's served hot like a tea and is said to help reduce bloat.

·2·

Fruit Salad

Gently blend 1 tsp of orange blossom water into a fruit salad to amp up the fragrance and boost the flavor of out-of-season fruits. Garnish with shredded fresh mint leaves.

·3·

Skin Toner

Because it is mild and is said to have antibacterial qualities, rose water works well as a facial toner applied straight from the bottle with a cotton ball. In the summer, dilute it with filtered water and store in the refrigerator in a spray bottle for a refreshing facial spritz. You can also use flower waters to scent a warm bath.

·4·

Winter Salad

Stir ½ tsp of orange blossom water into a mustardy vinaigrette and use it to dress a chicory or endive salad topped with orange segments and a few shreds of red onion.

·5·

Iced Tea

Flower waters are a sugar-free way to enhance your favorite iced tea. Steep a cinnamon stick with a black tea and a bit of orange blossom water for a spicy blend, or add a few drops of rose water to a glass of barely sweetened hibiscus tea.

·6·

Chocolate-Coated Fruit

Melt white, milk, or dark chocolate chips in the microwave just until melted. Stir in a bit of orange blossom water, then dip strawberries, dried apricots, or orange segments to coat. Roll the coated fruit in finely chopped pistachios, then let the fruit rest on a parchment paper–lined baking sheet until set.

·7·

Rosy Smoothie

Add ½ tsp of rose water to a blender with 1 cup [240 g] of vanilla yogurt, 1 cup [150 g] of frozen strawberries, and 2 or 3 fresh basil leaves. Blend until smooth, thinning with a little almond milk or water if too thick.

·8·

White Hot Chocolate

For two servings of decadent, grown-up cocoa, melt ½ cup [80 g] of grated or ground white chocolate into 1 cup [240 ml] of whole milk. Whisk until frothy and hot but not boiling. Stir in ½ tsp of either rose or orange blossom water. Top rose-scented cocoa with shavings of bittersweet chocolate; top orange-scented cocoa with a pinch of grated nutmeg. A shot of brandy never hurts, either.

·9·

Orange-Thyme Simple Syrup

Simmer 1 cup [200 g] of sugar with 1 cup [240 ml] of water and a few fresh thyme sprigs until the sugar dissolves. Cool, discard the thyme, and stir in 1 tsp of orange blossom water. Drizzle over ice cream or pancakes with fresh orange segments.

·10·

Strawberry Rose Parfait

Flavor strawberry yogurt with a bit of rose water; layer into glasses with chopped toasted almonds or pistachios and all-fruit strawberry preserves for breakfast or a light dessert.

Sesame-Apricot Granola

Apricots and sesame evoke all that is Middle Eastern for me, and they are the stars of this granola, the most traditionally flavored blend that we offer. We doubled down on the sesame flavor with a combination of toasted sesame seeds and tahini as well as nutritious hemp seeds. Sweetened with honey, this granola makes a delicious snack or topping for a fruit crumble.

MAKES ABOUT 6½ CUPS [650 G]

2¾ cup [275 g] old-fashioned rolled oats (not quick oats)
1 cup [140 g] toasted sesame seeds
2 Tbsp hemp seeds
¼ tsp fine sea salt
½ cup [170 g] honey
⅓ cup [75 g] well-stirred tahini
2 tsp vanilla extract
1 cup [180 g] diced dried apricots

Preheat the oven to 350°F [180°C] and line a rimmed baking sheet with parchment paper.

In a large bowl, mix the oats with the sesame seeds, hemp seeds, and salt. In a smaller bowl, whisk together the honey, tahini, and vanilla. Pour over the oat mixture and mix well, coating the entire mixture.

Turn the granola onto the prepared baking sheet and spread as thinly as possible. Bake for 10 minutes, then remove from the oven and stir and turn with a metal spatula. Spread out the granola again and return to the oven for 10 to 12 minutes longer, or until browned. Set aside to cool on the baking sheet until crisp. Stir in the apricots and toss to distribute.

Transfer the granola to airtight containers and store at room temperature for up to 3 months.

Semolina Breakfast Pudding

When my children were little, organic baby food wasn't produced commercially, and because I wasn't happy with what I found on the grocery shelves, I ended up making most of their food myself. This dish was a staple. It could be made with milk or water and sweetened with honey or agave for a natural, healthy breakfast that came together in 5 minutes. Dolling it up a bit with aromatic spices makes for a homey, comforting adult porridge that could also be a simple dessert. Revisiting this recipe brought back wonderful memories!

SERVES 2

1 cup [240 ml] whole milk
2 Tbsp semolina
1 Tbsp honey, plus more for serving
1 Tbsp fresh orange juice
⅛ tsp ground cardamom
⅛ tsp ground cinnamon
½ tsp orange blossom water
½ Cara Cara orange, sliced, for garnish

In a small saucepan, stir together the milk, semolina, honey, orange juice, cardamom, and cinnamon. Bring to a boil over medium heat, stirring constantly to prevent lumps from forming. When the mixture boils, lower the heat to a simmer, cover, and cook until thickened, 2 to 3 minutes, stirring occasionally with a fork.

Remove the pan from the heat and stir in the orange blossom water. Divide between two dishes and serve warm, garnished with orange slices and a drizzle of honey if desired.

Orange Blossom Cocktail

I am always looking for new ways to use the bright, floral flavor of orange blossom water, and that was the inspiration for this sophisticated libation. The aroma was so delicate, and the sugared rim added just the right touch. It's a crowd pleaser at our Industry City café for both brunch and happy hour. I find it's convenient to mix up a batch and then shake each cocktail to order; use about ½ cup [120 ml] of the mixture for each.

MAKES 4 COCKTAILS

¼ cup [50 g] sugar
1 orange, cut into slices
¾ cup [180 ml] freshly squeezed orange juice
½ cup [120 ml] gin
½ cup [120 ml] Triple Sec
2 Tbsp honey
2 Tbsp orange blossom water
Angostura bitters

Pour the sugar onto a saucer or sheet of wax paper. Use one of the orange slices to moisten the rims of four martini or coupe glasses. Dip the rims into the sugar to coat, then set aside to dry.

Combine the orange juice, gin, Triple Sec, honey, and orange blossom water in a cocktail shaker or lidded jar filled with ice. Shake vigorously until the cocktail is very cold and frothy and the honey has completely dissolved.

Strain into the prepared glasses. Add a dash of bitters to each glass and garnish with an orange slice.

Mahlab-Spiced Pecans

Mahlab's faint undertone of almond makes it a natural pairing for nuts of most any kind. Choose plump, whole pecan halves for this very special cocktail bite, and scatter a handful on your cheeseboard to round out your assembly of dried and fresh fruits, crackers, cured meats, and cheese.

MAKES 2 CUPS [250 G]

2 Tbsp light brown sugar

1 tsp ground mahlab

1 tsp ground nutmeg

Pinch of fine sea salt

Pinch of cayenne

2 tsp unsalted butter, melted

1 tsp vanilla extract

2 cups [240 g] pecan halves

Preheat the oven to 400°F [200°C]. Line a rimmed baking sheet with parchment paper.

Toss the brown sugar, mahlab, nutmeg, salt, and cayenne together in a small bowl. In another mixing bowl, stir together the melted butter and vanilla. Add the pecans to the butter mixture and stir to coat the nuts with the mixture. Sprinkle the spice mixture over the nuts and toss well to combine.

Turn the nuts onto the baking sheet and spread them in a single layer. Bake for 10 minutes, or until crisp and fragrant. Let the nuts cool on the pan, then transfer to an airtight container.

Cranberry Date Relish with Ginger

A raw fruit relish is a refreshingly punchy change from the typical jammy cooked cranberry sauce, and far less sweet, making it a great foil for roast meats as well as a holiday turkey. You can simply chop everything together in the food processor, but for a better texture and appearance, take the time to chop the dates and ginger by hand to ensure lovely pops of flavor in every bite. This makes a generous amount; halve the recipe if you prefer.

SERVES 8 TO 10

¼ cup [60 g] pitted dates
¼ cup [45 g] crystallized ginger
3 scallions
1 lb [455 g] fresh cranberries
3 Tbsp honey
Juice of 2 limes
1 jalapeño pepper, minced
¼ cup [10 g] chopped fresh cilantro
1¼ tsp minced fresh ginger
¼ tsp fine sea salt
¼ tsp freshly ground black pepper

Using a large, sharp knife, dice the dates and crystallized ginger into small, uniform dice. Thinly slice the scallions and then mince them finely.

Put the cranberries in the bowl of a food processor and pulse a few times until they are in rough pieces. Add the honey, lime juice, jalapeño, cilantro, fresh ginger, salt, and pepper and continue to pulse until finely diced. Add the dates, crystalized ginger, and scallions and pulse once or twice to combine.

Refrigerate overnight to allow the flavors to blend thoroughly. Serve at room temperature.

TEN MORE WAYS TO USE

MAHLAB

·1·

Cherry Pancakes

Add ½ to 1 tsp of mahlab to your favorite pancake or waffle batter; as they cook, they will fill the house with a lovely aroma. Serve simply topped with a shower of powdered sugar.

·2·

Cherry Hot Cocoa Mix

Whisk together 1 cup [120 g] of confectioner's sugar, ½ cup [40 g] of cocoa powder (preferably Dutch processed), 1½ tsp of mahlab, and a big pinch of salt. Store the mixture in a tightly sealed jar. To serve, blend 3 Tbsp of cocoa mix into 1 cup [240 ml] of warm milk (use a few tablespoons of the milk to make a paste before combining) and serve with a shot of amaretto to accentuate the almond notes if you like.

·3·

Cherry Shortbreads

Add ½ tsp of mahlab along with the vanilla in your favorite sugar cookie recipe. Roll in chopped natural almonds and top with a glacé cherry before baking.

·4·

Whipped Topping

Mahlab is wonderful for flavoring whipped cream, as it doesn't add any grittiness (or alcohol). Sprinkle ½ tsp of mahlab over 1 cup [240 ml] of heavy cream and whisk to combine. Add 3 or 4 Tbsp of confectioner's sugar and whisk or beat until the cream forms soft or stiff peaks, as desired. It's especially good on a summer berry cobbler or a slice of almond cake.

·5·

Overnight Oats

In a pint jar, combine ½ cup [50 g] of rolled oats with 2 Tbsp of chia seeds and ½ tsp of mahlab. Add 1 cup [240 ml] of almond milk, and agave or date syrup. Shake well and refrigerate overnight, shaking now and again if you think of it. Serve topped with slivered almonds.

· 6 ·

Cherry Cake Vodka

Add 1 Tbsp of whole mahlab seeds, 1 vanilla bean, and 2 Tbsp of superfine sugar to a fifth of vodka. Infuse the vodka for at least a week, shaking a few times. Shake 2 parts infused vodka with 1 part half-and-half and a splash of amaretto in a cocktail shaker with ice. Strain into a stemmed glass for a riff on a Birthday Cake Martini.

· 7 ·

Flavored Nut Butter

Grind lightly toasted pecans in a food processor until smooth, stopping to scrape down the sides once or twice. Add a pinch of sea salt and mahlab—about ¼ tsp for every cup of nuts is a good place to start—and blend again to combine.

· 8 ·

Breakfast Spread

Flavor 4 oz [115 g] of softened cream cheese or farmer's cheese with ½ tsp of mahlab, stirring until well combined. Add a drizzle of honey (or more if you prefer) and ¼ cup [30 g] of chopped toasted almonds. Serve with bagels or multigrain toast.

· 9 ·

Finishing Sugar

Mix up a batch of mahlab/cinnamon sugar by combining 2 Tbsp of cinnamon and 2 tsp of mahlab with 1 cup [200 g] of sugar. Store it in an airtight container to sprinkle on muffin tops or pie dough, mix with nuts to top a coffee cake, or roll inside cinnamon buns or frozen croissant dough before baking. Or just dust onto hot buttered toast and serve with a cup of tea.

· 10 ·

Simple Cherry Pudding

Spike a package of vanilla pudding mix (not instant; you want the kind that cooks on the stovetop) with 1 tsp of mahlab and prepare as directed. Serve topped with slivered almonds.

Fruited Farro Salad

Farro has a chewy texture and hearty flavor that makes it a great partner for dried fruit. It's a nice cold-weather accompaniment to a rich braise or roast chicken. I've specified quick-cooking farro, which is parboiled to reduce its cooking time, but regular farro is absolutely fine; just increase the cooking time by about 20 minutes, checking after 40 minutes to see if the grains are tender.

SERVES 4

2 Tbsp plus 2 tsp extra-virgin olive oil

½ cup [90 g] quick-cooking farro

1 tsp Aleppo pepper

1 tsp fine sea salt

½ tsp ground white pepper

¼ cup [45 g] Turkish dried apricots, cut into slivers with scissors

¼ cup [35 g] currants

¼ cup [35 g] minced red onion

¼ cup [10 g] chopped fresh cilantro

2 Tbsp pomegranate molasses

Heat the 2 tsp of oil in a 2 qt [2 L] saucepan over medium heat. Add the farro and toast, stirring often, for 5 minutes, or until it is just becoming fragrant. Stir in the Aleppo pepper, salt, and white pepper. Add 1½ cups [360 ml] of water, bring to a boil, then cover and reduce the heat to low. Simmer for 20 to 30 minutes, or until the liquid is absorbed and the farro is tender. Fluff the grains with a fork.

Transfer the farro to a mixing bowl and add the apricots, currants, red onion, and cilantro; toss to combine. Drizzle with the pomegranate molasses and the remaining 2 Tbsp of oil, and toss gently but thoroughly. Serve hot, warm, or at room temperature.

Red Kale Salad with Date Syrup Dressing

We sell a ton of kale salad at the store, and with good reason: these sturdy greens don't become limp or soggy even when prepped and dressed well ahead of time, and their robust flavor is a good foil for boldly seasoned dressings. The hint of sweetness and bite of Aleppo pepper in this one will make converts out of anyone still reluctant to hop on the kale train. Try the dressing on lentils and some feathery frisée; it adds depth of flavor and an elusive sweetness to salads of hearty grains like farro or barley, or legumes enriched with peppery greens.

SERVES 4

Date Syrup Dressing

¼ cup [85 g] date syrup

2 Tbsp balsamic vinegar

1 Tbsp chopped fresh mint or 1 tsp dried

½ tsp fine sea salt

½ tsp freshly ground black pepper

½ tsp Aleppo pepper

¼ cup [60 ml] extra-virgin olive oil

Red Kale

1 bunch red Russian kale, stems removed

1 tsp fine sea salt

½ tsp freshly ground black pepper

½ cup [110 g] pitted dates, sliced crosswise into rings

½ cup [60 g] toasted pecans (see Note)

¼ cup [35 g] slivered red onion

1 tsp sumac, plus more for garnish

Fresh mint leaves, for garnish

To make the date syrup dressing: Whisk the date syrup together with the vinegar in a small bowl until combined. Season with the mint, salt, black pepper, and Aleppo pepper. Add in the oil in a steady stream, whisking constantly, until thick and emulsified. (The dressing can be made ahead of time and stored in the refrigerator in a tightly covered container for up to 2 weeks; whisk again before serving to recombine.)

To make the red kale: Cut the kale leaves crosswise into small slices and sprinkle with the salt and pepper. With your hands, roughly massage the leaves to break down the membranes and soften them up a bit.

Transfer the kale to a large bowl and add the dates, pecans, red onion, and sumac. Toss to combine. Pour the dressing over the kale and toss well. Garnish with the mint and a sprinkle of sumac.

NOTE

Toast the pecans in a 350°F [180°C] oven for 5 to 7 minutes, stirring once or twice. Cool on a plate.

Curried Couscous Salad with Dried Fruit

Salads that can be served as either a main or a side are a year-round mainstay of our takeout business, and this is one of our most popular. It has lots of assertive flavors and textures that pair perfectly with everything from barbecued chicken to a savory pot roast. Consider doubling the amount of chickpeas if you plan to serve it on its own as a vegetarian entrée, or add a can of drained tuna for a nice lunch salad.

SERVES 6 AS A MAIN COURSE SALAD OR 8 TO 10 AS A SIDE

2 cups [360 g] instant couscous
¾ cup [180 ml] plus 1 Tbsp extra-virgin olive oil
1 bunch scallions, both white and green parts, thinly sliced
1 medium red bell pepper, cored, seeded, and chopped
½ cup [70 g] black raisins
½ cup [70 g] golden raisins
½ cup [80 g] cooked chickpeas
4 tsp curry powder
¾ tsp allspice
¾ tsp salt
¾ tsp freshly ground black pepper
¼ cup [60 ml] fresh lemon juice

Bring 2 cups [480 ml] of water to a boil in a medium saucepan. Stir in the couscous and the 1 Tbsp of oil. Cover the pan and set aside for 15 minutes to plump.

In a large bowl, toss together the scallions, red pepper, black and golden raisins, and chickpeas. In a small bowl, whisk together the curry powder, allspice, salt, and black pepper. Stir in the lemon juice, then slowly whisk in the remaining ¾ cup [180 ml] of oil until well combined.

Fluff the cooled couscous with a fork and add it to the bowl with the scallions, tossing to combine. Add ¾ of the dressing and mix well. Set aside at room temperature for 1 hour to blend the flavors. Just before serving, pour on the remaining dressing and mix one more time.

[4705]
[4630]
[4840]
[4815]

Roasted Cauliflower Salad with Lentils and Dates

When cauliflower began to trend with our customers, I responded to the demand with this hearty combination of cauliflower and lentils. I added plenty of warm spices and an addictive dressing that is sweet, tart, and creamy all at once.

SERVES 6

¼ tsp ground cumin

¼ tsp ground cinnamon

¼ tsp ground ginger

Pinch of cayenne or ¼ tsp Urfa pepper

¼ cup [60 ml] plus 1 Tbsp extra-virgin olive oil

1 head of cauliflower, cut into 1 in [2.5 cm] florets

1 tsp fine sea salt

1 tsp freshly ground black pepper

3 Tbsp fresh lemon juice

2 Tbsp tahini

1 tsp honey

1 cup [75 g] cooked green lentils (see Note)

½ bunch scallions, both white and green parts, separated and cut into slices

2 cups [40 g] loosely packed spinach, baby arugula, or chopped romaine

10 dates, pitted and chopped

½ cup [70 g] roasted unsalted almonds, coarsely chopped

Fresh mint, for garnish

Preheat the oven to 425°F [220°C].

In a mixing bowl, stir together the cumin, cinnamon, ginger, and cayenne. Add the ¼ cup [60 ml] of oil and stir to combine. Add the cauliflower florets and toss to coat with the spice mixture.

Turn the cauliflower onto a large rimmed baking sheet and spread in a single layer. Season with ½ tsp of the salt and ½ tsp of the pepper. Roast until the cauliflower is tender and golden brown, 25 to 30 minutes, turning the florets once or twice for even roasting.

In a large bowl, whisk together the lemon juice with the tahini, honey, and remaining 1 Tbsp of oil. Add 2 Tbsp of water and whisk until smooth. Stir in the lentils and white parts of the scallions, and season with the remaining ½ tsp each of salt and black pepper.

Arrange the greens on a large platter. Top with the lentil mixture and then the cauliflower. Scatter the dates and almonds over all, then sprinkle with the scallion greens and fresh mint.

NOTE

If you are pressed for time, you can use drained canned lentils for this recipe. If you want to make them from scratch, start with a scant ½ cup [90 g] dried green lentils. Cook them in 2 cups [480 ml] of lightly salted boiling water for 20 to 25 minutes, or until just tender. Drain well before adding to the bowl with the spices and oil as instructed.

Rose Risotto with Crab and Snap Peas

This delicate dish is rosy not by virtue of its color but from the hint of rose water that brings all the ingredients together into a luxurious celebration of springtime. It's important to use a subtle hand when deploying rose water, as its perfumy presence can be surprisingly assertive, overpowering other mild-tasting foods rather than quietly enhancing their sweetness. If you grow your own unsprayed roses, a few petals strewn on top would be a pretty garnish for a romantic evening.

SERVES 4 OR 6 AS A STARTER

8 oz [230 g] sugar snap peas, strings removed, cut into ½ in [12 mm] pieces

2 Tbsp unsalted butter

1 Tbsp extra-virgin olive oil

1 large shallot, minced

1 cup [200 g] short-grain rice, such as arborio or carnaroli

⅓ cup [80 ml] dry white wine

1½ tsp fine sea salt

3½ cups [840 ml] chicken stock or more as needed, preferably low-sodium, heated

1 to 1½ tsp rose water

Zest and juice of ½ lemon

8 oz [230 g] jumbo lump crabmeat

Fresh rose petals or snipped chives, for garnish

Bring a saucepan of salted water to a boil. Add the snap peas and cook until just barely tender, about 3 minutes. Drain and run under cold water to stop the cooking, then set aside.

In a deep skillet, melt 1 Tbsp of the butter together with the oil over medium heat. Add the shallot and cook just until softened, about 3 minutes. Do not allow the shallot to brown.

Add the rice to the skillet and stir to coat the grains with the fat. Toast over medium-high heat until the grains appear opaque, 2 to 3 minutes, then add the wine. Cook and stir until the wine is completely absorbed, then add the salt and 1 cup [240 ml] of the hot stock. Bring the liquid to a simmer, then reduce the heat to medium-low so the mixture bubbles briskly. Cook, stirring frequently, until most of the stock has been absorbed by the rice. Add another ½ cup [120 ml] of stock and continue to cook and stir for another 15 minutes or so, adding more of the stock every time the mixture starts to look dry, and stirring now and then. Cook only until the rice is al dente, with a tiny, uncooked center in each grain.

Add the rose water, ½ cup [120 ml] of the remaining stock, and the remaining 1 Tbsp of butter and stir for 1 to 2 more minutes to make a very loose, saucy mixture. Stir in the snap peas and the lemon zest and juice, then add the crab and stir very gently to incorporate. Cook until heated through, adding a little more stock if the risotto is too thick. Serve immediately, garnished with the petals or chives.

Glazed Chicken Legs with Curry and Dates

This is our version of chicken Marbella, the iconic Silver Palate dish. It's a bit sweet, a bit spicy, and great either hot or at room temperature—in other words, the perfect dish for easy entertaining. Choose an imported or California dried date for this; softer Medjool dates will disintegrate into the sauce. Organic Turkish mulberries, if you can find them, would be great in this, too.

SERVES 4

¼ cup [60 ml] extra-virgin olive oil
2 tsp hot curry powder
1 tsp fine sea salt
3 lb [1.4 kg] chicken legs
¼ cup [80 g] Major Grey's mango chutney
¼ cup [55 g] dried dates, coarsely chopped
¼ cup [10 g] chopped fresh cilantro

In a large bowl, combine the oil, curry powder, and salt. Add the chicken legs and turn them in the mixture to coat thoroughly. Cover the bowl and refrigerate for at least 2 hours and up to overnight.

Preheat the oven to 450°F [230°C] and spray a large rimmed baking sheet with nonstick cooking spray.

Arrange the chicken legs on the prepared baking sheet in a single layer. Spread a bit of the chutney on each leg. Bake for 25 to 30 minutes, or until the chicken is starting to look brown and crisp. Sprinkle the dates onto the chicken and cook an additional 5 to 10 minutes, or until the chicken is no longer pink near the bone when you cut into it with the tip of a sharp knife.

Transfer the chicken to a large platter and serve sprinkled with the cilantro.

Skillet-Roasted Chicken with Apricot Stuffing

We developed this stuffing as a side dish for the store's holiday menu, and we sell many trays of it each Thanksgiving. Here I've adapted it as a one-skillet comfort meal using chicken pieces. It has all the flavors of a holiday dinner but is easy enough to pull together on a weeknight. It looks especially nice made in a cast iron skillet.

SERVES 4 TO 6

¼ cup [55 g] (½ stick) unsalted butter

1 cup [140 g] diced onions

1 cup [120 g] diced celery

2 tsp za'atar

1 tsp dried sage, crumbled

1 tsp dried thyme

1½ tsp fine sea salt

1½ tsp freshly ground black pepper

1½ cups [360 ml] chicken broth

1 large egg

¼ cup [10 g] chopped fresh parsley, plus more for garnish

8 cups [720 g] cubed stale multigrain bread, from about 10 slices

¾ cup [135 g] diced dried apricots

½ cup [70 g] chopped roasted, salted hazelnuts

2½ lb [1.2 kg] chicken legs, thighs, or breasts, breasts cut into 2 pieces if very large

½ tsp Aleppo pepper, plus more for garnish

Preheat the oven to 375°F [190°C].

Melt the butter in a large ovenproof skillet over medium heat. Add the onions, celery, za'atar, sage, thyme, and 1 tsp each of the salt and black pepper. Sauté, stirring often, until the onions begin to soften, about 5 minutes. Add the chicken broth and stir to scrape up any browned bits from the pan. Allow to cool.

Beat the egg with the parsley in a large bowl; add the bread cubes and toss until the egg has been absorbed. Add the apricots, hazelnuts, and the sautéed onion mixture and combine thoroughly. Spread the stuffing over the bottom of the same skillet you cooked the onions in.

Season the chicken pieces with the remaining ½ tsp each of salt and black pepper and the Aleppo pepper. Arrange the chicken atop the stuffing, skin-side up. Cover the pan tightly with foil and bake for 20 minutes. Remove the foil and bake until the chicken is golden and the dressing is crisp and browned around the edges, another 40 minutes. Serve hot, directly from the skillet, garnished with chopped parsley and Aleppo pepper flakes.

Duck Breasts with Sweet Cherry Sauce

Duck breasts are one of those wonderful ingredients that seem restaurant-fancy but turn out to be incredibly easy to cook once you know a few tricks. While they rest after pan-searing to a perfect, rosy pink, it's a snap to turn the ras el hanout–flavored pan juices into an easy sauce studded with sweet cherries. Serve with roasted squash or sweet potatoes and a bitter green for contrast.

SERVES 2

½ cup [70 g] dried sweet cherries

½ cup [120 ml] tawny port or fruity red wine

½ tsp mustard seeds

1 large (12 to 16 oz [340 to 455 g]) duck breast or 2 small ones

1 tsp salt

1 tsp ras el hanout

1 shallot, chopped

½ cup [120 ml] chicken broth

Combine the cherries, port, and mustard seeds in a small microwave-safe bowl. Heat on high for 1 minute, then set aside to plump.

With a sharp knife, score the fat side of the duck breast in a cross-hatch pattern, making sure to cut into only the fat, not the meat. Sprinkle both sides of the breast with ½ tsp of the salt, then rub both sides with the ras el hanout.

Put the breast fat-side down in a heavy, dry skillet; cast iron works well. Place the skillet over medium heat and cook, without turning, until the fat is well rendered and the skin is deeply browned, about 10 minutes. Turn the breast and cook on the second side until the breast is cooked to your liking, about 5 more minutes for medium-rare. Transfer the breast to a plate and tent with foil.

Pour almost all of the rendered fat out of the skillet and return the skillet to medium heat. Add the shallot and cook until softened, about 3 minutes. Add the cherries and their soaking liquid to the pan, scraping up any browned bits, and bring to a simmer. Cook until the alcohol smell has dissipated, then add the chicken broth. Simmer for 2 or 3 minutes to reduce, then stir in any juices that have accumulated around the duck. Season with the remaining ½ tsp of salt.

Slice the duck breast diagonally and serve with the sauce spooned on top.

Pan-Roasted Pork Chop with Fruited Compound Butter

Compound butters are just about the easiest way I can think of to jazz up a weeknight meal, especially because they can be made ahead and stashed in the freezer until needed. I always have two or three different flavors on hand, ready to enhance a piece of grilled fish, veggies, or a steak. A fruity version like this one, made with a touch of curry powder, does wonders for your basic Tuesday night pork chops!

SERVES 4

4 center-cut bone-in pork chops (about 8 oz [230 g] each)
¼ cup [60 ml] extra-virgin olive oil
1 Tbsp hot curry powder
1½ tsp fine sea salt
½ cup [110 g] (1 stick) unsalted butter, at room temperature
1 Cara Cara or navel orange
½ cup [80 g] finely chopped dried apricots
½ cup [70 g] finely chopped dried cherries
½ tsp Aleppo pepper
2 Tbsp chopped parsley, for serving

Put the pork chops in a sealable plastic bag. In a small bowl, whisk together 2 Tbsp of the oil with the curry powder and 1 tsp of the salt. Add to the bag with the chops, make sure they are well covered with the mixture, and seal the bag. Refrigerate for at least 4 hours and up to overnight.

Mash the butter in a medium bowl until very soft. Grate 1 Tbsp of zest from the orange and add to the butter along with 2 tsp of the juice. Add the apricots, cherries, and Aleppo pepper and combine thoroughly.

Scrape the mixture onto a sheet of plastic wrap and form it into a log about 5 in [12 cm] long, using the plastic to shape and smooth the log. Refrigerate until firm, at least 1 hour. (The compound butter will keep for a couple of weeks in the refrigerator and can be frozen for 1 or 2 months.)

When ready to serve, preheat the oven to 450°F [230°C]. Heat the remaining 2 Tbsp of oil in a large ovenproof skillet (cast iron works well) over moderately high heat. When hot but not smoking, add the pork chops and sear on both sides until well browned, about 5 minutes per side. Transfer the pan to the oven and roast the chops until the internal temperature reaches 155°F [65°C] on an instant-read thermometer, 5 to 10 minutes, depending on the thickness of the chops.

Transfer the chops to individual plates and top each with 2½ in [6 cm] thick coins of compound butter (you will have some left over). Sprinkle with chopped parsley and serve hot.

Rosewater Marshmallows

So pretty, so delicate, these pink puffs are an unexpected and elegant addition to a bridal shower dessert tray or wrapped up for a Valentine's Day treat. They are also lovely in a cup of hot chocolate.

MAKES ABOUT 40 MARSHMALLOWS

¾ cup [90 g] confectioner's sugar, plus more as needed
2 packets unflavored gelatin
2 large egg whites
2 cups [400 g] granulated sugar
1 Tbsp rose water
2 tsp grenadine syrup

Spray a 9 by 13 in [23 by 33 cm] baking pan with nonstick cooking spray and dust with ¼ cup [30 g] of the confectioner's sugar. Don't dump out the excess sugar; just leave it in the pan.

Fill a small bowl with ½ cup [120 ml] cold water and sprinkle in the gelatin. Let stand for 10 to 15 minutes to soften.

Beat the egg whites in the bowl of a standing mixer on high speed until they form soft peaks. Set aside while you prepare the sugar syrup.

Stir the sugar together with ½ cup [120 ml] of water in a 4 qt [3.8 L] saucepan. Bring to a boil over high heat and continue to cook, without stirring—just swirling the pan now and then to prevent the mixture from burning—until the mixture reaches 250°F [120°C] on a candy thermometer, 10 to 12 minutes. Remove from the heat and stir in the softened gelatin.

With the mixer on low, slowly beat the sugar syrup into the beaten egg whites. Add the rose water. Turn the mixer to medium-high and beat until the mixture has cooled and grown in volume, about 5 minutes. Stir in the grenadine, a few drops at a time, until the mixture is tinted to your liking. Pour into the prepared pan and spread evenly, smoothing the top as well as you can with an offset spatula. Let stand, uncovered, overnight.

The next day, sift another ¼ cup [30 g] confectioner's sugar evenly over the pan of marshmallows. Cut into 40 pieces. Carefully separate the marshmallows and dust the exposed sides with the remaining confectioner's sugar (you can also use any that is left in the pan). Stored in an airtight container; these will keep for several weeks at least.

ROSE ALMOND
OLIVE OIL CAKE
page 322
TAHINI SWIRL
BROWNIES
page 265
SYRIAN SWEET
CHEESE PASTRIES
page 289
ORANGE
BLOSSOM
CUPCAKES
page 325
WHITE CHOCOLATE
CRANBERRY COOKIES
WITH SUMAC GLAZE
page 81

ROSEWATER MARSHMALLOWS
page 318

Rose Almond Olive Oil Cake

Semolina is used in many Middle Eastern desserts, giving them a pleasant, slightly coarse texture as well as a unique flavor. In this very moist cake, semolina combined with almond flour is the backdrop for a batter flavored with rose, mahlab, and more almonds. This cake keeps for 1 week in a tightly covered container at room temperature.

SERVES 8

Cake

½ cup [120 ml] extra-virgin olive oil, plus more for greasing the pan

3 large eggs

¾ cup [150 g] natural cane sugar

2 Tbsp fresh lemon juice

Zest of 1 lemon, preferably Meyer lemon

1 tsp rose water

1½ cups [240 g] fine semolina

½ cup [60 g] almond flour

2 tsp baking powder

1 tsp ground mahlab

¼ cup [25 g] sliced raw almonds

Glaze

½ cup [60 g] confectioner's sugar

1 tsp almond milk

1 tsp rose water

To make the cake: With the whisk attachment of an electric mixer, beat the oil, eggs, and cane sugar together until they are light and fluffy and look like pale yellow softly whipped cream. Switch to the paddle attachment. Add the lemon juice, lemon zest, and rose water and beat well. Add the semolina, almond flour, baking powder, and mahlab. Mix just until combined. Set the batter aside for 1 hour to hydrate the nut flour.

Preheat the oven to 350°F [180°C]. Trace the bottom of an 8 in [20 cm] springform pan onto parchment paper and cut out the circle, trimming it so it lays flat in the pan. Grease the bottom and sides of the pan with oil, then lay the paper circle on the bottom of the pan and grease it, too.

Pour the batter into the prepared pan. Bake for 30 minutes, or until the top no longer feels squishy to the touch and a toothpick inserted in the center comes out with crumbs attached. It will be golden brown. Without turning off the oven, set the pan on a wire rack to cool for 5 minutes, then release the sides of the pan and allow the cake to cool completely.

Spread the sliced almonds on a baking sheet and toast in the oven for 3 minutes, or until golden. Transfer to a plate to cool.

To make the glaze: In a small bowl, use a fork to stir together the confectioner's sugar, almond milk, and rose water until smooth. Drizzle over the cake, letting the excess run down the sides. Sprinkle evenly with the toasted almonds.

Orange Blossom Cupcakes with White Chocolate Orange Ganache

These elegant little beauties have an elusive orange aroma that comes from orange blossom water and a deep orangey flavor.

MAKES 18 CUPCAKES

Cupcakes

2 cups [400 g] sugar

1½ cups [210 g] all-purpose flour

1½ cups [180 g] cake flour

2 tsp baking powder

1 tsp fine sea salt

1 cup [220 g] (2 sticks) unsalted butter, cut into cubes

1 Tbsp orange blossom water

2 eggs, at room temperature

1½ cups [360 ml] milk, scalded and cooled

Candied Orange Peel

1 mandarin orange

⅓ cup [65 g] plus 2 Tbsp sugar

Ganache

4 cups [720 g] white chocolate chips

1⅓ cups [320 ml] heavy cream

2 tsp orange blossom water

1 Tbsp fresh orange juice

Preheat the oven to 350°F [180°C]. Grease two 12 cup muffin tins and insert eighteen paper liners.

To make the cupcakes: Combine the sugar, flours, baking powder, and salt in the bowl of a food processor. Add the butter and orange blossom water and pulse until small pea-size balls form. Beat the eggs and milk in a mixing cup, then add to the butter mixture. Process until the batter is smooth.

Divide the batter evenly among the prepared tins and bake for 30 minutes, or until a toothpick inserted in the center of a cupcake comes out clean. Cool for 5 minutes in the tins, then turn out onto a wire rack to cool.

To make the candied orange peel: Using a sharp knife, slice the peel off the orange in strips, avoiding the pith. Cut the strips into thin pieces. Place the ⅓ cup [65 g] of sugar in a small saucepan with 3 Tbsp of water. Add the peel and bring to a simmer over medium heat. Reduce the heat to low and simmer for 5 to 10 minutes, or until the peels are translucent and the syrup is thickening. With a slotted spoon, transfer the strips to a plate, reserving the cooking liquid. Toss with the remaining 2 Tbsp of sugar. Transfer to a wire rack to dry.

To make the ganache: Place the white chocolate chips in a mixer bowl. Place the cream in a saucepan and bring nearly to a boil over medium heat. Pour the hot cream over the chips and stir well until melted and smooth. Remove from the heat and let cool completely, stirring from time to time. Add the orange blossom water and use an electric mixer to beat until fluffy and light. Add the orange juice by the teaspoon until smooth.

To assemble, brush the cupcakes with the reserved orange syrup. Frost the cupcakes with the ganache and garnish each with a strip of candied peel.

Double Cherry Rice Pudding

Rice pudding might just be the ultimate comfort food, but that doesn't mean it's not ripe for an update. In this version, cherries are a definite upgrade from the usual currants or raisins, and a dash of mahlab adds an appealing note of burnt almond. Serve topped with a spoonful of mahlab-flavored whipped cream to underscore the cherry theme. Any short-grain rice will work just fine here; no need to break the bank on pricey arborio.

SERVES 4

2 cups [480 ml] whole milk
1½ cups [270 g] cooked short-grain rice
¼ cup [50 g] sugar
½ tsp mahlab
¼ tsp fine sea salt
½ cup [70 g] dried cherries
1 egg

In a medium saucepan, stir together 1½ cups [360 ml] of the milk with the rice, sugar, mahlab, and salt. Bring almost to a simmer over medium-high heat, then reduce the heat to medium-low and cook for 3 to 5 minutes, or until it starts to thicken, stirring often to prevent the bottom from scorching. Stir in the cherries.

In a small bowl, stir together the remaining ½ cup [120 ml] milk with the egg until combined. Stir into the rice mixture and cook over medium heat until very creamy and thick. Serve warm or chilled. The pudding will keep for up to 3 days in the refrigerator.

NOTE

The pudding with thicken and firm up as it cools. If you are making ahead and prefer a creamier consistency, transfer the rice pudding back to a saucepan and stir in about ½ cup [120 ml] milk or cream. Stir over medium heat for about 5 minutes before serving

Chocolate Chunk Halvah Cookies

It's hard to improve on a time-honored favorite like chocolate chip cookies, but I may have done exactly that. Just the right amount of chewy yet crisp around the edges, these complex cookies also boast nuggets of nutty halvah (see page 284) and a subtle richness that has everything to do with the brown butter base. If you want to double down on the pistachio flavor, you can substitute chopped pistachios for the chocolate bits. It makes for a cookie that is a little more sophisticated and no less delicious.

MAKES 2 DOZEN COOKIES

¾ cup [165 g] (1½ sticks) unsalted butter

2 cups [280 g] unbleached all-purpose flour

½ tsp baking soda

½ tsp fine sea salt

1 cup [200 g] light brown sugar

½ cup [100 g] granulated sugar

2 eggs

2 tsp vanilla extract

1 cup [180 g] bittersweet chocolate chunks

2 cups [450 g] pistachio halvah, cut into ½ in [12 mm] cubes

Maldon sea salt (optional)

In a skillet, melt the butter over medium-low heat. Continue to cook, swirling the pan now and then, until the butter smells nutty and is a deep golden brown, 10 to 12 minutes. Pour into a bowl, leaving behind as much of the dark sediment as possible, and let cool to room temperature.

Whisk the flour, baking soda, and salt together in a bowl. In the bowl of an electric mixer, combine the cooled butter with both sugars, the eggs, and the vanilla. Add the flour mixture, beating on low speed just until completely combined, scraping down the sides once or twice.

Stir in the chocolate bits and all but ½ cup [115 g] of the halvah pieces by hand, mixing gently just to distribute through the dough. Turn out the dough onto a large piece of plastic wrap and form into a flat disk. Refrigerate for at least 2 hours or overnight.

Preheat the oven to 325°F [160°C]. Line two rimmed baking sheets with parchment paper.

Roll the dough into roughly shaped balls, 2 Tbsp at a time, and arrange on the baking sheet. Press one of the reserved halvah chunks into the top of each cookie and sprinkle with a few flakes of Maldon salt. Bake the cookies until just set, 10 to 12 minutes. Cool on the pans for 10 minutes before transferring to wire racks to cool completely. Store the cookies in an airtight container for 3 to 5 days.

TEN MORE WAYS TO USE

HALVAH

•1•

Ice Cream Add-in

Chop nut halvah and bitter-sweet chocolate into fine pieces and fold into a pint of softened vanilla ice cream. Refreeze until firm, then scoop and serve topped with whipped cream and/or fudge sauce, and more crumbled halvah.

•2•

Easy Breakfast Pastries

Spread refrigerated dough with a thin layer of fruit preserves and crumble halvah on top. Roll, slice into pinwheels, and bake as directed. Serve sprinkled with confectioner's sugar for a less-sweet take on cinnamon rolls.

•3•

Cake Filling

Sprinkle crumbled halvah onto the buttercream frosting between the layers of a plain vanilla or chocolate cake for flavor and crunch. Use shards of halvah to decorate the top.

•4•

Pudding Topper

Crumble bits of plain, nut, or flavored halvah onto soft puddings to give a nice textural contrast. Try it with butterscotch pudding or a decadent dark chocolate mousse.

•5•

Halvah Sandwich

Do as my father does and slip a thin slice of halvah into a warmed pita for an afternoon snack.

•6•

Banana Smoothie

Whiz a frozen banana in a blender with ½ cup [120 g] of yogurt or milk (dairy or nondairy) and 2 to 3 tablespoons of crumbled halvah, any flavor. The sesame adds nice body and flavor.

·7·

Sesame Pancakes

Cut halvah into small cubes and stir into pancake batter as you would chocolate chips. Serve topped with a dollop of yogurt or labneh, drizzle with date or maple syrup, and crumble more halvah on top.

·8·

Halvah Fondue

Melt 1 lb [455 g] of chocolate with 4 oz [115 g] of plain halvah and ¼ cup [60 ml] of heavy cream over simmering water until smooth. Serve with fresh fruit or chunks of pound cake for dipping.

·9·

Baked Apples

Fill the center of a cored apple with crumbled plain or nut halvah and dot with butter. Set in a pan filled with a little water and bake at 350°F [180°C] until soft but not collapsing, about 30 minutes.

·10·

Cheese Board

Pair a slab of pistachio halvah with dried Medjool dates or figs, some nuts, and a creamy cheese like a Saint-André and a well-aged Cheddar or Gouda.

Apricot Ice Cream

For some, summer is evoked by the smell of hot dogs on the grill or maybe tomatoes on the vine. For me, it's the delicate scent of the apricot ice cream a neighboring store churned all summer long throughout my childhood. This ice cream has a unique stretchy texture from the mastic, and a lovely orange color. Because the ice cream base itself is not too sweet, the apricot flavor takes center stage. Whenever I mix up a batch, I am transported directly back to those sunny childhood days.

MAKES 2 QT [1.9 L]

4 cups [960 ml] whole milk, preferably organic
2½ tsp sahlab powder (see Note, page 273)
1 cup [200 g] sugar
1 lb [455 g] tart dried apricots
1½ tsp mastic "tears"
1 cup [240 ml] heavy cream
2 tsp orange blossom water

Pour all but ¼ cup [60 ml] of the milk into a large saucepan. In a small bowl, stir the sahlab into the reserved ¼ cup [60 ml] of milk until dissolved.

Stir the sahlab mixture into the saucepan of milk and bring to a boil, stirring frequently. When the mixture reaches a boil, add the sugar, reduce the heat to medium-low and cook, stirring frequently, for 25 minutes, until slightly thickened.

While the milk heats, combine the apricots with 1 cup [240 ml] water in a small saucepan. Bring to a boil, stir once, then cover and set aside to cool completely.

Using a small spice grinder or a mortar and pestle, grind or pulverize the mastic to a very fine powder. Transfer the powder to a small bowl and blend with 1 Tbsp of the heavy cream. Add to the hot milk mixture and cook for 5 more minutes, or until slightly thickened. Set aside to cool to room temperature.

While the milk cools, combine the apricots and cooking liquid in a blender or food processor. Purée until very smooth.

Strain the cooled milk mixture into a clean bowl. Stir in the remaining cream, the orange blossom water, and the apricot purée. Refrigerate until thoroughly chilled, at least 2 hours or overnight.

Pour the ice cream mixture into the canister of an ice cream maker and freeze according to the instructions. Transfer to freezer containers and freeze for at least 2 hours or until completely firm. Keep frozen until ready to serve.

Creole Seasoning
Cumin
RETAIL PRICE
$3.00
500190
Creole Seasoning
RETAIL PRICE
$2.50
500191
Cumin Ground
RETAIL PRICE
$2.50
500192
Cumin Whole
Ginger
Grains of Paradise
Greek Seasoning
Gumbo Powder
Harissa
RETAIL PRICE
$2.50
500210
Ginger Whole
RETAIL PRICE
$4.00
500212
Grains of Paradise
RETAIL PRICE
$5.00
508184
Greek Seasoning
RETAIL PRICE
$4.00
500213
Gumbo Powder
RETAIL PRICE
$4.00
500215
Harissa Spice
Matcha Tea Powder
Meat Shawarma Seasoning
Mulling Spice
Mustard

Curry
Curry Leaves
Hot Curry
Curry Vandouvan
RETAIL PRICE $2.50 500193 Curry
RETAIL PRICE $2.50 500195 Curry Leaves
RETAIL PRICE $2.50 500194 Curry Hot
RETAIL PRICE $6.00 500196 Curry Vadouvan
Hungry Harbor Seafood Seasoning
Italian Seasoning
Yemeni Hawaij Seasoning
Herbs de Provence
Hibiscus
RETAIL PRICE $3.00 508185 Herbs de Provence
RETAIL PRICE $2.00 500216 Hibiscus
RETAIL PRICE $3.00 500217 Hungry Harbor Seafood Seasonin
RETAIL PRICE $2.00 500218 Italian Seasoning
Brown Mustard Seeds
Nutmeg
Nutritional Yeast
Oregano

MENUS

There is really no wrong way to mix and match most of the recipes in this book; just aim for a nice variety of textures and colors, with a few contrasting flavor notes to keep the mix lively. Here are a few suggestions to get things started. Don't forget to put some spicy condiments like Green Zhug (page 164), Spiced Salt (page 157), or Turkish Pepper Paste (page 235) on the table for those who prefer some heat, a basket of warmed pitas or fresh Za'atar Bread (page 98), and a bowl of pickled vegetables to round things out.

Holiday Gathering

Cranberry Date Relish with Ginger **297**

Pan-Roasted Broccoli and Chestnuts **246**

Berbere Turkey (variation of Berbere-Spiced Chicken Thighs) **185**

Winter Squash with Roasted Pumpkin Seeds **176**

Pistachio Cheesecake with Kataifi Crust **275**

Outdoor Summer Party

Pomegranate Cranberry Sangria **37**

Mom's Million-Dollar Salad **241**

Deviled Eggs with Dukkah **229**

Fruited Farro Salad **300**

Layered Bulgur, Fennel, and Mint Salad with Pine Nuts **118**

Spatchcocked Chicken with Preserved Lemon Marinade **72**

Spicy Beef Kebabs with Tzatziki **199**

Apricot Ice Cream **333**

Chocolate Tahini Ice Cream **272**

Brunch

Za'atar Bloody Mary **97**

Pomegranate Mimosa **78**

Lebanese Breakfast **223**

Herbed Egg Bites (Ejjeh) **113**

Syrian Sweet Cheese Pastries **289**

Blueberry Melon Salsa **142**

Afternoon Tea

White Coffee **290**

Fresh Mint Tea **138**

Sahadi's Snack Mix **224**

Lebanese Sweet Pudding **269**

White Chocolate Cranberry Cookies with Sumac Glaze **81**

Meze Spread

Hummus with Moroccan Spices and Preserved Lemon **40**

Our World-Famous Olive Medley **102**

Crostini with Green Almond Relish **46**

Spiced Beet Dip with Za'atar, Goat Cheese, and Pistachios **104**

Red Pepper Walnut Spread (Mohammara) **226**

Zesty Calamari Skewers **167**

Za'atar Bread **98**

Spring Open House Buffet Supper

Shawarma-Crusted Roast Beef Tenderloin **204**

Slow-Roasted Harissa Salmon **193**

Roast Fingerlings with Burrata and Mint Salsa **125**

Sizzled Zucchini with Pepper Relish **175**

Spring Vegetable Salad with Mustard Seed Dressing **180**

Individual Spinach-Walnut Pies **232**

Fall Buffet Supper

Glazed Chicken Legs with Curry and Dates **310**

Seared Tuna Loin with a Sesame Mustard Seed Crust **257**

Za'atar-Roasted Vegetables **126**

Roasted Cauliflower Salad with Lentils and Dates **306**

Millet Pilaf with Almonds and Feta **115**

Game Day Get-Together

Margs, My Way **69**

Brooklyn Nachos **155**

Sahadi's Hot Wings **168**

Harissa Mac and Cheese **182**

Sweet-and-Sour Beef Hand Pies **76**

Cocktail Party

The Mediterranean Rose **39**

Mahlab-Spiced Pecans **296**

Whipped Feta Spread **103**

Great Green Tapenade **106**

Fiery Berbere Shrimp **160**

CRANBERRY DATE RELISH WITH GINGER
page 297

CHRISTMAS RICE
page 258

SHAWARMA-CRUSTED ROAST BEEF TENDERLOIN
page 204

PAN-ROASTED BROCCOLI AND CHESTNUTS
page 246

ACKNOWLEDGMENTS

Sahadi's has given me room to be as creative in the kitchen as I want to be, and that is truly a gift. I am proud to be a member of this vibrant, hospitable family, four generations of whom work, socialize, and explore food together.

SPECIAL THANKS GO TO · Mom, Dad, and Uncle Bob for their love and encouragement, and for allowing me to open my first kitchen. My grandmother, Adele Haddad, for fostering my earliest love of food and hospitality. Sonia and Aunt Yvonne, who allowed me to peek over their shoulders and pick their brains, and who taught me traditional techniques. Pam made my recipes come alive on the page, retesting until they were perfect. By the end, she knew my cooking style better than anyone. Kristin, Caitlin, Nidia, and Jess, the terrific team who cooked, styled, and photographed until my recipes became a book. Thanks also to our Sahadi kitchen teams, who contributed so significantly to the shoot. David Black and his team, who believed in this book from the beginning. Julie Scelfo helped kick-start this process and cataloged the history of the store. Chronicle Books and their amazing creative team, who have been a real pleasure to work with. (Camaren, sorry we didn't get to go the distance together!)

I AM ALSO GRATEFUL TO · Our management teams, who helped me find the time to complete this undertaking. Special thanks to Denissa, who held it all together at the shop while I focused on this project. My brother and partner Ron, your support of my career, especially during this project, has meant the world to me. Kerry, Victoria, and Amanda, who have taste-tested many a recipe in this book. Renee, Joel, Charles, and Gabrielle, who consumed dish after dish as we curated the selections. Michael and Caitlin, my children, whose adventurous and curious palates brought life and joy to our home test kitchen. So proud you have become essential parts of Sahadi's. Pat, who has had my heart and my back for nearly my entire life. You are a true life partner and work partner, someone to cook for and enjoy with, to travel and laugh alongside.

SAHADI IMPORTING CO.
HADI'S
718.624.4550
MIDDLE EASTERN
SAHADIS.COM
SAHADI'S
MORNING CRISP

INDEX

FOOD PRODUCTS
SAHADI IMPORTING CO
MIDDLE EASTERN
&
SPECIALTY FOODS
Sahadi's
MIDDLE EASTERN
SPECIALTY FOODS
Sahadi's
11-9-91